| | DATE DUE | | |
|---|---|---|---|
| | | | |
| | | | |
| | | | |
| | | | |
| | | | |
| | | | |
| | | | |
| | | | |
| | | | |
| | | | |

OVERDUE FINE
$0.10 PER DAY

# On Desire

# On Desire
## Why We Want What We Want

*William B. Irvine*

## OXFORD
UNIVERSITY PRESS

2006

# OXFORD
## UNIVERSITY PRESS

Oxford University Press, Inc., publishes works that
further Oxford University's objective of excellence
in research, scholarship, and education.

Oxford  New York
Auckland  Cape Town  Dar es Salaam  Hong Kong  Karachi
Kuala Lumpur  Madrid  Melbourne  Mexico City  Nairobi
New Delhi  Shanghai  Taipei  Toronto

With offices in
Argentina  Austria  Brazil  Chile  Czech Republic  France  Greece
Guatemala  Hungary  Italy  Japan  Poland  Portugal  Singapore
South Korea  Switzerland  Thailand  Turkey  Ukraine  Vietnam

Published by Oxford University Press, Inc.
198 Madison Avenue, New York, NY 10016
www.oup.com

Oxford is a registered trademark of Oxford University Press

Library of Congress Cataloging-in-Publication Data
Irvine, William Braxton, 1952–
On desire : why we want what we want / William B. Irvine
p. cm.  Includes bibliographical references and index.
ISBN-13: 978-0-19-518862-2
ISBN-10: 0-19-518862-4
1. Desire.  I. Title.
BF575.D4178  2005
128'.3—dc22  2005005938

9 8 7 6 5 4 3
Printed in the United States of America
on acid-free paper

*For Jamie*

# Contents

# Acknowledgments

If the hard drive of my computer can be trusted, I first got the idea to write a book on desire—succumbed, one might say, to the desire to write such a book—in September 2000. Between that time and when the final words were being written in the closing days of 2004, many people contributed to the book in a variety of ways. I would like to take this opportunity to thank them.

First, thanks to the students who signed up for the desire seminars I taught in the winter of 2001 and the winter of 2003; to Derek Vanhoose and Jason Phillips, who did independent study with me on desire; and especially to Nicholas Barnard, Chris Poteet, and Sarah Kaplan, who read the manuscript outside of class. These students were the guinea pigs on whom I tested my work in progress.

Thanks to my colleagues in Wright State University's College of Liberal Arts and Department of Philosophy for allowing me to lecture them about desire. Thanks to my colleagues Scott Baird and Don Cipollini in the Biology Department; Scott discussed the evolution of desire with me, and Don arranged for me to give a seminar on the topic. A special thanks to my colleague James McDougal in the Department of Pharmacology and Toxicology for reading and commenting on chapter drafts. Thanks also to Bruce LaForse of the Classics Department for answering questions about Greek and Latin, and to Carlos Lopez of the Religion Department for answering questions about Hinduism and Buddhism.

Thanks to Gary Klein for letting me give a presentation on the psychology of desire at Klein Associates, and thanks to Terry Stanard and David Malek at Klein for their feedback on my research. Gary also deserves a special thanks for his encouragement and his assistance in helping move this project forward.

Thanks to Connie Steele and Karen Chamberlain, who took a special interest in the desire project and offered encouragement.

Thanks also to Elda Rotor and Cybele Tom at Oxford for their first-rate editorial direction and for reminding me that an individual's progress as an author is measured not only in how many words are written each day but in how many of those words are subsequently deleted.

Finally, I am grateful for permission to reprint an excerpt from "Papyrus Chester Beatty I," from *Love Lyrics of Ancient Egypt*, translated by Barbara Hughes Fowler, copyright © 1994 by the University of North Carolina Press. Used by permission of the publisher.

Little is needed to make a wise man happy, but nothing can content a fool. That is why nearly all men are miserable.

—La Rochefoucauld

# On Desire

# Introduction

You are currently experiencing desire; otherwise, you wouldn't be reading these words. Even if you are reading them at the behest of someone else, you are motivated by your desire to please that person. And if you stop reading, you will do so not because you have stopped desiring but because your desires have changed.

We are awash in desire at virtually every waking moment. If we fall asleep, we temporarily subdue our desires—unless we dream, in which case our dreams will likely be shaped by our desires. Our skill at forming desires is truly remarkable. No one has to teach us how to do it. It is, furthermore, a skill we can exercise endlessly without tiring. When it comes to desiring, we are all experts. If there were an Olympics of desiring, we would all make the team. Sickness and old age may change what we desire, but they do not stop us from desiring.

Try, for a moment, to stanch the flow of desire. You will have to stop squirming, tapping your fingers, clenching your toes; you will have to let your tongue go slack in your mouth and let your eyelids close; you will have to slouch in your chair—or better still, lie down; to the extent possible, you will have to relinquish control of your breathing; you will have to let your mind go blank. You will, in other words, have to enter what we call a meditative state. And even then you will not have purged yourself of desire: you would not remain in this state unless you had an ongoing desire to do so. It takes desire to attempt, unsuccessfully, to extinguish desire.

If you try the above experiment, you will discover that it is almost impossible to keep your mind empty. New thoughts will arise, many of which express desire. You might notice that you are hungry and wish to eat, or that you are uncomfortable and wish to fidget. You might experience anger, which reflects disappointment of your past desires, or anxiety, which reflects your desires about the future. This experiment, by the way, resembles the Zen meditation known as zazen. By performing this meditation, Zen practitioners gain insight into the insidious process by which desires form within us.

Desire animates the world. It is present in the baby crying for milk, the girl struggling to solve a math problem, the woman running to meet her lover and later deciding to have children, and the old woman, hunched over her walker, moving down the hall of the nursing home at a glacial pace to pick up her mail. Banish desire from the world, and you get a world of frozen beings who have no reason to live and no reason to die.

Some people have far fewer desires than the rest of us. Some of them lack desire because they are depressed; others lack it because they have achieved enlightenment. This enlightenment, by the way, is typically the end result of years of conscious effort, brought on by an intense desire to free themselves, to the extent possible, from the grip of desire.

Because we continually experience desire, we are oblivious to its presence in us. It is like the noise made by the fan of a computer. The noise is always there, a low whisper, and because it is always there, we stop noticing it. Similarly, we are usually oblivious to our desires—to their ebb and flow within us, to the role they play in our lives. It is only when our desires are intense (like when we fall in love) or when they come into conflict (like when we want a bowl of ice cream but, because we are on a diet, simultaneously want not to want it) that we pay attention to our desires, with a mixture of puzzlement and vexation. And because we are oblivious to the workings of desire within us, we are full of misconceptions about it.

One consequence of reading this book may be that for the first time in your life you pay close attention to the operation of desire within you. When you do this, you will quickly become aware of the remarkable extent to which your desires have a life of their own. They pop into your head, seemingly out of nowhere. Indeed, in many cases, you don't so much *choose* your desires as *discover* them within you. You will also come to appreciate the extent to which these unbidden desires determine how you spend your days and, in the long run, how you spend your life.

Another thing: once you gain an understanding of how desire works, the desires you form are likely to change. This certainly happened to me over the course of my research. Once I came to understand the extent to which desires arise within me spontaneously and not as the result of rational thought processes, I grew suspicious of my desires. "Where did this desire come from?" I would ask. "Why do I want this thing that I want?" And having asked, I would in many cases end up discarding the suspect desire. (In many cases, but not in all! I certainly don't claim to have mastered desire.)

My goal in investigating desire was to turn it inside out—to understand how and why desires arise, how they affect our lives, and what we can do to master them. In pursuing this goal, I examined what Buddhists, Taoists, Hindus, the Amish, Shakers, and Catholic saints have said about desire, as well as what ancient Greek and Roman and modern European philosophers have said. Besides being multicultural, my examination of desire was multidisciplinary. After examining the writings of philosophers and religious thinkers, I investigated scientific research into how and why we form the desires we form.

Lots of people have thought and written about desire in the last few millennia. The reader might therefore wonder what, if anything, is left to say about the subject. As it turns out, this is an auspicious time for a reexamination of desire. In the last three decades, evolutionary psychologists have made a number of discoveries concerning why we want what we want. During that same period, neuroscientists have made discoveries that help us understand, for the first time ever, the mechanism by which we desire. This understanding allowed them to develop drugs such as Prozac that rekindle desire in depressed patients.

In the following pages, I will attempt to reconcile classical views on desire with the scientific research done in the last few decades. As we shall see, this research substantially confirms many of the prescientific observations of philosophers and religious thinkers about the workings of desire. It also validates much of the advice on mastering desire offered by the likes of Buddha, Epictetus, and Thoreau.

The social and economic developments of recent decades also make this an ideal time to reexamine desire. Around the world, rising levels of affluence have not translated into increased levels of personal satisfaction. In particular, the citizens of affluent nations enjoy a level of material well-being unimaginable to their great-grandparents. Even those citizens labeled impoverished by government statisticians have antibiotics, reliable contraception, CD players, Internet access, and indoor plumbing. But although they "have it all" compared to their ancestors, they remain dissatisfied.

Most people spend their days pursuing worldly success—fame, fortune, and all the things that go with them. (And if not fame and fortune, at least social status and relative affluence.) They imagine that on gaining this success, they will also gain satisfaction—they will at last feel satisfied with their accomplishments, relationships, possessions, and most importantly, with their lives. And with this satisfaction, they think, will come lasting happiness. What they fail to realize, as I shall argue in the following pages, is that it is entirely possible to gain satisfaction without pursuing, much less gaining worldly success. Indeed, in pursuing worldly success, people generally impair their chances of gaining personal satisfaction.

People commonly think that the best way to attain happiness is to change their environment—their house, their clothes, their car, their job, their spouse, their lover, their circle of friends. But those who have thought carefully about desire—the people whose views we will examine in the following pages—have unanimously drawn the conclusion that *the best way—indeed, perhaps the only way—to attain lasting happiness is not to change the world around us or our place in it but to change ourselves*. In particular, if we can convince ourselves to want what we already have, we can dramatically enhance our happiness without any change in our circumstances. It simply does not occur to the typical person that satisfaction can best be gained not by working to satisfy the desires we find within us but by selectively suppressing or eradicating our desires. As we shall see, throughout the ages and across cultures, thoughtful people have argued that the best way to attain happiness is to master our desires, but throughout the ages and across cultures, ordinary people have ignored this advice.

Perfect mastery of our desires is probably impossible. Even Buddha did not succeed in extinguishing desire: after his enlightenment, he retained a number of desires—to breathe, to eat, and most notably, to share with others the source of his enlightenment. What we should therefore seek is relative mastery: we should learn to sort through our desires, working to fulfill some of them, while working to suppress others.

How will we know when we have "mastered" desire? We will experience what, as we shall see, has been the goal of most of those who have thought carefully about desire—a feeling of tranquility. This should not be confused with the kind of tranquility brought on by ingestion of a tranquilizer. It is instead marked by a sense that we are lucky to be living whatever life we happen to be living—that despite our circumstances, no key ingredient of happiness is missing. With this sense comes a diminished level of anxiety: we no longer need to obsess over the things—a new car, a bigger house, a firmer abdomen— that we mistakenly believe will bring lasting happiness if only we can obtain them. Most importantly, if we master desire, to the extent possible to do so, we will no longer despise the life we are forced to live and will no longer daydream about living the life someone else is living; instead, we will embrace our own life and live it to the fullest.

The remainder of this book is divided into three parts. In Part One, I consider the secret life of desire. I begin by describing cases in which people find themselves suddenly and unaccountably in the grip of desire, as well as cases in which the desires people took for granted—that for decades had shaped their lives—suddenly abandon them. I also examine our intense need to interact with and win the admiration of other people.

If we are to win our battle against undesirable desires, it helps to understand them. It is for this reason that, in Part Two of this book, I take a look at what scientists have discovered about desire—about how we form desires and why we form the desires we do. I begin with a discussion of the structure of desire and the sources of desire within us. I go on to describe some of the research, undertaken by neuroscientists and psychologists, on what takes place in the brain when we desire. Then I speculate on how we evolved the ability to desire and on what specific desires came to be "hardwired" into us as the result of our evolutionary past. Because of this wiring, we tend to form certain desires, but it is by no means clear that by working to satisfy these desires we will have a life that is either happy or meaningful.

In Part Three, I examine the advice on mastering desire that has been given over the millennia and across cultures, including religious, philosophical, and what can best be described as eccentric advice.

Readers should be warned at the outset that I will not, in the following pages, provide a "magic bullet" with which they can instantly and effortlessly eradicate unwanted desires. What

I instead offer is insight into how desire works, the role it plays in human life, and the connection between desire formation, desire fulfillment, and human happiness. The hope is that readers armed with this insight will achieve a greater level of personal satisfaction than if they were afflicted, as most people are, with misconceptions about the workings of desire.

Readers might also benefit from my discussion of the advice thoughtful people have offered, over the millennia, on how we can prevent undesirable desires from arising within us and expel them from our minds when, despite our best efforts, they do arise. Again, I have no magic bullet to offer: following any of this advice will take time and effort. If we like what the Zen Buddhists have to say about mastering desire, we might want to spend hours in silent meditation; if we like what the Amish say, we might want to join an Amish community (if they will have us); if we like what the Stoic philosophers say, we might want to spend time studying their writings. But having said this, I should add that the time and effort we spend trying to master desire are probably considerably less than the time and effort we will expend if we instead capitulate to our desires and spend our days, as so many people do, working incessantly to fulfill whatever desires float into our head.

# PART ONE

# THE SECRET LIFE OF DESIRE

To think that I've wasted years of my life, that I've longed to die, that I've experienced my greatest love, for a woman who didn't appeal to me, who wasn't even my type!

—Marcel Proust

# The Ebb and Flow of Desire

Some desires are formed as the result of rational thought processes. Suppose I want lunch. I conclude that the best way to get it, given that my refrigerator is empty, is to drive to a nearby restaurant. As a result, I form a desire to drive to the restaurant in question. This process is perfectly, admirably rational.

It would be a mistake, though, to suppose that all our desires are formed in this manner. To the contrary, many of our most profound, life-affecting desires are not rational, in the sense that we don't use rational thought processes to form them. Indeed, *we* don't form them; they form themselves within us. They simply pop into our heads, uninvited and unannounced. While they reside there, they take control of our lives. A single rogue desire can trample the plans we had for our lives and thereby alter our destinies.

If we are to understand desire—indeed, if we are to understand the human condition—we need to acknowledge the possibility of spontaneous desire. Let us, then, examine some cases in which perfectly rational people have had their lives turned upside down by the sudden, inexplicable onset of desire.

Falling in love is the paradigmatic example of an involuntary life-affecting desire. We don't reason our way into love, and we typically can't reason our way out: when we are in love, our intellectual weapons stop working. Falling in love is like waking up with a cold—or more fittingly, like waking up with a fever. We don't decide to fall in love, any more than we decide to catch the flu. Lovesickness is a condition brought upon us, against our will, by a force somehow external to us.

What force is this? Some would, half seriously, point an accusing finger at Cupid. We fall in love because Cupid selects us as his target without first asking our leave to do so and lets fly an arrow that infects us with lovesickness. This, I realize, is just a myth, but it is nevertheless a myth with impressive explanatory power.

Lovesickness, we should note, is different from lust. A lustful person experiences intense sexual desire that can be satisfied indiscriminately, with any number of people. A lovesick person, on the other hand, experiences an intense desire, generally sexual in nature, that has a target—a specific human being.

When we are lovesick, we lose a significant amount of control over our lives. We start acting foolishly—indeed, we become fools for love. Roman Stoic philosopher Seneca described love as "friendship gone mad."[1] French aphorist François duc de La Rochefoucauld declared, "All the passions cause us to make mistakes, but love is responsible for the silliest ones."[2] Freud called lovesickness "the psychosis of normal people."[3]

Humorist Fran Lebowitz sums up the foolishness of lovesickness in the following terms: "People who get married because they're in love make a ridiculous mistake. It makes much more sense to marry your best friend. You *like* your best friend more than anyone you're ever going to be in love with. You don't choose your best friend because they have a cute nose, but that's all you're doing when you get married; you're saying, 'I will spend the rest of my life with you because of your lower lip.'"[4]

Although romantic love has had its ups and downs over the centuries, lovesickness seems to have been around forever. The poetry of ancient Egypt describes something indistinguishable from modern-day lovesickness. One poem, written more than three thousand years ago, begins as follows:

> It's seven whole days since I
>     have seen my [love]. A sickness
> pervades me. My limbs are lead.
>     I barely sense my body.
> Should physicians come,
>     their drugs could not cure
> my heart, nor could the priests
>     diagnose my disease.
> Should they say, "Here
>     she is," that would heal me.[5]

We can likewise find in Plutarch descriptions of lovesickness as a medical condition. He tells us that in the third century B.C., Erasistratus was asked to diagnose Prince Antiochus, the son of King Seleucus. The symptoms: "his voice faltered, his face flushed up, his eyes glanced stealthily, a sudden sweat broke out on his skin, the beatings of his heart were irregular and violent, and, unable to support the excess of his passion, he would sink into a state of faintness, prostration, and pallor." Erasistratus's diagnosis: the lad was lovesick.[6]

Robert Burton, in his *Anatomy of Melancholy,* published in 1621, has much to say about lovesickness as a medical condition. He observes that "of all passions . . . Love is most violent."[7] He also offers a cure for lovesickness: "The last refuge and surest remedy, to be put in practice in the utmost place, when no other means will take effect, is, to let them go together, and enjoy one another."[8]

The symptoms of lovesickness are well known to anyone who has been afflicted by it. First comes a fixation on a person— a crush. (The common use of the word *crush,* by the way, is syntactically backward: we speak of having a crush on someone, but what really happens is that we feel crushed by them— we feel as if there were a heavy weight on our chest.) With this crush, we lose control of part of our thought processes inasmuch as we cannot stop thinking about the object of our desire. We experience what psychologists call intrusive thoughts.

When we are lovesick, our love makes sense to us, much as our delusions make sense to us when we are in the grip of a high fever or our nightmares make sense to us while we are asleep. To our friends and relatives, though, our infatuation might make no sense at all: "What can he possibly see in her?" they will ask. And in the same way as a fever can pass or we can awaken from a nightmare, lovesickness can end, at which point we might go up to our friends and relatives, bewildered, and ask, "What did I see in her?" In the words of French philosopher and mathematician Blaise Pascal, "The heart has its reasons, which reason does not know."[9]

The departure of love can be as puzzling as its arrival. Philosopher Bertrand Russell, for example, was a happily married man until, during a bicycle ride along a country road, he suddenly realized that he no longer loved his wife. This realization came as a complete surprise: "I had had no idea until this moment that my love for her was even lessening."[10] In love, then, we have a dramatic illustration of the role desire can play in human life. It can grab us by the scruff of the neck, shake us for a spell, and then discard us.

Falling in love is only one instance in which we don't choose our desires, but they choose us. The same thing can happen with material desires.

Consider, for example, the predicament of the consumer who one day detects in himself a desire to own one of those absurdly oversized cars known as sport utility vehicles. Although SUV buyers attempt to give rational justifications for their purchase, the justifications rarely ring true—unless the buyer happens to be, say, a geologist or a fur trapper. The recent popularity of SUVs is particularly puzzling. SUVs have been around for decades: it has been possible to buy a Chevy Suburban since the mid-1930s. Why are so many people getting them now? What changed? You can, of course, ask exactly the same question about any other consumer fad.

At the time of this writing, the consumer craving for SUVs showed signs of having crested, only to be replaced by an even more inexplicable automotive craving—to own a Hummer, the modified version of the vehicle designed to transport soldiers across war zones. The first consumers who bought Hummers looked a bit foolish—they weren't, after all, living in a war zone. But then a funny thing happened. Like a contagious disease, the desire for Hummers spread: one by one, the neighbors of Hummer owners found themselves afflicted with Hummer envy.

Affluent individuals have no end of goods on which to spend their money. It is possible, for example, to spend $450,000 on a wristwatch, $15,000 on stereo headphones, and $6,000 on a Sub-Zero refrigerator. (I recently toured the home of someone who owns one of these refrigerators. "Why do they call it Sub-Zero?" I asked, thinking that perhaps its interior was unusually cold. "They call it Sub-Zero," the homeowner replied, "because that's what my IQ had to be to spend six grand on a refrigerator.") And when people aren't affluent, they don't let this stop them from acting as though they were. They form and act on material desires with reckless abandon. Consider the unmarried, unemployed mother of three who, four days after buying a used Ford Mustang, spent $2,736—over half the car's Blue Book value—to replace its plastic hubcaps with chrome wheels: "Nothing's worse than plastic hubcaps," she explained.[11]

In America, the insatiable craving for consumer goods is in large part responsible for more than a million of us going bankrupt each year. It is also responsible for our having, in recent years, a negative national savings rate, meaning that the average American, in the average month, not only saves nothing but borrows to finance his lifestyle. All this, even though today's Americans enjoy a level of material prosperity that would have astonished their great-grandparents.

For another example of the sudden onset of desire and how it can transform our lives, consider the case of Thomas Merton. Merton was born in 1915. In his college years, he was a typical student, awash in pleasures of the flesh. He drank hard and ran around with a fast crowd. He became a father out of wedlock.[12] He was, in his own words, "an extremely unpleasant sort of a person—vain, self-centered, dissolute, weak, irresolute, undisciplined, sensual, obscene, and proud. I was a mess."[13] In less than a decade, he was not just a devout Catholic, and not just a monk in a monastery, but a monk in a Trappist monastery, meaning that he had taken a vow of silence and agreed to live an ascetic life.

Whenever anyone travels far—in the personal as opposed to the physical sense—in the course of a lifetime, the interesting question is, how did that person get from point A to point B? In the case of most travelers, the motivations for their journey must remain a mystery to the rest of us since the travelers are either oblivious to their own motivations or conscious of them but unable or unwilling to put into words what it was that drove them down the path their lives took. In the case of Merton, we are lucky: his autobiographical *Seven Storey Mountain* lays out in great detail the psychology of a man in transition.

Let us first consider Merton's desire to convert to Catholicism. It is a classic example of a spontaneous desire: "All of a sudden, something began to stir within me, something began to push me, to prompt me. It was a movement that spoke like a voice."[14] The voice told Merton to go find a priest and express a desire to become a Catholic. He sacrificed his old amusements in order to take instruction, and before he knew it, he burned with a desire to be baptized. Conversion, he hoped, would make him subordinate his desires to God's will.

For most people, this would have been the end of the story, but Merton soon came to realize that "there had been another thought, half forming itself in the back of my mind—an obscure desire to become a priest."[15] After a night of drinking, Merton and his friends were sitting on the floor playing records, smoking cigarettes, and eating breakfast, when this "obscure desire" revealed itself. "The idea came to me: 'I am going to be a priest.'" The desire, says Merton, "was a strong and sweet and deep and insistent attraction that suddenly made itself felt." It was "a new and profound and clear sense that this was what I really ought to do."[16]

After deciding to become a priest, Merton had to decide which religious order to join. He rejected the Cistercians of the Strict Observance, commonly known as the Trappists, as being too ascetic, what with their vow of silence and their vegetarianism. (He says that their very name made him shiver.) He instead gave the Franciscans a try but found them unsatisfying, inasmuch as their order gave him too much freedom to form and pursue desires. He decided that perhaps he was not cut out to be a priest and set out to live the most religious life a layperson could live.

Not long after this, he was struck with a new desire: "I suddenly found myself filled with a vivid conviction: 'The time has come for me to go and be a Trappist.'" He didn't know where this desire came from, but it was nevertheless "powerful, irresistible, clear."[17] Why join the Trappists rather than some other religious order? Because sometime before, in a moment of crisis, he had opened the Bible randomly, put his finger down, and read what was there: "Behold, thou shalt be silent." Merton took this as a sign. (Cynics might point out that his decision to join a monastery coincided with his receiving a letter from the draft board; World War II had just begun.)

Merton was not surprised by these sudden onsets of desire and by his inability to explain them. To the contrary, he unhesitatingly rejected the claim that our desires—and in particular, our most important, life-affecting desires—are formed as the result of rational thought. The intellect, he tells us, "is constantly being blinded and perverted by the ends and aims of passion, and the evidence it presents to us with such a show of impartiality and objectivity is fraught with interest and propaganda." We are, he says, masters of self-delusion. Our desires "are fruitful sources of every kind of error and misjudgement, and because we have these yearnings in us, our intellects . . . present to us everything distorted and accommodated to the norms of our desire."[18] As we shall see in later chapters, Merton is not alone in thinking that reason tends to be the servant rather than the master of desire.

It is, by the way, instructive to contrast Merton with Bertrand Russell. When people hear about how Merton's life was transformed by sudden desires, they are tempted to think that Merton must have had a mystical side that made him susceptible to this sort of thing. A more rational person, they suggest, would not likewise allow himself to be bandied about by desire. The thing to realize is that Russell was one of the least mystical, most analytical persons ever to have walked the earth, and yet his desires had a secret life. No one, it would seem, is immune to the sudden onset and equally sudden departure of desire.

Where do spontaneous desires come from? How do they get into our heads? Some of our desires are a consequence of our evolutionary past. We fall in love because, evolutionary psychologists argue, our ancestors who tended to fall in love were more likely to make babies and raise them successfully than those who didn't. Other desires arise because someone has skillfully planted the seeds of desire within us. Why does a consumer suddenly find himself wanting an SUV? In most cases, advertising plays a role. Advertisers are experts in transforming an individual who is basically satisfied with life into someone who craves the product they are selling—indeed, into someone who might be willing to part with half a year's wages to get it. Other spontaneous desires are more difficult to explain. It seems unlikely, for example, that Thomas Merton's sudden desire to become a Trappist monk was due either to evolutionary programming (the claim that our ancestors who became Trappist monks were more likely to reproduce than those who didn't is wildly implausible) or to advertising (the Trappists don't advertise).

The mysterious origin of spontaneous desires and their resulting unpredictability are troubling. Any thoughtful person will be disturbed by Merton's tale. It raises the possibility that we are all just three spontaneous desires away from life in a Trappist monastery—or if not this, then three spontaneous desires away from some other life that we would have trouble imagining for ourselves.

Indeed, chances are that the reader *has* experienced a life-affecting spontaneous desire. Has the reader ever fallen in love? Did the onset of love result in marriage? If so, did it subsequently result in a divorce? And whether or not it resulted in marriage, did the onset of love result in the birth of a child? If you have experienced love and its aftermath, your subsequent life is doubtless profoundly different from the life you would have lived if you had never succumbed to love. And yet you did not choose to fall in love.

Usually in life, our desires change with the passage of time, as one desire displaces another. Compare your fondest desires when you were ten years old with your fondest desires today. There should be a difference. What has happened is that slowly, with the passage of time, some of your earlier desires were fulfilled and you went on to form new desires, while other desires seemed impossible to fulfill and you abandoned them in favor of new desires. This is the natural state of man: a head full of desires, but with the desires in question changing from year to year and even from minute to minute, like the water in a river.

Sometimes the flow of desires ceases, and a person experiences what I call a crisis of desire. Before I go any further in my examination of such crises, let me explain the difference between a crisis of desire and a mere conflict of desire. Suppose someone has a drug addiction. At first he will enjoy the addiction, but the day might come when he hits bottom and realizes that his desire for his drug of choice is doing him great harm. This is *not* what I mean by a crisis of desire; it is only a conflict of desire.

Conflicts of desire are specific: one particular desire or cluster of desires causes us trouble by interfering with our other desires. Thus, the drug addict may complain that his desire for drugs keeps him from accomplishing his other desires—say, to be a good husband and father. We deal with a conflict of desires by dealing with the troubling desire. In the case of drug addiction, we might undergo treatment or join a twelve-step program. In a crisis of desire, on the other hand, it isn't some one desire that is giving us trouble, it is our whole set of desires. Or perhaps it is our ability to desire, or the loss of this ability, that is giving us trouble.

Crises of desire, in the sense I have in mind, are of three sorts. In the first you suddenly lose your ability to desire. In the second you retain your ability to desire but experience a sudden disgust, not with respect to a single desire—that would be a conflict of desires—but with respect to your whole collection of desires. In the third you experience a meaning-of-life crisis in which you retain the ability to desire but can no longer see any point in desiring. Let me now illustrate these three crises.

We have all experienced an inability to desire. We have a name for this state, boredom—and by this I don't mean the kind of boredom you experience when you are, say, bored by a job. In that kind of boredom, you are still able to desire. In fact, you desire intensely to do something other than the job that bores you; thus, desire is not dead within you. What I mean by boredom is the condition in which there are many things you can do; it's just that you don't want to do any of them. You are bored: desire is dead within you.

Fortunately for us, this sort of boredom is usually a temporary condition, rarely lasting longer than a Sunday afternoon. Soon enough, our ability to desire reappears. Suppose, however, that you lost your ability to desire and that this condition lasted not just for an afternoon but for years. This is what happened to Pulitzer-prize-winning novelist Larry McMurtry, of *Lonesome Dove* fame.

McMurtry underwent heart surgery. His recovery went well for the first two months, but then disaster struck: he could no longer read. It isn't that his eyes or brain failed him. He had simply lost the desire to read, a desire that had been one of the dominating, defining desires of his life up until then. McMurtry's life had revolved around books—reading them, writing them, and buying and selling them in his role as rare-book collector. And then, out of the blue, books meant nothing to him. Here is his description of the situation: "The content of my life, which has been rich, began to drain rapidly away. I had been leading a typical type-A East Coast life, reading three newspapers a day, reading many magazines, and in general, trying to stay informed. But more or less overnight, staying informed ceased to matter to me. Though I subscribed to the *New York Times* in three cities I put it aside one day and didn't read another issue for seven months." McMurtry found himself transformed by the disappearance of desire: "From being a living person with a distinct personality I began to feel more or less like an outline of that person—and then even the outline began to fade, erased by what had happened inside. I felt as if I was vanishing—or more accurately, had vanished. . . . I became, to myself, more and more like a ghost, or a shadow. What I more and more felt, as the trauma deepened, was that while my body survived, the self that I had once been had lost its life."[19] He says he felt like an imposter, impersonating himself.

Three years after the surgery, he slowly recovered his ability to desire, and with it, his old self. By the fourth year, he could again pick up a first edition of Hemingway's *The Sun Also Rises* and take delight in finding a well-known typographical error—the word *stopped* spelled with three *p*s on page 181.[20]

McMurtry's crisis of desire raises a broader medical question. In a true crisis of desire, a person's world is shattered. The personal transformation can be greater than in many other of life's crises, as when a person is in a terrible accident or is sent away to prison. And yet, seen from outside, nothing happened to cause the transformation. For this reason, people are inclined to equate crises of desire with the onset of mental illness.

Loss of desire, the inability to sleep through the night, and sudden terrors, such as those experienced by McMurtry, are classic symptoms of depression. Furthermore, depression is not unusual after heart surgery, which gives a whole new meaning to the old cliché about the mental anguish associated with a "broken heart." One is therefore tempted to chalk up McMurtry's crisis of desire to mental depression. McMurtry, however, rejects the suggestion that his loss of interest in reading and writing was a symptom of depression: "That's complete bull. I've often been depressed; I had years of depression. They didn't stop me from reading, from running a bookshop and writing. This was different."[21] Whether McMurtry's self-diagnosis is correct is anyone's guess.

Sometimes a crisis of desire, rather than being taken by the world as a symptom of mental illness, is taken as a sign of enlightenment. Along these lines, consider the crisis of desire experienced by Siddhartha Gautama, the man we know as Buddha. In his time of crisis, Siddhartha was not troubled by some one desire, as a drug addict might be, and he did not lose the ability to desire, as McMurtry did; to the contrary, he was troubled by his whole set of desires and resolved his predicament by renouncing desire.

Siddhartha was born in 563 B.C. in what is now Nepal. His father raised him in a palace, cut off from all the world's suffering, so Siddhartha would not know of the evil in the world. And when Siddhartha, at age twenty-nine, asked to leave the palace and see the world, his father tried to arrange things so he would still be shielded from evil: he commanded that Siddhartha's route be prettified. Siddhartha nevertheless encountered "the three woes": an old man, a sick man, and a dead man. Because he had to wait twenty-nine years for his first encounter with suffering, it made a very great impression upon him and pushed him toward a crisis of desire.

What finally triggered the crisis? Accounts vary, but according to one, Siddhartha went to bed in the palace one night and "awoke to find his female musicians sleeping round him in disgusting attitudes." It was then, "filled with loathing for his worldly life," that he decided to leave the palace and seek wisdom.[22]

In a crisis of desire like Siddhartha's, a person first experiences a growing dissatisfaction with life that might last for weeks, months, or years. Then comes a triggering event, which might or might not itself be extraordinary. In many cases, the event that triggers the crisis is a familiar event—such as waking up surrounded by female musicians in disgusting attitudes—that suddenly becomes unendurable.

Here is how one Buddhist scholar characterizes the process people undergo when they experience a crisis of desire: our suffering triggers "an inner realization, a perception which pierces through the facile complacency of our usual encounter with the world to glimpse the insecurity perpetually gaping underfoot. . . . When this insight dawns, even if only momentarily, it can precipitate a profound personal crisis. It overturns accustomed goals and values, mocks our routine preoccupations, leaves old enjoyments stubbornly unsatisfying."[23]

It is instructive to contrast what Siddhartha experienced with what we today call midlife crises. People undergoing a typical midlife crisis aren't disgusted by their current desires as Siddhartha was; to the contrary, they are disgusted by the meager extent to which their current desires are being satisfied.

Thus, a male undergoing a garden-variety midlife crisis is disturbed not by his sexual appetites but by the lack of variety in his sexual partners. He is disturbed not by the crass materialism of his life but by the fact that he is still driving a Ford when he could and should be driving a Porsche.

Or consider the empty nest syndrome, which is experienced by parents whose children have gone off to college. In most cases, the crisis triggered by an empty nest is not a crisis of desire in the sense I have in mind. Nevertheless, by examining the empty nest syndrome, we can gain insight into the operation of desire.

Parents, if they are good parents, typically supplant their own desires with those of their children. They get up in the morning and think not "What do I want?" but rather "What do my children need?" After doing this for two decades, their ability to selfishly desire atrophies. They are simply no good anymore at thinking about what *they* want, the rest of the world be damned. When their children finally leave the nest, though, this "external" source of desire dries up, and parents are faced with the task of relearning how to desire selfishly. This is the challenge that confronts empty-nesters—how to jump-start the engine of desire.

In other cultures, the empty nest syndrome is handled differently. In Hindu culture, for example, empty-nesters are counseled not to restart the engine of desire but to junk it. The Hindu Laws of Manu divide life into four stages: student, householder, retired person, and ascetic. Empty-nesters are typically making the transition from householder to retired person. The job of a householder is to make money and spend it wisely, in accordance with Hindu law. But when his skin starts to wrinkle, his hair grows gray, and he has met his son's son, the householder is ready to enter the next stage of life. Rather than relearning how to desire selfishly, he turns his reduced level of desire to his advantage: "Abandoning all food raised by cultivation, and all his belongings, he may depart into the forest, either committing his wife to his sons, or accompanied by her. Taking with him the sacred fire and the implements required for domestic [sacrifices], he may go forth from the village into the forest and reside there, duly controlling his senses."[24]

The crises of desire described above are bad enough, but one can imagine more serious crises than these. Consider, for example, Russian author Leo Tolstoy's "arrest of life." When he experienced his crisis of desire in his mid-forties, Tolstoy was rich, in perfect health, and at the height of his fame. He was, as most people are, filled with desire, but then something strange began to happen: he began to experience "moments of perplexity." They would pass, only to recur. These moments, he says, "were always expressed by the questions: What is it for? What does it lead to?"[25]

At first he ignored these questions, but they kept forming themselves in his mind. When, for example, he considered the needs of his children or of the peasants on his estate, he would suddenly say to himself, "What for?" Even his literary fame ceased to be a source of delight: "I would say to myself, 'Very well; you will be more famous than Gogol or Pushkin or Shakespeare or Molière, or than all the writers in the world—and what of it?' And I could find no reply at all."[26]

Soon Tolstoy was experiencing a full-blown crisis of desire: "I felt that what I had been standing on had collapsed and that I had nothing left under my feet. What I had lived on no longer existed, and there was nothing left." He continues:

> My life came to a standstill. I could breathe, eat, drink, and sleep, and I
> could not help doing these things; but there was no life, for there were no
> wishes the fulfilment of which I could consider reasonable. If I desired
> anything, I knew in advance that whether I satisfied my desire or not,
> nothing would come of it. Had a fairy come and offered to fulfil my de-
> sires I should not have known what to ask. If in moments of intoxication
> I felt something which, though not a wish, was a habit left by former
> wishes, in sober moments I knew this to be a delusion and that there was
> really nothing to wish for. I could not even wish to know the truth, for I
> guessed of what it consisted. The truth was that life is meaningless.[27]

It seemed to Tolstoy as if someone had played an evil and stupid joke on him by placing him in the world and that this someone watched in amusement as Tolstoy achieved worldly success,
only to discover that it all meant nothing. Tolstoy's only surprise, he tells us, is that he didn't realize this from the start. For
all his life, he had been happy to let his desires run free; only
now did he realize the foolishness of doing so.

Tolstoy's crisis of desire was different from those discussed
earlier. Larry McMurtry found himself unable to desire but
still desired to desire. Siddhartha was able to desire but desired
not to desire. Tolstoy didn't lose the ability to desire and didn't
want to renounce desire. He just no longer saw any point in
desiring. What Tolstoy experienced was that most serious crisis of desire, a meaning-of-life crisis. Such crises are dangerous
because they can end in suicide. And indeed, during his crisis
Tolstoy contemplated suicide.

It took years for Tolstoy's crisis of desire to develop. In another
well-documented case involving a sixty-five-year-old woman
who must remain nameless, it took a matter of minutes. The
woman in question had battled with Parkinson's disease for
thirty years, and although her symptoms had become quite
severe, she was, psychologically speaking, fighting a good fight:

she was not depressed and did not experience mood swings. Then one day in 1999, all this changed: within a period of five minutes, she went from being her normally cheery self to being profoundly depressed. Doctors witnessed the episode, videotaped the change in her expressions, and recorded her utterances: "I no longer wish to live, to see anything, hear anything, feel anything. . . . I'm fed up with life, I've had enough. . . . I don't want to live anymore, I'm disgusted with life." The doctors were convinced that these feelings were genuine and sincere. The woman had simply lost the will to live. It had vanished in a matter of minutes, before their very eyes.[28]

What had happened to the woman? Had she received some profoundly sad news? Had she been reading the works of some pessimistic philosopher? No such thing. At the time she fell into her meaning-of-life crisis, doctors, in an attempt to relieve the symptoms of Parkinson's disease, had been electrically stimulating a region of her brain. Researchers have found that if they stimulate the right spot, victims of Parkinson's disease can enjoy remarkable improvement; but for doctors to find the right spot, the patient has to be awake when they are doing their exploratory stimulations. In the case of this woman, doctors inadvertently stimulated the wrong spot. One interpretation of what happened is that doctors inhibited the part of the brain that generates the will to live, and as a result the woman experienced instant depression. I will have more to say about this woman and her fate in Chapter 6, when I examine the biological basis of desire.

The crises described in this chapter are troubling. They demonstrate the possibility that when we wake up tomorrow morning, we, like McMurtry, will have lost our ability to desire, or that we, like Siddhartha, will discover that we no longer desire the things we desired the night before. In either case, we will experience a crisis of personal identity that might transform us as human beings. It is also possible that we will experience a meaning-of-life crisis like the one experienced by Tolstoy. Readers who are inclined to discount these possibilities should realize that McMurtry, Siddhartha, and Tolstoy were likewise unconcerned about them—until they found themselves in the grip of a crisis of desire.

Undergoing a crisis of desire is excruciatingly painful, but it can have a beneficial outcome: as a result of his crisis, for example, Siddhartha gained enlightenment. Is it possible to gain enlightenment without undergoing a crisis of desire? Perhaps. In particular, we might hope that by taking to heart the advice offered by those who, like Siddhartha, survived a crisis of desire, we, too, can gain a degree of enlightenment. We will examine some of this advice in Part Three.

To be alone is one of the greatest evils for man.

—William James

Hell is—other people!

—Jean-Paul Sartre

# Other People

Most people seek fame and fortune. If universal fame eludes them, they seek regional fame, local renown, popularity within their social circle, or distinction among their colleagues. Likewise, if they can't amass a fortune in absolute terms, they seek relative affluence: they want to be materially better off than their co-workers, neighbors, relatives, and friends.

At first glance, our desire for fame (more generally, for social status) and our desire for fortune (for material things) seem to be distinct: the former involves people, the latter does not. A bit of reflection reveals, though, that our social and material desires are very much connected: it is largely because we live among other people and want them to admire us that we want the material things we do. If we were indifferent to social status, it is unlikely that we would want the car, the jewelry, and the house that we find ourselves dreaming of. Indeed, if our neighbors ridiculed rather than admired the owners of SUVs, expensive wristwatches, and fifteen-thousand-square-foot mansions, it is unlikely that we would put ourselves out trying to acquire these things.

From this it follows that if we wish to understand why we experience the desires we do—understand, that is, why we want what we want—it is essential that we appreciate the role other people play in our lives. In particular, we need to understand what it is that we want from other people. Let us, therefore, take a look at our social desires.

Man, said Aristotle, is a political animal.[1] By this he meant not that we are intrinsically interested in politics—many of us obviously aren't. He meant that man is suited by his nature to live in a *polis,* or community. We are by nature gregarious. We surround ourselves with family and friends. Most of us would find it difficult to be deprived of human contact for an extended period. Indeed, most of us have never, in our entire lives, gone twenty-four hours without human contact; if we have, it probably wasn't by choice.

People need people. It is a need that is arguably surpassed only by our need for air, water, and perhaps food. (Some people would prefer a day without food to a day without people.) Deprive the average person of human contact for an extended period, and we will have to fear for his sanity.

Why do we need other people? What do we get from them? In part, they are a source of pleasure. We need them if we want to make conversation, play tennis, or have sex. We also need them for the goods and services they offer. My grocer provides me with food, and my doctor keeps me healthy. My contact with these individuals makes perfect sense, inasmuch as it is far easier to buy food from a grocer than to grow my own and inasmuch as I am not competent to diagnose my own illnesses. And to earn money with which to purchase these goods and services I deal with yet other people, in the context of my job. Other people are also a source of useful information. They know things I don't know but would benefit from knowing. I talk to them in part to obtain these nuggets of information—such as that the local grocer is giving away free samples of ice cream. But these practical social needs are only part of the story. Even if we have everything we need to sustain a comfortable life, we will still seek out other people.

In part we seek them out for the social feedback they provide. Most of us are insecure. We worry that the choices we have made about how to live our lives are the wrong choices. We turn to others for reassurance. We might tell a friend our thoughts, activities, plans, desires, and fears because we want the friend's reaction. We want our friends to approve of our choices—or if not approve, then straighten us out.

Sometimes the social feedback is direct and unambiguous: "That haircut is atrocious." Often, though, the feedback is couched in euphemism: "It isn't as bad as the haircut you got last Christmas." The feedback can also be nonverbal. A spouse's facial reaction on seeing our new haircut may be more important to us than any reassuring remarks she might subsequently make. Because social feedback is so important to us, we develop considerable skill at reading our fellow humans: we learn how to see through their expressed reaction and detect their true feelings.

Although friends, relatives, and lovers are all important sources of feedback, we also pay attention to the feedback provided by enemies and even complete strangers. In fact, we might even value their feedback more than that of friends, since our friends have an incentive to lie to us—to tell us what we want to hear and thereby preserve our friendship—that enemies and strangers don't. One enemy pointing out a shortcoming of ours might loom larger in our mind than ten friends denying that we have any such shortcoming. One stranger snickering at our haircut might send us back to the barber, even though our relatives tell us that nothing is wrong with it.

Even if we were utterly self-confident—even if we felt no need to check our decisions with others—we would probably still care very much about what other people think of us. We want them to acknowledge our existence, take account of us, and react to us. We might want them to love us, and if not love us then at least admire us. And if we can't have people's admiration, we seek their respect or recognition.

In all but exceptional cases, we seek the admiration or recognition not of a chosen few individuals but of the masses. Deep down, most of us would love to be famous—to have not only our friends, relatives, and neighbors admire us, but complete strangers as well. Indeed, according to Plato, we will be puzzled by men's behavior unless we understand "how they are stirred by the love of an immortality of fame. They are ready to run all risks greater than they would have run for their children, and to spend money and undergo any sort of toil, and even to die, for the sake of leaving behind them a name which shall be eternal."[2] Samuel Johnson remarked, "Every man, however hopeless his pretensions may appear to all but himself, has some project by which he hopes to rise to reputation; some art by which he imagines that the notice of the world will be attracted."[3] Philosopher David Hume wrote of the "love of fame; which rules, with such uncontrolled authority, in all generous minds, and is often the grand object of all their designs and undertakings."[4] And novelist Anthony Trollope wrote that the desire for fame "is so human that the man who lacks it is either above or below humanity." He then admits his own desire for fame—his desire to be not just a clerk in the post office, but *somebody*.[5]

And it isn't just that we *want* to be famous; most of us imagine that we *will* be famous. Consider, for example, sociologists. Few would accuse them of being a fame-hungry group. Nevertheless, a survey of nearly two hundred sociologists found that about a hundred of them expected to become one of the ten leading sociologists of their time—obviously a mathematical impossibility. The survey also found that more than half of them hoped to achieve immortality via their sociological research: they thought their writings would still be read after they died.[6]

Philosophers also seek fame in their own low-key fashion. I don't have a survey to prove this, but I do have Cicero's observation that "those very philosophers even in the books which they write about despising glory, put their own names on the title-page. In the very act of recording their contempt for renown and notoriety, they desire to have their own names known and talked of."[7] A case can be made, then, that even those who openly scorn fame secretly crave it. In the words of Tacitus, "The lust of fame is the last that a wise man shakes off."[8]

Sociologists and philosophers have to work hard to achieve fame; tyrants can accomplish it through legislation, even though they have done nothing to deserve either fame or infamy. A recent example of this is Saparmurat Niyazov, the dictator of Turkmenistan, self-declared "Father of All Turkmen." He named cities, streets, mosques, farms, the main airport, and even celestial bodies after himself. He erected statues of himself around the country and put his face on billboards and the currency. He even renamed a month in the Turkmen calendar for himself—the headline in the *New York Times* read, "Turkmen Leader, Wishing to be August, Settles for January." And to ensure that his state-enforced fame would not fade during his lifetime, he named himself president for life—twice.[9]

If we gain fame, what then? We are likely to be miserable. The problem with fame is that it resides in other people's heads, and as the nineteenth-century German philosopher Arthur Schopenhauer observed, "other people's heads are a wretched place to be the home of a man's true happiness."[10] Because fame requires the cooperation of other people, it puts us at the mercy of those same people. In particular, when a person is inflated with fame, the rest of us have it in our power to deflate him, and perhaps plunge him into misery and anguish, with a few well-chosen words. This is not to say that it is impossible for a famous person to be happy, but when this happens, Schopenhauer suggested, it is usually because the activity that brought the person fame also brought him happiness—meaning that his fame and happiness are not directly connected and that he would remain happy if his fame were to diminish.[11]

It would be a mistake to think that the responses we seek in other people are invariably positive—that we seek only their love, admiration, or respect. To the contrary, a considerable portion of human behavior is motivated by a desire to generate negative feelings in others. Most people, for example, have a desire to cause feelings of envy in those around them—I will have more to say about this in a moment. We might also have a desire to defeat other people: when we enter a tennis tournament, our goal might be not merely to win a trophy but to take delight in the physical and emotional suffering of our opponents. (In the words of novelist Gore Vidal, "It is not enough to succeed. Others must fail.") We might have a desire to disgust other people. This desire might motivate a male to belch in the presence of a female who has spurned his advances. Or we might have a desire to frustrate other people. This is presumably what motivates children to tantalize their younger siblings with toys. Finally, a person might seek the ultimate negative response in those around him: he might want others to fear him. Presumably, this is the social desire that drives totalitarians such as Stalin. They seek not fame but infamy.

It is tempting to play down the existence of negative social desires and argue either that they are rare or that only unbalanced or mentally ill people experience them. If we accept this view, though, we will be unable to explain a considerable part of human behavior. In a perfect world, everyone would want to be loved, admired, and respected. In our world, lots of people have given up on being loved, admired, and respected but nevertheless want other people to acknowledge their existence: "If others won't love me, then let them fear me. If others won't respect me, then they will have to put up with my disgusting or belligerent behavior. I will not be ignored!"

Consider, by way of illustration, someone who runs amok—who, to use the slang expression, "goes postal"—killing several co-workers and then himself. Such a person, it might be suggested, has no need for people; his antisocial behavior demonstrates as much. I would argue, to the contrary, that many social misfits have an intense need for people; it's just that the need in question is grotesquely negative. If the above individual had no need for people, he could simply commit suicide or live in seclusion. He kills people because he needs something from them, perhaps their attention or respect. And since he can't gain their respect, he is willing to settle for their fear. He will force them to acknowledge his existence, even if doing so requires his own death.

Another negative reason we need other people is so we can feel superior to them. This, I realize, is a horribly cynical thing to suggest, but at the same time, many thoughtful observers of desire have seen fit to suggest it. According to Schopenhauer, "what every one most aims at in ordinary contact with his fellows is to prove them inferior to himself." He adds, "Politeness is a tacit agreement that people's miserable defects, whether moral or intellectual, shall on either side be ignored and not made the subject of reproach."[12] According to philosopher Thomas Hobbes, "all the heart's joy and pleasure lies in being able to compare oneself favourably with others and form a high opinion of oneself."[13] And according to theologian John Calvin, each of us "seeks to exalt himself above his neighbour, confidently and proudly despising others, or at least looking down upon them as his inferiors. The poor man yields to the rich, the plebeian to the noble, the servant to the master, the unlearned to the learned, and yet every one inwardly cherishes some idea of his own superiority. Thus each flattering himself, sets up a kind of kingdom in his breast."[14]

Mark Twain was not an intellectual, but he found himself in agreement with Schopenhauer, Hobbes, and Calvin on our need to look down on those around us: "Good breeding," he wrote, echoing Schopenhauer's claim about politeness, "consists in concealing how much we think of ourselves and how little we think of the other person."[15] And finally, Ambrose

Bierce defines *hatred* as "a sentiment appropriate to the occasion of another's superiority."[16]

Because we care very deeply about what other people think of us, we go to considerable trouble and expense to create and project a certain image of ourselves. Thus, according to La Rochefoucauld, "in every walk of life each man puts on a personality and outward appearance so as to look what he wants to be thought: in fact you might say that society is entirely made up of assumed personalities."[17] The image we project, however, will typically be quite unlike the "real" us: in the words of Schopenhauer, "A man can be *himself* only so long as he is alone; and if he does not love solitude, he will not love freedom; for it is only when he is alone that he is really free."[18]

We take great care in constructing this false image of ourselves. In conversation we are careful what we do and don't reveal to others. We might tell someone that we just bought a car, but we withhold the information that we had to borrow from our parents to make the down payment and that lately we have been receiving dunning notices from our creditors. We might tell someone about the award-winning novel we just finished reading but not about our ongoing addiction to a certain soap opera. We try to project an image of happiness even if we are miserable. Indeed, as La Rochefoucauld observes, "we go to far less trouble about making ourselves happy than about appearing to be so."[19]

The social mask we wear, however, is uncomfortable. We cannot wear it twenty-four hours a day but must periodically remove it so our skin can breathe—so our real selves can emerge. This is why we value privacy. When we are alone, behind closed doors, we can finally quit acting and be ourselves.

When someone invades our privacy—in particular, when some-one drops by without warning, enters our house, and gets a glimpse of how we really live—we are upset. We have been unmasked. The effort we invested in creating an image has been undermined.

We project our self-image not only to those we know but to complete strangers as well. In high school, we wear jackets to show all we encounter that we lettered in track. When we turn eighteen, we get tattoos to make it apparent to everyone that we possess a trait that would not otherwise be obvious—such as the fact that we experience "no fear!" Later, when we have saved enough to buy a car, we buy vanity license plates that inform perfect strangers who happen to be driving behind us on the interstate that we are a CATLUVR. Why isn't it enough that this driver loves cats and enjoys having them as pets? Why does she feel compelled to share this personal fact with us? Because she wants other people, even perfect strangers, to form the "right" idea about who she is.

And the cars to which these vanity plates are attached are themselves vanity objects, chosen to tell others something about us. Someone who drives a late-model Ferrari Spyder con-vertible obviously has a different self-image than someone who drives a rusted-out pickup. We can easily imagine the Ferrari owner refusing to be seen driving a rusty truck; doing so would destroy the image he had worked so hard and spent so much to create.

Even in trivial consumer choices such as whether we drink Pepsi or Coke, we are potentially making a declaration to the world. Because these soft drinks, through the skillful use of advertising, project different images, consumers can use them in their effort to project a certain image to the world around them. In a curious sense, then, in our own lives we behave like advertising executives: we carefully build a brand—the image we project to the world—and then work hard to maintain it.

It is only a slight exaggeration to say we live for other people— that the bulk of our time, energy, and wealth is spent creating and maintaining a certain public image of ourselves. The best way to appreciate the truth of this claim is to consider how our behavior would change if other people vanished.

Suppose you woke up one morning to discover that you were the last person on earth: during the night, aliens had spirited away everyone but you. Suppose that despite the absence of other people, the world's buildings, houses, stores, and roads remained as they had been the night before. Cars were where their now-vanished owners had parked them, and gas for these cars was plentiful at now-unattended gas stations. The electricity still worked. It would be a world like this world, except that everyone but you was gone. You would, of course, be very lonely, but let us ignore the emotional aspects of being the last person, and instead focus our attention on the material aspects.

In the situation described, you could satisfy many material desires that you can't satisfy in our actual world. You could have the car of your dreams. You could even have a showroom full of expensive cars. You could have the house of your dreams—or live in a palace. You could wear very expensive clothes. You could acquire not just a big diamond ring but the Hope Diamond itself. The interesting question is this: without people around, would you still want these things? Would the material desires you harbored when the world was full of people still be present in you if other people vanished? Probably not.

Without anyone else to impress, why own an expensive car, a palace, fancy clothes, or jewelry?

If you found yourself alone in a materially abundant world, chances are your desires would take a utilitarian turn. You might try living in a palace, but move out and take up residence in a dwelling that was emotionally cozier and easier to keep clean. You might try expensive suits but revert to clothes that were more comfortable. Indeed, you might even stay in your pajamas all day long or, on fine spring days, walk around in your underwear or in the nude. You might acquire an expensive wristwatch, only to realize that without other people to meet, you don't need to know what time it is.

Your life would also change in more mundane ways. For one thing, if you are a woman, why wear makeup? Most makeup, after all, is worn not for the sake of the wearer but for the sake of those who encounter the wearer. But without other people, why worry about how you look to other people? And if the last woman would dispense with makeup, the last man would stop worrying about how his haircut looked—and in particular wouldn't worry about how his haircut looked from behind. Presumably, he would care only about practical matters, such as how a haircut felt and how easy his hair was to keep clean—assuming that he keeps his hair clean for his own sake and not to impress other people.

If we compare the lifestyle of the last person with our own, we will quickly recognize the impact the presence of other people has on our lives. We dress, choose a house, and buy a wristwatch with other people in mind. We spend a small fortune to project an image calculated to gain the admiration of these other people—or perhaps to make them envy us. We suppress ourselves and our desires in conformance with the image we wish to project. And to finance our image-projection activities, we might spend our adult life working at a job we hate.

Were we to find ourselves in the situation described in the last-person scenario, we would be freed from humanity, and as a result our material existence would be radically simplified. At the same time, we probably wouldn't relish our newfound freedom. To the contrary, we would soon come to appreciate Seneca's comment that "there is no enjoying the possession of anything valuable unless one has someone to share it with."[20]

Living without people can be devastating, but living with them is no picnic either. Schopenhauer complains that society "compels us, for the sake of harmony, to shrivel up, or even alter our shape altogether." Society "demands an act of severe self-denial; we have to forfeit three-fourths of ourselves in order to become like other people."[21] He adds that "there is nothing to be got from [people's] society which can compensate either for its boredom, annoyance and disagreeableness, or for the self-denial which it renders necessary."[22]

According to Schopenhauer, "almost all our sufferings spring from having to do with other people." He adds that "the Cynics renounced all private property in order to attain the bliss of having nothing to trouble them; and to renounce society with the same object is the wisest thing a man can do."[23] Yet it is generally difficult for people—even great thinkers such as Schopenhauer—to live without others. We poor humans are therefore on the horns of a dilemma: we find it hard to live with other people, and we find it even harder to live without them.

Envy is one of the things that makes living with other people so difficult. The envy we feel toward others is like a corrosive liquid, eating away at our happiness and destroying our tranquility: according to the Cynic philosopher Antisthenes, "as iron is eaten away by rust, so . . . the envious are consumed by their own passion."[24] And when others feel envy toward us, it can likewise poison our lives. British philosopher and economist John Stuart Mill calls envy "that most anti-social and odious of all passions."[25] According to Buddha, it is "the deadliest poison."[26]

Although *envy* and *jealousy* are often given as synonyms, it is possible to tease apart a difference in meaning. Someone is jealous because he fears the loss of something he already "possesses." A jealous husband, for example, might fear losing his wife to another man. Someone experiences envy, on the other hand, when he wants something he currently lacks: the husband just mentioned might envy a neighbor for having such a beautiful wife. Only if he succeeds in stealing the wife away from the neighbor will he be able to experience jealousy with respect to her. (In distinguishing between envy and jealousy in this manner, by the way, I am following in the footsteps of La Rochefoucauld: "Jealousy is in some measure just and reasonable, since it merely aims at keeping something that belongs to us or we think belongs to us, whereas envy is a frenzy that cannot bear anything that belongs to others.")[27]

Envy involves an element of admiration: if I am envious of someone's house, it follows that I admire it. (Philosopher Søren Kierkegaard characterizes envy as failed admiration.)[28] In cases of envy, though, these feelings of admiration are mixed with a sense of injustice. If I envy someone's house, I will feel, deep down, that it is unfair that he owns such a house but I do not. I can justify this feeling in many ways. I might think that I work harder, am a better person, have a purer heart, have had a harder life, or have greater needs than he. If the world were fair, I would live in such a house.

We are susceptible to feelings of envy for the simple reason that we are far better acquainted with our own lives than with others' lives. We are acutely aware of our own efforts, needs, acts of kindness, and so forth. Because of this, whenever good things happen to us, it seems obvious to us that we deserve them. Even if, through dumb luck, we win millions of dollars in a lottery, it seems perfectly fair. At the same time, we are largely oblivious to the efforts, needs, and acts of kindness of the people around us. Therefore, when good things happen to them, it is far from obvious to us that they deserve these good things—or, at any rate, deserve them as much as we do.

Sometimes it *is* unfair that someone else has something that you lack. In such cases, complaining about the situation is not a manifestation of envy. Suppose, for example, that you are competing with another employee for a promotion. Suppose that even though your job performance is better than hers in every measurable respect, she gets the promotion because she sleeps with the boss. If you begrudged this employee her promotion, you would be experiencing righteous indignation, not envy. Given the rules of the workplace, she doesn't deserve the promotion; you do. In most cases in which we begrudge others what they have, though, the argument from unfairness, if we examine it carefully, is without merit. Our complaints about unfairness are really nothing more than a cover for our feelings of envy, although we may not realize as much.

Imagine the following scenario. You receive an anonymous letter listing the salaries of the people in the office in which you work. Your salary listing is correct, but you notice that you are way down on the pay scale. In fact, people who have been there a shorter time and have less experience than you nevertheless draw a bigger salary. You are angry and depressed. You consider quitting.

Then you notice that your co-workers are massed around a memo your boss has posted on the office bulletin board. According to the memo, someone, in order to stir up resentment at the workplace, has been sending people false salary listings. And to make things even worse, the person in question has apparently obtained the actual list of salaries to work from, since he always correctly gives the salary of the letter's recipient, thereby adding an element of authenticity to his letter. To restore office harmony, the boss adds, he is posting, this one time only, a listing of everyone's salaries.

Your eyes turn to the listing in question. You find your own salary. And when you look at the salaries of your co-workers, you realize that compared to them, you are very highly paid. You then notice that your co-workers, who have also made this realization, are giving you a certain look. You return to your desk. As you sit there, you are likely to be a changed person. You are delighted that your boss recognizes and rewards the talents that are—to you, at any rate—so obvious. Your self-esteem soars. In fact, you take on a mildly condescending attitude toward your co-workers.

(This scenario is hypothetical, of course. In most workplaces, what people make is a carefully guarded secret, inasmuch as employers realize that knowledge of what others make gives rise to invidious comparisons, which in turn disrupt workplace harmony.)

Think of it—the same salary is capable of making you depressed or elated. It all depends on how your salary compares to that of your co-workers. Your salary, besides having a dollar value, has what economists call "positional" value: when you pick up a paycheck, you are interested not just in its dollar amount but in how your pay compares to that of your fellow workers.

We are also more interested in the positional value of our possessions than in their absolute value. When we buy a house, for example, whether it is *big* matters less than whether it is *bigger*. If everyone in our neighborhood owned smaller houses, we would probably have been content with a smaller house than the one we own. Conversely, if our house, although enormous, is significantly smaller than those of our neighbors, we might feel dissatisfied with it.

More generally, what we want is affected by what the people around us want. Sometimes we come to want something because others want it. Suppose, for example, we buy an SUV because we notice how popular it is with people in our socioeconomic group. This is the so-called bandwagon effect. Other times, we stop wanting something because others want it. Thus, we might stop buying a certain brand of clothing that we had bought for years. It isn't that the quality or style of the clothes has changed; our problem is that too many people—more precisely, too many of the wrong sort of people—are buying them. This is the so-called snob effect.

Why do we care about what other people earn or own? Because we tend to regard life as an ongoing competition for social status. When others gain status, it will in no way affect our absolute level of status, but it will necessarily affect our relative level: they will have risen compared to us. The competition for status is therefore a zero-sum game: when someone wins, someone else must lose.

If someone goes on to ask why we feel compelled to compete for social status, I would point to our evolutionary past: our ancestors who valued social status were more likely to attract a mate and therefore more likely to reproduce than those who did not. In particular, a socially dominant male was likely to have sexual access to many more females than a male at the bottom of the social hierarchy.

Our biggest rivals in the competition for status tend to be those who are closest to us, either in geographical terms or in terms of status. In other words, familiarity breeds envy. A person is more likely to feel envious of his co-workers, neighbors, or relatives than of a multibillionaire he has never met. It doesn't bother him that the multibillionaire owns seven homes, twelve luxury cars, and two private jets. What irks him is the fact that a co-worker has an office with a window and he doesn't, that his neighbor has a bigger hot tub than his, and that a relative just bought a new car, while his own car is decrepit. (Along these lines, H. L. Mencken defined *wealth* as "any income that is at least one hundred dollars more a year than the income of one's wife's sister's husband.")

When a man envies, say, someone for his car, it does not necessarily follow that he wants to do this other person harm. He could be perfectly happy to let the other person keep his car; his complaint is that if the world were fair, he would have a car like that, too. And if a man, in his envy, does wish to harm the owner of the car, he can accomplish this goal in two ways. He might steal the other person's car and make it his own, or he might destroy the other person's car and thereby remove the source of his envy. In either of these cases, he will have committed a crime of envy, which crimes form an interesting sub-set of crimes of passion.

Suppose, on the other hand, that we envy someone's car and that, through no fault of ours, it is destroyed in an acci-dent. We might then experience schadenfreude—joy at the loss of another. In the words of La Rochefoucauld: "We all have strength enough to endure the troubles of others,"[29] and "A neighbour's ruin is relished by friends and enemies alike."[30] Along similar lines, Ambrose Bierce defines *happiness* as "an agreeable sensation arising from contemplating the misery of others."[31] But the agreeable sensation in question is generally mixed with pain, since the feelings of envy that give rise to schadenfreude can destroy a person's happiness. According to Schopenhauer, "a covetous, envious and malicious man, even if he be the richest in the world, goes miserable."[32]

Besides envying others, we ourselves can become the tar-get of someone's envy. When this happens, we are relatively powerless to mitigate their feelings. Suppose, for example, a relative envies us because of the car we own, and suppose we try to placate this relative by giving him the car he so admires. Will our kindness win him over? Probably not. If anything, it will make matters worse. The envier will interpret our kind-ness as condescension, and if he envied us for being wealthy enough to own this car, he will likely envy us even more now: the fact that we can afford to give him the car demonstrates that we are even wealthier than he thought. Chances are that the only thing that will end the envier's envy is our own ruin-ation, at which time he will switch from envying us to pitying us or even despising us.

German sociologist Helmut Schoeck did an exhaustive study of envy. He found that "envy is much more universal than has so far been admitted or even realized,"[33] but although envy is ubiquitous, it is largely invisible. Indeed, it is perhaps the best disguised of all human emotions. According to La Rochefoucauld, "we often pride ourselves on even the most criminal passions, but envy is a timid and shamefaced passion we never dare acknowledge."[34] Or, in the words of Herman Melville, "Though many an arraigned mortal has in hopes of mitigated penalty pleaded guilty to horrible actions, did ever anybody seriously confess to envy? Something there is in it universally felt to be more shameful than even felonious crime."[35] Thus, someone whose envy drives him to commit murder is subsequently more likely to confess to the murder than to the envy that triggered it.

In his research, Schoeck looked hard for cases in which "the envious man . . . admits publicly to his own envy and confesses that he has harmed another person from that motive." He could find only one such case![36] (Schoeck, we should note, did his research on envy in the 1960s, when people were much less willing publicly to admit personal flaws than they are today.) Schoeck's conclusion: "Envy does not explain everything, but it throws light on more things than people have hitherto been prepared to admit or even to see."[37] Fail to appreciate envy, and we will fail to understand many aspects of human behavior.

This brings our discussion of the secret life of desire to an end. The reader should by now appreciate the extent to which we don't control our desires, but they control us. Indeed, we tend to have the least control over those desires that have the greatest impact on our lives: we get to choose what cereal we have for breakfast, for example, but not whether and with whom we fall in love. The reader should also appreciate the extent to which what we want is determined by our desire to gain social status: if we were the last person on earth, our desires would be dramatically different.

To gain further insight into why we form the desires we do, let us now turn our attention to what science has to say about our desires. In Part Two of this book, I will first map out the structure of desire and introduce some terminology that I think will facilitate our discussions. I will then examine the sources of desire, the psychology of desire, and the evolutionary process by which we gained the ability to desire.

Starting with the next chapter, then, readers will notice a change in the tone of this book. Some readers might wish that I dispensed with the science of desire and instead got on with advice on mastering desire. Rest assured that this advice is forthcoming, in Part Three. In the meantime, I think anyone wishing to master desire would do well to take a look at what science tells us about it. After all, to defeat the enemy—in this case, undesirable desires—we need to understand the enemy, and the information provided by science, though incomplete and doubtless mistaken in some respects, is the best we have.

# PART TWO

# THE SCIENCE OF DESIRE

> It is far easier to stifle a first desire than to satisfy all
> the ensuing ones.
>
> —La Rochefoucauld

# THREE

# Mapping Our Desires

We can categorize our desires according to why we want what we want. Sometimes we want something not for its own sake but so we can fulfill some other desire. For example, I might drive to a restaurant not because I enjoy driving—my car is fifteen years old, and its radio no longer works—but because I want to eat dinner. Indeed, if I didn't want to eat, I would have no desire at all to drive to the restaurant. Let us refer to desires that are desired so we can fulfill some other desire as *instrumental* desires.

Our desires can't all be instrumental. Suppose I want A because I want B, which I want because I want C, which I want because I want D, and so on. This chain of desires can be very long, but it must finally end in something I want for its own sake. Otherwise, there will be an infinite regress of desire, and the whole chain of desires will be unmotivated. (Analogously, consider a chain of paper clips: the bottom clip is supported by the one above it, which is supported by the one above it, and so on, but at some point, there must be a clip that is supported by something other than another clip; otherwise, the whole chain would fall to the ground.) Thus, besides instrumental desires, there must be what we shall refer to as *terminal* desires. These are things we want for their own sake and not for the sake of something else. They are things we desire intrinsically (and for this reason are sometimes called intrinsic desires).[1]

If someone asks why I want to drive to the above-mentioned restaurant, I will answer, "Because I want dinner." If someone asks why I want dinner, I will answer, "Because I want my hunger pangs to end." My wanting to drive to the restaurant and to eat dinner are, in this case, examples of instrumental desires: I want these things not for their own sake but so that I can fulfill some other desire. Now suppose someone asks why I want my hunger pangs to end. The best I can do by way of answering this foolish question is to point out that hunger pangs feel bad. And if someone goes on to ask me why I want to avoid feeling bad, there is nothing I can say, except to offer the obviously circular reply, "Because it feels bad to feel bad, and I want not to feel bad. Things that feel bad are intrinsically undesirable." If my questioner doesn't already understand this, nothing I can say will convince him. My wanting my hunger pangs to end is therefore an example of a terminal desire. It is something I want for its own sake, and not because getting it will enable me to fulfill some other desire.

My terminal desires can further be divided into two subcategories, those that are hedonic and those that aren't. My desire that my hunger pangs end is an example of a *hedonic* terminal desire. More generally, the desires I form to feel good or avoid feeling bad are hedonic, and here I mean "feel good" and "feel bad" in a broad sense, to include not just physical feelings, such

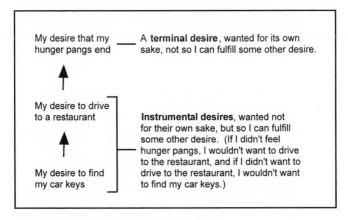

Figure 1. A Chain of Desire

as the pleasurable feeling of satiety at the end of a meal or the pain of hunger, but mental feelings, such as the experience of joy or humiliation.

For an example of a *nonhedonic* terminal desire, consider the desire to click my tongue that I formed and acted on a moment ago. This desire was terminal because I formed it not so that I could fulfill some other desire but for its own sake, and it was nonhedonic because I formed it "just because"—I clicked my tongue not because I thought doing so would feel good or not doing so would feel bad, but simply because I wanted to click it. As philosopher Harry Frankfurt points out, there are things I can do just because I make up my mind to do them: "Desires of this sort," he says, "are not aroused in us; they are formed or constructed by acts of will that we ourselves perform." He adds that we are capable of forming these desires "quite apart from any emotional or affective state."[2]

Having said this, some clarification is in order. To begin with, if I had clicked my tongue because of some strange obsession—if, for example, I feel unaccountably anxious when I go a full minute without clicking it—then my desire to click my tongue will no longer count as a nonhedonic terminal desire. For one thing, it won't be a terminal desire: it will instead be instrumental, since I want to click my tongue not for its own sake but so that I can fulfill another desire—namely, to make my unpleasant feeling of anxiety go away. And because this other desire is hedonic, my desire to click my tongue will also be (indirectly) hedonic. In this case, I won't be clicking my tongue "just because"; I will be clicking it because I want to feel better. Likewise, if I click my tongue to win a bet, my desire to click it won't count as a nonhedonic terminal desire: to the contrary, I want to click it because I want to experience the pleasure of winning the bet.

Suppose someone tells us she wants to donate a kidney to a complete stranger whose kidneys have just failed. Is this an example of a nonhedonic terminal desire? It depends on her motivation for forming this desire. If she formed it because she wants others to admire her or wants to feel good about herself, this will be another example of an indirectly hedonic instrumental desire. Suppose, on the other hand, she formed it because she wants to fulfill what she takes to be a moral duty. This raises the further question of why she wants to do her moral duty. If it is because doing her duty will win her the admiration of others, make her feel good about herself, or earn her a heavenly reward, the desire again won't count as a nonhedonic terminal desire. But if she says she wants to do her moral duty because she has simply made up her mind to do it, this desire, like my desire to click my tongue, will count as a nonhedonic terminal desire.

Notice that, as desires go, nonhedonic terminal desires are relatively unmotivated. Thus, contrast my desire to click my tongue "just because" with my desire, when I have missed dinner, that my hunger pangs end. I am unlikely to go to great lengths to click my tongue, and if something or someone stops me from clicking it—my wife, for example, might ask me to stop making that bothersome clicking noise—I might be a bit annoyed, but I will not feel intensely frustrated. But if I am experiencing hunger pangs and something or someone stops me from eating, I will be quite frustrated and will devote considerable effort and ingenuity to getting food. I do not feel driven to click my tongue the way I feel driven to relieve my hunger pangs.

My nonhedonic terminal desire to click my tongue is also less motivated than many of the instrumental desires I form. Suppose that because I want my hunger pangs to end, I want to drive to a restaurant, and that because I want to drive to a restaurant, I want to find my car keys. This last desire is instrumental: I want my car keys not for their own sake but so that I can fulfill my desire to drive to the restaurant. Nevertheless, it will be a highly motivated desire—indeed, almost as highly motivated as my desire to make my hunger pangs go away. If I cannot find my car keys, I will become deeply frustrated.

To summarize, our desires fall into two categories: instrumental desires that we desire for the sake of something else, and terminal desires that we desire for their own sake. Our terminal desires can in turn be divided into two subcategories: hedonic terminal desires, which we desire because we want to feel good or avoid feeling bad, and nonhedonic terminal

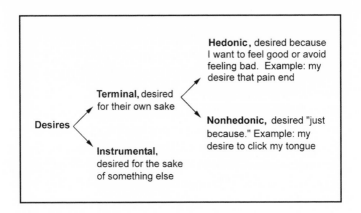

Figure 2. The Taxonomy of Desire

desires. Our hedonic terminal desires are motivated by our feelings; our nonhedonic terminal desires, on the other hand, are motivated by our willpower.

We can, with some effort, map our desires. (Figure 1 contains a very simple example of such a map.) Sometimes in the classes I teach, I demonstrate the mapping process. I pick a student at random and ask why he chose to attend my lecture. A typical response: "So I can pass your class." And why does he want to pass? "So I can graduate." Why graduate? "So I can get into law school." Why go to law school? "So I can become a lawyer, obviously." And why become a lawyer? "So I can buy an Arrest-Me Red Dodge Viper RT/10, with a 415 horsepower engine that will go from 0 to 60 in 5.0 seconds."

If we mapped the above student's desires, they would form a chain, the top link of which is his desire to own a Dodge

Viper, below which is his desire to become a lawyer, below which is his desire to go to law school, below which is his desire to graduate from college, and so on. Chains of desire can be quite complex. It is possible, for example, for the chain just mentioned to branch out below a given link. The above student is probably taking classes other than mine, and if asked why he is taking them, he would answer, "So I can graduate." Consequently, in our map of this student's desires, several desires will be directly below his desire to graduate—namely, his desires to pass the various classes he is currently taking. And in the same way as his desire to pass my class has a chain of desire below it, his desires to pass these other classes will have chains of desire below them.

It is also possible for chains of desire to interlock. This happens when a single instrumental desire does double duty—when fulfilling it will help a person fulfill two other desires. Consider again the student's desire to attend my class. As we have seen, he wants to attend because he wants to pass my class. It could also be, though, that he wants to attend because a fellow student in whom he has a romantic interest also attends my class. (We can suppose that when I asked this student why he wanted to attend my class, he neglected to mention this second motivation because he didn't want to embarrass the object of his affections.) In this case the student, in attending my class, is working on *two* chains of desire: one leads to ownership of a Dodge Viper, and the other leads to the affections of a fellow student. These two chains happen to interlock at his desire to attend my lecture.

We stopped mapping the above student's desires when we got to his desire for a Dodge Viper, but we can go further. Suppose I ask him why he wants a Viper. He might look at me in astonishment: to him it is obvious why such a car is desirable. But if pressed, he might tell me that it would give him a great deal of pleasure to drive such a car. If I ask why he wants to experience pleasure, he can't say much: pleasure is inherently desirable. This chain of desire, like all chains of desire, will end in a terminal desire—in something he wants for its own sake, and not so he can fulfill some other desire. This chain happens to end in a hedonic terminal desire; other chains will end in nonhedonic terminal desires.

The above-described student doubtless has desires other than the ones we have discussed. Each of these can give rise to chains of desire that in turn will branch out and interlock. For this reason, the structure of human desire is enormously complex. Furthermore, any attempt to map our desires will be frustrated by their changeability: a person's desires at the end of the mapping process will almost certainly be different than they were at the beginning. (Indeed, the process of asking a person repeated why-questions in order to map his desires will probably bring a new desire into existence—that we stop pestering him with why-questions.)

Even if we could overcome these problems and construct a map of someone's desires, it probably wouldn't be reliable: as we shall see in Chapter 5, people's answers to our why-questions aren't entirely trustworthy, inasmuch as people often don't really know why they want what they want. Furthermore, such a map would be of theoretical interest only. Certainly the person whose desires we mapped would not need to consult our map in order to make decisions. Nor does he need to keep a copy of the map in his head. All he needs is to keep a few basic desires in mind. By referring to these he can, by means of causal reasoning, generate new (instrumental) desires as circumstances require.

If we take a census of our desires, we will find that the vast majority of the desires we form are instrumental. Most of the time, we are working toward some goal, and for this reason we form desires, the fulfillment of which will enable us to reach that goal. As I sit here, for example, my overriding goal is to write this book. As a result, I form an ongoing stream of desires to write certain sentences, to read certain books, and so on. Interspersed with these instrumental desires are occasional terminal desires, including the hedonic terminal desire, when lunchtime draws near, to put an end to the hunger pangs I am experiencing and the nonhedonic terminal desire to pause in my writing to click my tongue or tap my fingers.

Because hedonic terminal desires are highly motivated, they typically give rise to far more instrumental desires than nonhedonic terminal desires do. For this reason, when we examine the desires we form in the course of a day, we find that they tend to be links on chains of desire that terminate in hedonic desires.

Suppose, by way of illustration, that it is early in the morning and I am getting dressed. I put on my left shoe. Why do I want to wear it? Because it feels better to wear shoes than not to wear them, particularly in winter. Thus, my desire to wear shoes is an indirectly hedonic instrumental desire. Now suppose that after I have put on my left shoe, I realize that I got the wrong right shoe out of the closet. At this point, the easiest thing to do would be to put on the nonmatching right shoe. (Doing this, after all, would fulfill my desire to wear shoes.) Chances are, though, that I will not put on the right shoe but will instead form a desire to go to the closet and get the shoe that matches the one I have on. At first it might seem as though this last desire is nonhedonic, but when we analyze my motivations, we will find that it is. Why, after all, do I want to wear matching shoes? Because if I wear mismatched shoes, I will experience humiliation when other people see what I have done. I want to wear matching shoes because I want to avoid humiliation, and I want to avoid humiliation because it feels bad. Thus, my desire to go to the closet to get the matching right shoe is another example of an indirectly hedonic instrumental desire.

If we similarly analyze the other desires we form in the course of a day, we will find that most of them are hedonic. Some, including my desire that my hunger pangs end, are directly hedonic; others, such as my desire to wear matching shoes, are indirectly hedonic. Because they outnumber and are more highly motivated than our nonhedonic desires, our hedonic desires will have a far greater impact on our lives than our nonhedonic desires do. Someone's nonhedonic terminal desire to click his tongue will have little impact on his life; his hedonic terminal desire to experience sexual pleasure, by way of contrast, can have a huge impact. Because he has this desire, he will go to great lengths to make himself attractive to members of the opposite sex. Likewise, his hedonic terminal desire to avoid hunger pangs means that he will go to great lengths to keep a certain bank balance. Indeed, if sex didn't feel good and starvation didn't feel bad, he would form far fewer instrumental desires than he currently does, and as a result, his life would be rather simpler than it is.

Imagine a person incapable of feeling good or bad. This person would never form hedonic terminal desires. To the contrary, the only desires he would be capable of forming would be nonhedonic desires, such as a desire to click his tongue. This person, it should be clear, would be quite unmotivated. He would not feel compelled to eat, to care for himself, or to seek companionship, fame, or fortune. He would resemble a deeply depressed individual. Unless others looked after him, he would soon perish.

If, however, a person is capable of enjoying sex or experiencing hunger pangs, he is likely to form corresponding terminal desires, and having formed them, he will form instrumental desires, fulfillment of which will enable him to enjoy sex and avoid hunger. Furthermore, he will feel highly motivated to fulfill the instrumental desires he forms. His days will therefore be full of activity. As we will see in Chapter 6, nature has wired us so that some things feel good and some things feel bad, and as a result, we are not only active but active in a way that increases the chance that we survive and reproduce.

How do desires form within us? To better understand the desire formation process, consider again the above pre-law student. Suppose he visits his academic adviser. The adviser looks at the courses he has taken and offers some advice: "You'll have to take Professor Irvine's logic course if you want to graduate." Up until this moment, the student probably had no desire to take my logic course; indeed, he might have had a desire not to take it, having heard how difficult logic is. But now he forms a new desire—to take my logic course in the coming quarter. When the adviser informs him that the course is already filled to capacity and that, unless I am willing to sign him in, he will have to wait to take it, thereby delaying his graduation, the student's desire to get into my course becomes intense. Soon the student is at my door, begging me to sign him into my logic class. "I really, really want to get in," he implores, and after a pause he adds, disingenuously, "because I hear it's a great class."

In this case, the desire formation process is admirably rational: given his desire to graduate from college, it makes perfect sense for him, as soon as he realizes that the only way he can fulfill this goal is to take my logic course, to want to take it. Furthermore, the desire in question is formed consciously—in broad daylight, as it were. If asked, the student can easily recount the steps involved in the formation of this desire.

In other cases, the desire formation process is rather more mysterious. Suppose that after I sign him into my class—would I turn away a student who thinks my class is great?—the student goes home and lies down to relax and watch some television. Even though he is at rest, the process of desire formation continues apace. Although he just finished lunch an hour ago and isn't particularly hungry, he finds himself thinking about the donuts in the kitchen. Soon he gets up and eats not just one of them but half a dozen. He returns to the couch and is again resting comfortably when he realizes that rather than paying attention to television, he is thinking about a girl he knows: "Wouldn't it be nice," he says to himself, "if she would go out with me? And wouldn't it be even nicer if she would go to bed with me?" Then his thoughts turn to his summer employment prospects: it looks as though he will once again be a lifeguard at the local swimming pool. His roommate, on the other hand, has lined up a high-paying internship at the company owned by his father. (This same roommate *already* owns a Dodge Viper: his father gave it to him as a high-school graduation present.) Before he knows it, the student is in the grip of an envy attack: he finds himself fantasizing that his roommate's father's company goes bankrupt and that the roommate is forced to sell his Viper and work this summer selling snacks and cleaning toilets at the local swimming pool.

The process by which the student formed the above desires is clearly different from the process by which he formed a desire to take my logic class. He didn't so much *decide* that he wanted to eat donuts, to date a certain girl, and to see his roommate in humbled circumstances as *discover* these desires within him. Indeed, he might tell us that he wishes he didn't want donuts, inasmuch as he has been trying to lose weight lately; that he wishes he didn't want to date the girl, inasmuch as she is his roommate's girlfriend (all the more reason, by the way, to envy the roommate); and that he wishes he didn't want to see his roommate in humbled circumstances, since this is an unchristian thing to want and he is trying to be a better Christian. Nevertheless, these desires are indisputably and annoyingly present within him, and he must deal with them. In a sense, then, *he* didn't form these desires, not consciously and voluntarily, at any rate; instead, they foisted themselves on him. He is at a loss to explain how they got there and is relatively powerless to make them go away.

What soon becomes clear when we consider cases such as this is that if we want to live the life of our choosing, rather than allowing our destinies to be determined by desires we did not choose to have, we need to learn how to control the desire-formation process, and to this end, we need to develop an understanding of why we form the desires we do. Let us, therefore, turn our attention to an investigation of the sources of desire within us.

Man often thinks he is in control when he is being controlled, and while his mind is striving in one direction his heart is imperceptibly drawing him in another.

—La Rochefoucauld

# FOUR

# The Wellsprings of Desire

What is the source of our desires? Think again about the student described in the previous chapter. He wanted donuts, and at the same time he wanted not to want them. Because a person's desires can conflict, there is reason to think we have multiple sources of desire within us, sources that can disagree about the desirability of something.

What are these multiple sources of desire? It is hard to say, but let me offer a theory of desire formation based on the writings of philosopher David Hume. The theory in question is rudimentary, and my fellow philosophers will doubtless take issue with it. (Indeed, it is entirely possible that even Hume would find it wanting.) The theory I am about to describe nevertheless merits our attention for a pair of reasons: it is easy to comprehend, and although it doesn't explain everything about how we form desires, it explains a lot.

One source of desires is our emotions—Hume called them the passions. The emotions, I would like to suggest, are the source of our hedonic terminal desires—our desires to feel good and avoid feeling bad. (I am again using "feel good" and "feel bad" in a broad sense, to include not only physical pleasure and pain but also things that are mentally pleasant, such as the feeling of joy, or mentally unpleasant, such as feelings of anxiety or humiliation.) Things that feel good are inherently desirable; otherwise, we wouldn't describe them as feeling good. Likewise, things that feel bad are inherently undesirable. This means that when asked why they want what they want, the emotions always have a ready answer: "It is desirable because it feels good," or "It is undesirable because it feels bad." This also means that the desires formed by the emotions will be terminal desires: the emotions want to feel good for the sake of feeling good, not so they can fulfill some other desire.

Although they are expert at forming terminal desires, the emotions are thickheaded when it comes to forming instrumental desires, the fulfillment of which will enable them to fulfill their terminal desires. Fortunately for us, though, we have within us a second source of desire: our intellect. (Hume called it reason.) The intellect is skilled in the formation of instrumental desires. This is what happened when the student described in the previous chapter was informed that he needed to take my logic class in order to graduate. He quickly formed an instrumental desire to take my class. It is a desire that his intellect will have no trouble justifying. Why did he want to get into my logic class? Because he wants to graduate.

Now consider the above student's sudden craving for donuts. According to my theory of desire formation, something like the following happened. The student's emotions formed a hedonic terminal desire to experience pleasure—in particular, to experience the gustatory sensations to be derived from eating something sweet and fattening. His intellect not only concurred in the desirability of this but quickly pointed out that donuts were available in the kitchen; indeed, so quick was the intellect in its response to the emotions that the two desires I have described might seem like one. Nevertheless, these desires are clearly separable. If the emotions had not formed a desire to experience pleasure, it is unlikely that the student's intellect would have formed a desire to go to the kitchen and eat donuts. (The student, it will be remembered, had just finished lunch and was resting comfortably when the craving for donuts struck him; he therefore had no reason to eat donuts.) Likewise, if the student's intellect had not known that there were donuts in the kitchen, it is unlikely that his desire to experience pleasure would have triggered in him a specific desire for donuts.

Readers who are skeptical about this account of how the student came to want donuts are encouraged to pay attention to their own desires. The next time you develop a sudden craving, think about what just happened. You will notice the presence within you of something that periodically tempts you, in a low whisper, with possibilities for pleasure: "Wouldn't sex feel good right now? Wouldn't drunkenness feel good?" Sometimes you act on these suggestions. Other times you either dismiss a suggestion or you act on it, even though at some other level you don't want to act on it. What you are witnessing, in these last cases, is the battle between your emotions—which, I think, are the source of these whispered suggestions—and your intellect. Unless you are an exceptional individual, your intellect all too often ends up losing these battles.

Although the forte of the intellect is the formation of instrumental desires, it can also form terminal desires: my intellect, I would like to suggest, is the source of my nonhedonic terminal desire to click my tongue. Notice, however, that my intellect will have a hard time justifying the terminal desires it forms. In particular, it cannot say it formed the desire to click my tongue because doing so would feel good. My intellect will be unable to come up with anything more profound, by way of justifying my desire to click my tongue, than a feeble "I just wanted to." Indeed, my intellect could as easily have formed the opposite desire—to keep my tongue still—and it knows it. For this reason, nonhedonic terminal desires tend to be pale, insubstantial things.

The desires formed by emotions, by way of contrast, are highly motivated. (The words *emotion* and *motivate* derive from the Latin *movere,* meaning "to move.") If we fail to fulfill these desires, we will pay a price: we will either feel bad or forgo an opportunity to feel good. Therefore, we typically feel driven to fulfill the desires formed by our emotions.

Chains of desire, then, are formed cooperatively by the emotions and the intellect. They divide the labor of desire formation, with the emotions specializing in the formation of terminal desires and the intellect specializing in the formation of instrumental desires; and in forming terminal desires, the emotions are concerned with feeling good and avoiding feeling bad. Something like this view can be found in Hume, who tells us that it is "from the prospect of pain or pleasure that the aversion or propensity arises toward any object: And these emotions extend themselves to the causes and effects of that object, as they are pointed out to us by reason and experience."[1]

My intellect and emotions often work in tandem. Generally when my emotions form a terminal desire—say, that my hunger pangs end—my intellect will quickly form an instrumental desire—to eat lunch—fulfillment of which will cause my hunger pangs to end. And when my intellect has formed this instrumental desire, my emotions will generally put their stamp of approval on it. Because they do, I will feel quite frustrated (frustration being an emotional state) if something or someone obstructs my efforts to fulfill the instrumental desire I have formed.

In other cases, the emotions form a terminal desire at the prompting of the intellect. My emotions don't need help from my intellect to realize that hunger pangs feel bad and consequently to form a desire that these pangs end. But suppose someone walks up to me and says something. My emotions will sit there calmly until my intellect points out that these words, uttered by this person under these circumstances, count as an insult. I will thereupon experience a painful feeling of humiliation, followed by anger, with the emotions being the source of both these feelings. Notice that if the same or an even worse insult was delivered in a language my intellect does not comprehend, my emotions would not be aroused.

The cooperation between the emotions and the intellect, although considerable, is not perfect: as we have seen, they sometimes disagree about the desirability of things. The relationship between the intellect and the emotions can best be viewed as an uneasy alliance. To better understand this relationship, it is useful to think about how laws are made in a bicameral legislature. Legislation that originates in one chamber might or might not subsequently be approved by the other. Similarly, the emotions might approve or reject desires formed by the intellect, and conversely.

Consider first cases in which my intellect wants something but my emotions object. My intellect, for example, might want to cross the country by airliner because it is the safest, most convenient way to do so. But if I have a fear of flying, my emotions will object, and if they object strongly enough, I will find it impossible even to set foot aboard an airliner.

Because my emotions can veto them, the terminal desires my intellect gets to form and act on tend to be inconsequential. My emotions will, for example, stand by idly and let my intellect form and act on a desire to click my tongue. But they won't likewise stand by if my intellect forms a desire to pierce my tongue with a thumbtack (since doing so would cause me pain) or to use my tongue to insult the mean-looking, muscular fellow who just rode up on a motorcycle (since doing so would probably cause me more pain still).

There is a simple experiment you can do if you want to witness the veto power possessed by your emotions: hold your breath. Your desire to hold it, under these circumstances, is a nonhedonic terminal desire formed by your intellect. At first your emotions will stand by and let you act on this desire. But after thirty seconds they will begin to protest, and after a full minute they will shout at you to put an end to the burning sensation you feel in your lungs. Before long, your emotions will win the battle: your intellect will capitulate, and you will again breathe.

In other cases, although the emotions don't veto a desire formed by the intellect, they fail to lend their support to it and thereby undermine it. Intellectually, we know what we need to do with our lives, and we set goals accordingly—to swim ten miles each week, to write a page a day, to learn to play the banjo, to terminate a relationship that is causing us grief. But unless our emotions cooperate, unless they commit to the goals our intellect sets, it is unlikely that we will accomplish these goals: our heart won't be in it, and a mind operating without the support of a heart is singularly impotent. And notice that the intellect cannot command the emotions to commit. Emotional commitment has a life of its own: it either happens or it doesn't.

In earlier chapters, I suggested that we tend to have the least control over those desires that have the greatest impact on our lives. We may be able to choose which cereal we have for breakfast, but we cannot likewise choose whether and with whom we fall in love. This is because our emotions are relatively indifferent to our breakfast menu but care very much about whether and with whom we have sex. (And even when we make a trivial decision, such as what cereal to have for breakfast, our emotions are at work: the cereal I choose will be determined, to a considerable extent, by things over which I have no control, such as my mood—I did not choose to be in the mood for cereal, I just am—and my cereal preferences—I did not choose to like a particular brand of cereal, I just do.)

The emotions, then, can effectively veto desires formed by the intellect. Does the intellect likewise have veto power over desires formed by the emotions? Often it doesn't: think about someone acting in a blind rage. But sometimes, if our willpower is sufficiently strong, our intellect can override desires formed by our emotions. The intellect's best strategy for dealing with the emotions is to use emotions to fight emotions. The intellect might point out, for example, that what the emotions want would in fact feel bad, that what they want may feel good now but will feel bad later, or that although what they want would feel good, there is something else that would feel even better. The intellect can also help sort through conflicting emotions and determine which will be acted on and which won't. The emotions are perfectly willing to listen to the intellect as long as the intellect isn't trying to impose its views but is merely trying to help the emotions get what they want.

The intellect can also use emotions not to fight emotions but to arouse them. Artificial intelligence researcher Marvin Minsky, for example, describes a situation in which he is having trouble concentrating on his research. In order to stay focused, he imagines that a competing researcher is on the verge of solving the problem Minsky is trying to solve. The trick works: Minsky stays focused even though he knows, intellectually, that the other researcher is unlikely to solve the problem, inasmuch as he has never shown the least interest in it.[2] Thus, although the intellect cannot command the emotions to commit to one of its projects, it might be able to trick them into committing.

The intellect has the greatest power over the emotions when it was responsible for triggering a particular emotion. Consider again the case in which my intellect informs my emotions that I have just been insulted, and I subsequently experience a flash of anger. Because my intellect played a key role in forming this desire, it retains the ability to extinguish it. Suppose, for example, someone says, within my hearing, "Irvine is a bad philosopher." I might feel insulted and hurt, but if I subsequently discover that she said not that I am a *bad* philosopher but that I am a *baaad* philosopher—meaning, in slang, that I am a good philosopher—my anger will quickly subside. Likewise, consider cases in which my intellect forms an instrumental desire and my emotions subsequently commit to that desire: suppose that because I am experiencing hunger pangs, my intellect forms an instrumental desire to go to a certain restaurant and my emotions quickly concur in the desirability of going there. If my intellect subsequently discovers that it was mistaken in forming this desire—that today is Monday and the restaurant in question is closed on Mondays—my intellect will abandon the desire, and my emotions will acquiesce.

(I mentioned above that my theory of desire formation is based on that of David Hume. Hume's own views are complex and possibly even contradictory. He tells us, on one hand, that reason alone "can never oppose passion in the direction of the will."[3] He nevertheless seems to recognize that when the emotions commit to a desire formed by the intellect, they will abandon that desire if the intellect does: "The moment we perceive the falsehood of any supposition, or the insufficiency of any means our passions yield to our reason without any opposition.")[4]

The relationship between the intellect and the emotions is therefore asymmetrical. Although the emotions have veto power over the intellect, in most cases the intellect has only the power of persuasion in its dealings with the emotions, and it can persuade them only if it can invoke a stronger emotion than the one it wants to suppress. Conversely, the intellect can form a desire, but if the emotions don't commit, the resulting desire will be feeble. And if the emotions object, the resulting desire will be stillborn.

Why does the intellect play second fiddle to the emotions? Why, in battles between the emotions and the intellect, do the emotions generally win? For the simple reason that they refuse to fight fairly. The emotions, in their dealings with the intellect, don't use reason to gain its cooperation. Instead, they wear it down with—what else?—emotional entreaties. They beg, whine, and bully. They won't take no for an answer. They won't give the intellect a moment's peace. In most cases, the best the intellect can hope for is to withstand these entreaties for a spell. Then it succumbs.

Our emotions are also capable of incapacitating our intellect by clogging our mind with intrusive thoughts. Our emotions might, for example, fill our mind with the recurring image of the person with whom we are infatuated, or if not that, with a recurring anxiety or a recurring thirst for an alcoholic beverage. Because of these intrusive thoughts, our intellect is simply too distracted to string together a coherent argument against the desire formed by the emotions: we can no longer think straight. If it wishes to regain its ability to function, the intellect has little choice but to capitulate.

The relationship between the intellect and the emotions is like the relationship between parents and their headstrong five-year-old. Such a child knows what he wants, and he will demand, whine, and whimper until he gets it. So it is with our emotions. When we are trying to lose weight, they will scream: "I don't care about any damn diet. I want chocolate!" If our intellect denies their request, our emotions might start whining—and might keep whining for hours. Likewise, when we are publicly insulted, our intellect might shrug it off, but our emotions, like a headstrong five-year-old, will complain that so-and-so called us a name. If our intellect tries to comfort our emotions with a bit of playground Stoicism—"Sticks and stones can break your bones, but names can never hurt you"—our emotions are likely to interrupt it with a tantrum.

Actually, dealing with our emotions is even worse than dealing with a headstrong five-year-old. We can avoid his whining by plugging our ears or locking him in his bedroom, we can punish him in hopes of modifying his behavior, and in an extreme case we can put him up for adoption. We can do none of these things with respect to our emotions. (In particular, we can't avoid the whining of our emotions by plugging our ears, inasmuch as they do their whining inside our head.) And while the five-year-old will tire of whining after an hour or so, our emotions can carry on their whining for days, months, even years.

Notice that the presence of a whining five-year-old in their lives does not deprive parents of their freedom. They can reject the child's requests. Indeed, they can give him absolutely nothing that he wants. They can, but they will pay a price for doing so. Thus, the parents of a headstrong five-year-old remain free but, understandably, use their freedom to placate their child. The same can be said of our intellect in its relations with our emotions.

Now imagine an ultra-headstrong five-year-old, who never tires of whining, whose whining can't be avoided, and whose behavior can't be modified. The parents of such a child would quickly realize the futility of resisting the child's entreaties. They would realize that in the long run, their life will be tolerable only if they give the child what he wants most of the time and save their energy for a few well-chosen battles. These parents will quickly get into the habit of saying yes to their child. Indeed, so quickly will they say yes that we—and maybe they as well—might forget that they have the power to say no.

Something like this happens with the intellect. It can't avoid the whining of the emotions and can't hope to modify their behavior. The intellect quickly figures out that the only sensible way—indeed, the rational way—to deal with the emotions is to unhesitatingly give them what they want most of the time and thereby conserve its strength so it can fight and win the battles that really matter—namely, to overcome the most undesirable of those desires generated by the emotions.

Here is another analogy that illuminates the relationship between the intellect and the emotions. The emotions are like a decadent voluptuary whose body has been bloated and whose brain has been addled by years of dissolute living. He doesn't know much, but he knows what he wants—namely, to feel good and avoid feeling bad. The intellect, on the other hand, plays the role of lackey to this voluptuary. The voluptuary sits there all day forming an incessant stream of desires: "I want women. I want whiskey." The lackey is himself indifferent to these things but is very good at devising strategies by which he can obtain them for the voluptuary.

If the voluptuary nods off, the lackey is at a loss for things to do. Although he is very good at carrying out the wishes of the voluptuary—doing so is his raison d'être—he has a hard time figuring out what, if anything, he wants for himself. The lackey sits there trying to think of something he wants, but before he has come to a conclusion, the voluptuary awakens and starts shouting out new demands. The lackey heaves a sigh of relief.

The lackey will sometimes try to reason with the voluptuary and talk him out of what he says he wants. Suppose, for example, the voluptuary demands whiskey. If the lackey replies that the voluptuary has already had a lot to drink, the voluptuary will be unfazed: he will simply gaze at the lackey with clouded eyes and repeat the demand. If the lackey ignores him, the voluptuary might start chanting, "Whiskey! Whiskey!" until the lackey can't take it anymore. A better strategy for the lackey, if he wants the voluptuary to forgo whiskey, is to point out that if he drinks any more, he won't be able to enjoy the women who will later be arriving for his amusement. This reminder might make the voluptuary drop his demand for whiskey.

The picture just presented is, to be sure, a caricature: most of us aren't decadent voluptuaries. Some would suggest that this proves we aren't ruled by the hedonic terminal desires formed by our emotions. I would argue, to the contrary, that it proves no such thing. Notice, after all, that our desire for social status is itself a hedonic desire formed by our emotions: we seek social status because it feels good when others admire us and feels bad when they despise us. It is in part because we find this desire within us that we don't live dissolute lives: what would the neighbors think if we spent our days in hedonistic excess?

Although our emotions dominate our intellect, it might seem, to the casual observer, as if our intellect has the upper hand. Most of our desires, after all, are instrumental, and since instrumental desires are formed by the intellect, it follows that most of our desires are formed by our intellect. Someone might cite this as proof of the dominance of our intellect, but in this case, appearances are misleading.

If we examine our instrumental desires, we will find, as we saw in the previous chapter, that the majority of them belong to chains of desire, the terminal member of which is a desire formed by the emotions. The instrumental desires in these chains may indeed have been formed by the intellect, but in forming them the intellect was doing the bidding of the emotions: it was helping them fulfill some hedonic terminal desire. Had the emotions not formed the terminal desire in question, none of the associated instrumental desires would have been formed by the intellect.

The supporting role played by the intellect becomes apparent when a person is mentally depressed. Those who slip into depression are just as intelligent as they used to be. (If their score drops on an IQ test, it is because they don't feel motivated to take the test, not because they became less rational.) But because of their depressed state, the flow of terminal desires formed by their emotions slows to a trickle. They no longer feel like eating, having sex, listening to music, or going to parties. In such cases, the intellect doesn't generate terminal desires to take up the slack. Rather, it sits there idle. If the emotions formed terminal desires, the intellect would gladly form appropriate instrumental desires; but in the absence of a steady flow of terminal desires generated by the emotions, the intellect, like the lackey described above, doesn't know what to do with itself.

Depressed individuals rarely respond to logic. We can argue that they should eat or get out of bed. They might agree with us that it would be in their best interests to do so, but because their emotions are incapacitated, they no longer feel compelled to do what is in their best interests. A depressed individual is still capable of forming nonhedonic terminal desires (such as my desire to click my tongue), but as I have noted, such desires are pale, insubstantial things compared to the robust desires formed by the emotions. These latter desires are potent enough to make us get out of bed and do all the things necessary to survive and thrive; terminal desires formed by the intellect generally aren't.

Consider again the pre-law student described in the previous chapter who wants, eventually, to buy a Dodge Viper. Suppose it is early in the morning. As this student lies in bed trying to decide whether to attend my class or sleep in, various thoughts will run through his mind. He knows he would enjoy driving a

Viper, but this enjoyment will come years from now—if it comes at all, there being no guarantee that his career ambitions will be successful. Sleeping in not only feels good but feels good now and is a "sure thing."

The student might succumb to these thoughts were it not for other, contrary thoughts running through his mind: "Yes, it is comfortable lying here, but what are the consequences of not attending lecture? Maybe Professor Irvine will notice my absence and hold it against me. Maybe I will miss important material and have trouble on the upcoming test, which in turn might affect my course grade. Maybe a lower course grade will undermine my chances of getting into law school—as will the slightly weaker letter of recommendation Professor Irvine might write because of my repeated absences." The student will experience these and other anxieties as he lies there in bed. He knows he can allay these unpleasant feelings by getting up and going to class—and so he does.

(I would argue, by the way, that the emotions are the source of these anxieties. Besides tempting us with possibilities for pleasure—"Wouldn't sex feel good right now?"—the emotions are also capable of apprehensive whispers: "Think of how bad it would feel to miss your airline flight!")

When our emotions form a terminal desire, we feel motivated to fulfill it: to do so will feel good, or at any rate, will feel better than not fulfilling it. But what about the instrumental desires our intellect forms so we can fulfill this terminal desire? Fulfillment of these instrumental desires won't itself feel good; indeed, for the pre-law student to drag himself out of bed will feel distinctly bad. More generally, although the objects of terminal desires formed by the emotions are inherently desirable, the objects of instrumental desires formed by the intellect aren't. What is it, then, that motivates us to fulfill these instrumental desires?

The intellect, as we have seen, cannot command the emotions, but it can channel currently existing emotional energy. If, for example, the emotions want X, the intellect might talk them into wanting to do Y by pointing out that doing it will get them X. As soon as the emotions are convinced that doing Y will get them X, the anxiety they felt with respect to X will transfer to Y. The intellect can then point out to the emotions that by doing Z, they can get Y; again, the anxiety will transfer. In this manner, anxiety flows down the chains of desire formed by the intellect. We thereby become motivated to fulfill the instrumental desires in these chains, even though doing so won't itself feel good—indeed, even though doing so will feel bad.

We have already encountered an example of this anxiety transfer process. Because I am experiencing hunger pangs, I form an instrumental desire to drive to a restaurant. My anxiousness to end my hunger pangs transfers: I become anxious to drive to the restaurant. And because I want to drive to the restaurant, I form a desire to find my car keys, and again my anxiety transfers. This last anxiety will be almost subliminal unless I have trouble finding my keys. Then it will spike upward, and I might turn the house upside down in an effort to find them.

Above I spoke about the emotions "committing to" a desire formed by the intellect. The commitment in question generally takes the form of attachment of a feeling of anxiety to that desire. The emotions are quite willing to do this if the desire formed by the intellect is an instrumental desire that will enable them to fulfill some terminal desire they formed, but they will be much less willing if the desire is a nonhedonic terminal desire formed by the intellect. Consider again my desire to click my tongue. It is unlikely, when I form a desire to do this, that I will experience any anxiety with respect to doing it. At any rate, the anxiety will be insignificant compared to the anxiety I experience when I am hungry and unable to find my car keys.

To appreciate how strong a motivating force anxiety can be, consider those individuals whose feelings of anxiety are out of control—namely, those with obsessive-compulsive disorder. Such individuals, driven by feelings of anxiety, might spend the day repeatedly washing their hands. Their lives have been hijacked by anxiety.

An acquaintance who is subject to a hand-washing compulsion describes it in these terms. If he hasn't washed his hands in a while, he experiences an uncomfortable feeling of tension or anxiety. He knows he can make this feeling go away by washing his hands. He also knows that after he washes them, the feeling will return. People who find out about his compulsion ask him why he can't just decide that he isn't going to wash his hands. This question misses the point. Intellectually, he knows there is no good reason for washing his hands as often as he does. But he also knows that his intellect is powerless against the feeling of anxiety he experiences. Indeed, the rational thing for him to do, given that he is subject to this anxiety and can make it go away by washing his hands, is to wash them. It is as rational as it is for him, on experiencing hunger pangs, to eat.

We might pity the person with a hand-washing compulsion, but at least there is something he can do to make his anxiety go away, if only for a time. Those subject to free-floating anxieties are not so lucky. Because anxieties are usually attached to specific desires, people know what they must do to extinguish them—satisfy the desires to which they are attached. (This is true even in the case of a hand-washing compulsion.) Free-floating anxieties, however, are not attached to any specific desire; therefore, a person experiencing a free-floating anxiety has no idea of what action on his part will quell his feeling of anxiety.

When anxieties attach themselves to the desires in a chain of desire, they play a very useful role, inasmuch as they motivate us to ascend the chain in question. But when anxieties attach themselves to desires we wish we didn't have—such as a desire to wash our hands—they become troublesome, and when they fail to attach themselves to any desire at all, they become a source of considerable distress.

If anxiety is what drives us to achieve our goals, and if we have many goals, as most people do, we should be in a constant state of anxiety—but we aren't. Most of the time, most of us are perfectly calm. How can we resolve this paradox?

People have, as we have seen, a tendency to form long-term desires that they will probably never fulfill. We want to be rich and famous, for example, even though the odds are stacked against us. But although our long-term desires may be unrealistic, the short-term desires we form tend to be utterly pragmatic. The things we want in daily living are for the most part things easily within our power to obtain. We want to check our e-mail; we turn on the computer, confident that it will display our daily mix of junk mail and messages. We want breakfast; we open the refrigerator confident that the bagels we bought will be there. We want to drive to work; we turn the key of our car, confident that it will start and confident that the roads will be open.

In those cases in which, because of circumstances beyond our control, we can't be confident of getting what we want, we typically develop a contingency plan that will enable us to get, if not exactly what we want, then something pretty close to it. A woman wanting an outdoor wedding, for example, might develop a backup plan in case there is a rainstorm on her wedding day. She might not be confident that her wedding ceremony will take place out of doors, but thanks to her contingency plan, she can be confident that the ceremony will take place.

We normally get what we want for the simple reason that, despite our insatiability with respect to the big things in life, such as fame and wealth, we are quite satiable with respect to the little things, such as having breakfast. We restrict ourselves, in everyday living, to wanting things we can be confident of obtaining. We do this in large part because we recognize that insatiability with respect to the little things in life—constantly wanting things we were unlikely to obtain—would be too painful, inasmuch as it would involve constant frustration. By restricting ourselves to wanting things within our power to obtain, we keep our daily level of frustration to a minimum.

Another reason we normally get what we want in daily living is because it is the job of our intellect to devise effective, low-risk strategies for getting what we want. Many of those who find daily living to be a constant source of frustration are in this predicament either because they lack intellectual ability or possess it but fail to make use of it.

By playing it safe in our formation of short-term desires, we spare ourselves considerable worry. But even in those cases in which we are confident of getting what we want, anxiety lurks unperceived, ready to spring into action at a moment's notice. It reveals itself if we are unexpectedly prevented from getting what we were confident of getting. Suppose, for example, that when I turn on my computer to check my e-mail, I get an error message: my computer is unwilling to let me access any of the files or programs that reside on its hard drive. I will feel frustrated—I will, that is, experience anger along with a sudden spike in my anxiety level. My wife might witness an astonishing transformation. Before sitting down at my computer, I was calm and content; after trying to turn it on, I am angry and distraught. I might even let loose a string of obscenities.

The anguish associated with frustration is often wildly disproportionate to the significance of the setback that frustrates us. Schoolyard bullies everywhere understand this. They can punch their victim but in doing so run the risk of getting caught and punished. Alternatively, they can frustrate their victim— say, by blocking a doorway or refusing to give him something he needs—and thereby cause considerable distress without laying a finger on him. But when they frustrate their victim, bullies must take care not to frustrate him too much. People can experience frustration only when they expect to get what they want. If bullies create in someone the feeling that all his efforts are doomed to fail, his frustration level will decline, and the bully's attempt to frustrate him will itself be frustrated. (Bullies also understand the anguish associated with anxiety: by making someone worry that they will punch him, they can cause almost as much misery as if they actually punch him but with much less chance of getting into trouble.)

When we form a chain of desire, there is always a chance that some of the links in the chain will be broken—that we will discover that we cannot fulfill them and thereby ascend the chain. When this happens, we experience frustration, and the feeling of frustration pushes us to find a detour around the broken link. We do this by using our intellect to forge new links in our chain—that is, we generate new instrumental desires, the fulfillment of which will enable us to circumvent the broken link and allow us once again to ascend the chain we have formed. Thus, the frustration caused by my dysfunctional computer will push me to think about other ways I can gain access to my files: I will spend hours, days, or even weeks of fairly intense intellectual effort trying to circumvent this broken link in my chain of desire.

If the feeling of anxiety is the stick that drives us up chains of desire, the feeling of success is the carrot that awaits us at the top of the chain. Consider again the pre-law student described above. Suppose that despite various setbacks, he succeeds in ascending his chain of desire: he ultimately buys a Viper and drives it off the showroom floor. He is likely to experience a double pleasure. He will, for one thing, experience the pleasure of driving the car around, which includes the pleasure that comes from accelerating quickly when the light turns green and from being an object of admiration. He will also experience a pleasurable feeling of having accomplished his goal—a feeling of success. This feeling might be considerably more intense than the pleasure he gets from accelerating quickly and being admired.

When we accomplish a long-standing and personally significant goal, we experience the rush of success. It has both a mental component (a profound feeling of well-being and perhaps a kind of giddiness) and a physical component (a feeling of tightness or fullness in our chest). Because of our success, our self-esteem will rise, and as a result, we will gain social confidence. We might now look down on people to whom we formerly kowtowed.

Success is very much like a drug: it makes you feel good; you don't know what you are missing until you experience it; once you experience it, you want more; and in your attempts to recapture that first high, you will have to resort to ever bigger "doses." And if success is like a drug, some drugs are like success: a cocaine high, I am told, very much resembles the rush of success.

Once people experience success, something strange happens. They recognize that success feels very, very good: it may not be as intense as an orgasm, but it is longer-lasting and, unlike an orgasm, is multidimensional in the way it feels good. Having recognized this, people form a new goal for themselves—to obtain the feeling of success for its own sake.

Our evolutionary ancestors who formed and successfully ascended long chains of desire were more likely to survive and reproduce than those who didn't. But in forming such chains, they exposed themselves to periodic frustration and the possibility of failure. Presumably the rush of success was an evolutionary counterbalance to these negatives: it was the carrot that induced them to plan for their future well-being by forming and working to ascend long chains of desire.

According to the above theory of desire formation, we have two sources of desire within us, our emotions and our intellect. Although the emotions and intellect can disagree about the desirability of something, they generally work in tandem: the emotions form terminal hedonic desires, and the intellect forms instrumental desires, fulfillment of which will enable the emotions to get what they want. And in order that the instrumental desires formed by the intellect not be feeble things, as was my desire to click my tongue, the emotions attach feelings of anxiety to them. In emphasizing the battle between the emotions and the intellect the above theory rings true: we have all witnessed within ourselves the battle between our heart and our head.

Let us now take a look at what science has discovered about the process of desire formation. Psychological research suggests that there are indeed multiple sources of desire within us, that many desires arise out of our unconscious mind, that the desire formation process is much less rational than one might think, and that when our emotions stop functioning, our intellect finds it hard to form desires. And as we shall see in the next chapter, this same research demonstrates that the wellsprings of desire are indeed mysterious.

> When making a decision of minor importance, I have
> always found it advantageous to consider all the pros
> and cons. In vital matters, however, such as the choice
> of a mate or a profession, the decision should come from
> the unconscious, from somewhere within ourselves.
>
> —Sigmund Freud

# FIVE

# The Psychology of Desire

The choices we make typically reflect our desires: we choose
what, all things considered, we want. According to the conventional view, the process by which we make choices is rational. We consider the pros and cons of a particular choice or
maybe even do a more formal cost-benefit analysis. After weighing our options, we choose. For the most part, it is a process
carried out in our conscious mind.

A growing body of evidence suggests, however, that many
of our choices are not made in this fashion. *We* do not make
them, if by "we" is meant our conscious minds. To the contrary, the choices are made unconsciously, and it is only after
they have been made "for us" that we are informed of them, at
which point we put our stamp of approval on them.

For evidence in support of this claim, we can turn to the work
of experimental neurologists. Joaquim Brasil-Neto and his

colleagues, for example, appear to have created desires in people.[1] Subjects' heads were placed in a transcranial magnetic stimulator, which made a clicking noise and randomly stimulated the motor area on one or the other side of a subject's brain. Subjects were asked to move, at their discretion, either their left or right index finger when they heard the click. Subjects thought *they* were deciding which finger to move, but 80 percent of the time they moved the finger opposite the side of the brain that was stimulated. This meant that scientists could predict which finger a subject would "choose" to raise with 80 percent accuracy. In this experiment, magnetic stimulation apparently affected brain processes of which subjects were unaware and thereby caused them to want to move a particular finger. In other words, investigators influenced a subject's choice without disrupting the subject's feeling that the choice was voluntary.

For even more striking evidence of the unconscious control of conscious choice, consider the work of neuroscientist Benjamin Libet. He wired people to detect electrical activity in their brains and instructed them to initiate a voluntary motion—a flick of the wrist—at a time of their choosing. Libet recorded what took place in their brains before, during, and after the decision to move was made.

We would naturally expect the decision to flick one's wrist to precede the resulting flick, since it takes time for the signal to get from the brain to the wrist and for the muscle to contract, and this is what Libet found: on average, a person's wrist flicked 200 milliseconds after the person decided to flick it. What is striking is that Libet detected a buildup of activity in a person's brain 350–400 milliseconds *before* the person "decided" to flick his wrist—that is, before the person was consciously aware that he was going to flick his wrist. This makes it look as though the desire to flick began in the unconscious brain, which started preparing for the move and, after about a third of a second, informed the conscious brain of its decision. In other words, it wasn't the conscious decision to flick a wrist that caused it to flick; instead, a deeper mental event first caused the person to "choose" to flick his wrist and then caused the wrist to flick. In the words of Libet, "The initiation of the freely voluntary act appears to begin in the brain unconsciously, well before the person consciously knows he wants to act!"[2] Libet's work, I should add, is controversial, and his results are open to other interpretations.[3] Nevertheless, experimental work by others appears to confirm the core of Libet's findings.[4]

Experiments such as these suggest that our choices are not formed in a conscious, rational manner. Instead, they bubble up from our unconscious mind, and when they finally reach the surface of consciousness we take ownership of them. Psychologist Daniel M. Wegner has gone so far as to argue that conscious will is an illusion—that despite appearances, what causes my finger to rise is not my consciously willing that it rise but something else.[5]

At first glance, such claims seem preposterous. My willing that a finger rise is, after all, strongly correlated with its rising: my fingers rise almost always when I will that they rise, and rise almost never when I will that they not rise. But of course, a correlation alone is no proof of causation. It is entirely possible for event B invariably to follow event A without A having been the cause of B. Suppose, for example, that a third event C, of which we are unaware, causes A and, a little time later, causes B. In such a case, it will certainly look as though A is causing B, but this will be an illusion.

Consider, by way of illustration, the onset of a cold. First comes the scratchy throat. A day later comes the runny nose. It looks as though the scratchy throat is causing the runny nose, but this is an illusion: both the scratchy throat and the subsequent runny nose are caused by an unseen virus. Or consider software that simulates a game of billiards on a computer screen. A ball crosses the screen and contacts a second ball, which rolls off. It certainly looks as though the first ball is the cause of the second ball's motion, but this again is an illusion. The real cause of the motion of the two balls is unseen software.

Wegner and other psychologists argue that something like this happens when we will that a finger move. It may look as though the act of willing is the cause of the finger movement, but in fact a third "unseen" event both causes the experience of willing and, a split second later, causes the finger to move. The event in question takes place in our unconscious mind.

It is disturbing enough to think that our "choices" are really just reflections of deeper mental processes that are hidden from us and over which we—that is, our conscious selves—have little or no control. Even more disturbing is the suggestion, supported by a variety of experimental data, that these internal processes are often in conflict with each other. We do not have one inner self; we have several, and they are capable of making contrary choices.

That our will is not a solitary thing becomes apparent when we consider cases of so-called alien hand syndrome. In one such case, a forty-year-old man experienced a brain hemorrhage that interfered with his brain's internal communications: one hemisphere of his brain could not communicate with the other. As a result, his left hand came to have a mind of its own, a mind resembling that of an obstinate two-year-old. During dinner, his left hand would refuse to give the fork to his right hand. During a game of checkers, his left hand would make a move he didn't want to make. He would correct the move with his right hand, only to have his left hand move it back. When he was reading, one hand would turn the pages of the book while the other hand attempted to close it. His legs were also somewhat affected: once he found one leg trying to go down some stairs while the other leg was trying to go up.[6]

In another case of alien hand syndrome, a thirty-nine-year-old woman had been the victim of a gunshot wound to the head. The injury partially severed her corpus callosum, the function of which is to allow the two hemispheres of the brain to communicate. As a result, her left hand came to have a will of its own. It had an annoying tendency to grab her throat during sleep, and to prevent this she kept her left hand tied up when she was in bed.[7] In yet another case of alien hand syndrome, a woman's left hand tried to stop her right hand from smoking cigarettes.[8]

Cases like these suggest that our brains have not one center of control, not one part that wills, but multiple decision-making centers that independently come to decisions about what we should be doing with ourselves. They are like army generals who each has his own idea about what the battle plan should be. In most armies, a supreme commander listens to his generals' ideas and decides what should be done, thereby coordinating their behavior. But if a general is unable to communicate with the supreme commander, he might initiate a combat action on his own—an action that might be at odds with the actions of the other generals and with the battle plan set forth by the supreme commander. In cases of alien hand syndrome, it is as if a general is cut off from main headquarters and is undertaking actions on his own authority.

In schizophrenia we see an extreme case of a divided mind. Those suffering from schizophrenia sometimes hear voices instructing them to do things that "they" don't consciously want to do. Evidence suggests that these voices are being produced by one part of the schizophrenic's brain and heard by another, not in the usual way—by being spoken with the mouth and being heard by the ears—but through the brain's internal communication circuitry. Thus, schizophrenics hear voices no one else hears. They spend their days in self-conflict, with the conscious, hearing part of the brain trying to resist the suggestions made by the unconscious, speaking part.

This isn't the only evidence of the existence of multiple sources of desire within the brain. Neuroscientists Michael Gazzaniga and Joseph LeDoux have studied the consequences of corpus callosotomies, operations in which the brain's corpus callosum is cut, thereby preventing one hemisphere from communicating with the other. (The goal in such surgery is to prevent an epileptic seizure from spreading from one hemisphere to the other; this operation, though radical, is less radical than a hemispherectomy, in which seizures are treated by the removal of one entire hemisphere of the brain.) They discovered that the brain's two hemispheres process information differently and can therefore come to different conclusions about what should be done in response to the information in question.

Gazzaniga and LeDoux devised an apparatus that flashed words on a screen at which split-brain subjects were staring. Words flashed on the left side of the screen would go into the right hemisphere of a subject's brain (because of the way the optic nerves "cross" on their way to the brain), and words flashed on the right side would go into the left hemisphere. When Gazzaniga and LeDoux flashed the command *laugh* on the left side of the screen—thereby sending it to the right hemisphere of a subject's brain—the subject would laugh. When they asked the subject why he was laughing, the subject's brain directed the question to the speech-processing area in the subject's left hemisphere. Because the subject's inter-hemispheric communication was compromised, the left hemisphere had no idea what the right hemisphere had "seen."

One might therefore expect the patient to say he didn't know why he was laughing, but this isn't what happened. Instead, the patient's left hemisphere made up a reason for laughing— like that the patient found the experiment amusing.[9] Likewise, when the right hemisphere was presented with the word *wave,* the patient would wave; when asked why he was waving, he would rationalize his behavior and claim to have seen someone he knew.[10] LeDoux and Gazzaniga concluded that people routinely don't know why they do what they do, inasmuch as the behavior in question is caused by brain systems that operate without their conscious knowledge. One of the main jobs of consciousness, they argue, is to confabulate—to generate a coherent story that ties together the operations of the various brain systems, and one way to generate this story is to hazard a guess about why a particular brain system is doing something.[11] In short, we figure out our own desires the way we figure out the desires of other people—by observing our behavior and drawing inferences from it. And in the same way as we can be utterly mistaken about the motivations of other people, we can be mistaken about our own motivations: the inference we draw about our behavior can have little bearing on reality.

Readers might concede that schizophrenics, people who have developed alien hand syndrome as the result of a gunshot wound to the head, or people who have had their corpus callosum cut may have divided wills. But what about those of us who are in perfect mental and physical health? What evidence is there that our brain processes are in conflict?

Unless we are exceptional individuals, we are daily presented with evidence of a divided will. We experience what philosophers call weakness of the will: our emotions seduce our intellect. We find ourselves wanting to do things—such as get drunk, have sex, or express anger—that at a higher, more rational level we don't want to do. On New Year's Eve, we might resolve to give up alcohol, a resolution that is broken before the first week of January is over. That our resolutions are so quickly broken suggests that we are not in control—that elemental forces within us give rise to desires that, at a conscious level, we desire not to have but are nevertheless powerless to resist. Indeed, the mere fact that we make resolutions shows that we are not in control of our desires. In making them we are, in effect, announcing to the various sources of desire within our brains that we, not they, are in charge. If we were truly in charge, though, we wouldn't need to announce the fact. (Analogously, an adult who is truly in control of a group of children doesn't need to announce that he is, and the more he feels compelled to announce it, the less in control he is likely to be.)

Gazzaniga and LeDoux illustrate the phenomenon of discordant desires with the following imaginary case. George, a married man, believes that men should be faithful to their wives but nevertheless finds himself involved in an extramarital affair. At first he passes the affair off as a fling, but as it continues, he finds that it is causing him much mental distress: he realizes that his behavior is at odds with his expressed values, and this bothers him. George's distress will continue until he either terminates the affair or changes his values—or continues the affair and retains his belief that married men should be faithful to their spouses but divorces his wife.

George's situation raises two questions: why did the discordant desires arise in the first place, and why does George find the situation so distressful? In response to the first question, Gazzaniga and LeDoux offer a theory, based on their work with split-brain patients. They suggest that different desire-generating systems (or "functional modules") operate within the brain. Some of these systems work in conjunction with and are under the control of the brain's dominant verbal system and thereby give rise to conscious, "rational" desires. Other desire-generating systems operate without the knowledge of the brain's verbal system and are therefore outside its control. We become aware of the existence of these systems only when they give rise to desires that we—that is, the "we" represented by our dominant verbal system—find to be objectionable.[12] In the case of George, the desire to have an affair was generated by one of these other systems.

Sometimes the dominant verbal system doesn't fight desires it had no part in generating but instead tries to justify them. It notices that we are engaged in a certain sort of behavior and then concocts a plausible-sounding reason why we should behave in that fashion. This is what LeDoux and Gazzaniga observed in their split-brain research, and this, Gazzaniga argues, is also what happens in those of us whose corpus callosa are intact.[13]

Consider again the army-general analogy presented in our discussion of alien hand syndrome. In a perfect world, the army is rational: the supreme commander decides what should be done, and his generals carry out his orders. In the case of the brain, though, the "supreme commander"—which LeDoux and Gazzaniga think is on the left side of our brain and is connected with the brain's speech-processing region—doesn't so much give orders as come up with plausible-sounding reasons why his generals are doing what they are doing. This supreme commander sees one of his subordinate generals attempting a frontal assault against an impregnable fortress and responds not by expressing his astonishment but by calmly muttering, "Good idea. That must be what I want him to do."

To answer our other question about George—why he is distressed by his discordant desires—we can invoke evolutionary psychology. When our desires conflict, we are in effect at war with ourselves, and this makes it harder for us to cope with the world around us. One side of us will try to undo what the other side accomplishes. Our evolutionary ancestors who were at war with themselves were unlikely to survive. For this reason, evolution has given us an incentive to avoid internal discord: we experience the feeling of distress psychologists call cognitive dissonance. The only way to eliminate this feeling is to declare a winner of the internal debate and proceed with life.

Evolutionary psychologists Leda Cosmides and John Tooby argue that our mind's systems, or modules, were designed by adaptive evolution for particular purposes. The mind, they like to say, resembles a Swiss Army knife. In the same way as the knife has different blades and tools that perform different functions, the mind is composed of different modules, each of which performs a different mental function that, in our evolutionary past, proved conducive to survival and reproduction.[14]

Psychologist Timothy Wilson refers to the collection of psychological modules that operate without our conscious knowledge as our adaptive unconscious.[15] One function of the adaptive unconscious, Wilson claims, is to set goals and initiate action. Another is to interpret the world around us: in particular, when the adaptive unconscious detects danger, it warns us. And the adaptive unconscious not only interprets, says Wilson, but feels. According to him, what goes on in our conscious mind is just a small part of what is going on in our head at any given moment. Much of our "thought" instead takes place in our adaptive unconscious.

The conscious mind, says Wilson, relegates many thought processes to the adaptive unconscious, the way the pilot of a jumbo jet relegates operation of many of the plane's functions to "invisible" computer systems. The adaptive unconscious processes information in "rapid, nonconscious, involuntary ways"[16]—and a good thing, too, since otherwise we would be overwhelmed with information. Wilson suggests, quite plausibly, that the adaptive unconscious was already fully functional in animals before they gained consciousness.

Although our adaptive unconscious is part of our mind, it is inaccessible to us. We can know of it only by inference—by watching ourselves behave and then forming conjectures about what must be going on in our adaptive unconscious to account for that behavior. As a result, writes Wilson, "There is a great deal about ourselves that we cannot know directly, even with the most painstaking introspection."[17] The maxim "Know thy-self" might therefore be harder to act on than one might wish.

When we make decisions, we are typically susceptible to influences of which "we"—our conscious selves—are utterly unaware, but to which our unconscious selves respond. Timothy Wilson, together with psychologist Richard Nisbett, devised a number of experiments to reveal this phenomenon. In one of these experiments, college students memorized lists of word pairs and were then asked to name a detergent. Students whose word pair list included the pair *ocean-moon* were twice as likely to name the detergent Tide as those whose word pair list did not. And when Nisbett and Wilson asked students why they had named Tide, they almost never said it was because they had been exposed to the *ocean-moon* word pair. Instead they might have said that Tide was the best-known detergent, that Tide was the detergent their mother used, or that they liked the Tide box. They had demonstrably been influenced by exposure to the *ocean-moon* word pair but were oblivious to how the exposure had influenced them.[18]

In another experiment, Nisbett and Wilson, under the guise of doing a consumer survey, asked people to evaluate four pairs of nylon stockings: which of the four did they think was of the highest quality? The four pairs were in fact identical, so one might expect people to say they were of equal quality. The subjects in the experiment claimed, however, that they could detect significant differences in quality. (Curiously, they tended to think that the stockings on the right side of the display were of the highest quality, while the stockings on the left side were of the lowest quality; indeed, four times as many people favored the rightmost stockings as favored the leftmost.) Subjects were able to give reasons for their choice, even though their choice was unreasonable, given that the stockings were identical.[19]

One might think that we would have considerable—indeed, complete—knowledge of how we come to make certain decisions. After all, we have direct access to our minds, and our minds are what make the decisions. Experiments such as those described above, however, indicate that in an important sense, we don't know our own minds: it is entirely possible for us to make a decision without fully understanding why we made the decision we did. Indeed, according to Nisbett and Wilson, our understanding of why we make certain decisions may be no better than our understanding of why other people, to whose minds we lack direct access, make decisions. In short, your understanding of why I made a decision might be as good as, or possibly even better than my understanding of why I made a decision.

The above-described research has obvious applications in commerce. When, in our role as consumers, we decide to buy a particular product, the decision is typically quasi-rational. A desire to buy something emerges from deep within us, and once we are aware of the existence of this desire, we set about concocting reasons why it is a sensible desire and one we should act upon. Advertisers, of course, realize this. They design ads that will trigger the unconscious desire formation process within us and then help us rationalize the desire the ad has created.

We spend our days working to attain the objects of our desires, thinking that if only we had the things we want, we would find lasting happiness. Our efforts pay off and we get what we wanted, but time and again we find that getting it brings us only temporary happiness—or no happiness at all. Why can't we, on getting what we wanted, live happily ever after? Why are we so insatiable? Psychological research offers a partial answer to these questions.

According to psychologists Daniel Gilbert and Timothy Wilson, we have an unfortunate tendency to "miswant"—to want things that we won't like once we get them. "In a perfect world," they observe, "wanting would cause trying, trying would cause getting, [and] getting would cause liking."[20] But ours is not a perfect world. In particular, our predictions about what we will like tend to be mistaken, and as a result, we tend to want things that, when we get them, will make little difference to our level of happiness. (The problem, quips Gilbert, isn't that you can't always get what you want; it's that you can't always *know* what you want.)[21]

Sometimes we miswant because the desire we form is based on an incorrect theory of what will make us happy. Because we are overworked, for example, we might fantasize about a vacation during which we could lie on the beach with nothing at all to do; but when we are actually lying on the beach, we might find that we are bored. Or we might miswant because feelings triggered by events in our life "contaminate" the desires we subsequently form. Suppose that moments after hearing we have won a prestigious award, someone calls to ask whether we can work at a local soup kitchen for the next four weekends. Our excitement about winning the award might spill over into our thoughts about working in the soup kitchen: we might imagine that while working there, we will feel the excitement we currently feel. In this state of mind, we might agree to work in the soup kitchen, but while working there, we might feel anything but excitement and wonder how we got ourselves into this predicament.[22]

Besides misjudging how getting or not getting what we want will affect us, we also, say Gilbert and Wilson, tend to misjudge how long it will affect us: "People tend to overestimate the duration of their emotional reactions to future events—especially negative events—and . . . this can lead them to miswant in the long term." Ask an assistant professor how failing to get tenure will affect him, and he will probably say, correctly, that it would be emotionally devastating, but he will go on to claim that the emotional devastation will last for an extended period. Research shows, however, that assistant professors who fail to get tenure recover fairly quickly and before long are no less happy than those assistant professors who got tenure.[23]

Someone might suggest that it is understandable that assistant professors would incorrectly predict how failing to get tenure would affect them: most assistant professors have never failed to get tenure and therefore make their prediction on the basis of inadequate data. But even when we turn our attention to events people have often experienced, they make mistaken predictions about how the events in question will affect them in the future. Thus, we can ask sports fans how having their favorite team lose the big game or ask voters how having their preferred candidate lose the election will affect them emotionally. Even though they have experienced these sorts of losses in the past, they will tend to misjudge the effect this next loss will have on them: they think that the agony of defeat will be more intense and longer-lasting than it is.[24]

Suppose we can avoid miswanting. Suppose we can teach ourselves to want only those things that, when we get them, we will like having. Even then our insatiability will not be cured. This is because of the psychological phenomenon known as adaptation: we tend to get used to what we have and therefore like it less with the passage of time.[25] We grow indifferent to the spouse, home, or car that was once our pride and joy, and because we are no longer satisfied with what we have, we form new desires in the belief that satisfying them—unlike when we satisfied our previous desires—will lead to lasting happiness.

These two psychological phenomena, miswanting and adaptation, lie at the heart of human insatiability. We work hard to fulfill the desires we find within us in the belief that doing so will bring us satisfaction. In some cases, we get what we want only to discover that, thanks to miswanting, we don't really want it. As a result, we experience at best momentary satisfaction. In other cases, when we get the thing we wanted, we do find it desirable, but its desirability diminishes with the passage of time, as we adapt to its presence in our life. Soon our old feeling of dissatisfaction returns. Thanks to miswanting and adaptation, most people spend their lives on what economic psychologist Daniel Kahneman calls a satisfaction treadmill.[26]

How can we get off the treadmill? How can we enjoy a degree of tranquility that is impossible as long as we are running to satisfy the next desire in what will turn out to be a never-ending series of desires? We can, to begin with, take steps to avoid miswanting: we can study the way we form desires and learn to distinguish those things that are really desirable, given our life plan, from those things that, because of our present circumstances or our present state of mind, merely seem desirable. We can also take steps to impede the adaptation process. In particular, we can consciously strive to keep wanting the things we already have. As we shall see in Part Three of this book, although the terms *miswanting* and *adaptation* are contemporary, thoughtful people have understood for thousands of years that these phenomena lay at the root of much human dissatisfaction.

Psychologist Arthur S. Reber offers the following summary of the psychological research on decision making: "During the 1970s . . . it became increasingly apparent that people do not typically solve problems, make decisions, or reach conclusions using the kinds of standard, conscious, and rational processes that they were more-or-less assumed to be using." To the contrary, people could best be described, in much of their decision making, as being "arational": "When people were observed making choices and solving problems of interesting complexity, the rational and logical elements were often missing."[27]

Psychologist Robert Zajonc takes this claim one step further: "For most decisions, it is extremely difficult to demonstrate that there has actually been *any* prior cognitive process whatsoever."[28] It isn't that the decisions people make are irrational; it's that the process by which decisions are made are utterly unlike the step-by-step rational process that might be used to solve, say, a math problem. Decisions are typically made in the unconscious mind, by means of some unknown process. Indeed, according to Reber, people not only don't know how their decision-making process works, they don't even know what information it takes as input.[29]

Daniel Wegner agrees that the decision-making process is less than rational: "We just don't think consciously in advance about everything we do, although we try to maintain appearances that this is the case. The murkiness of our intentions doesn't seem to bother us much, though, as we typically go right along doing things and learning only at the time or later what it is we are doing. And, quite remarkably, we may then feel a sense of conscious will for actions we did not truly anticipate and even go on to insist that we had intended them all along."[30]

According to Wegner, people have "an ideal of conscious agency."[31] We are convinced that we consciously control our actions, that we are in charge of ourselves. When it looks as though we are falling short of this ideal—when we find ourselves doing something we did not choose to do—we hide the fact from ourselves by creatively revising our beliefs about what it is we want.[32] This strategy, says Wegner, eventually "leads us to the odd pass of assuming that we must have been consciously aware of what we wanted to do in performing actions we don't understand or perhaps even remember—just to keep up the appearance that we ourselves are agents with conscious will."[33]

This is not to say that our decision making is utterly irrational. Consider again what I have called instrumental desires. Suppose I want X and know that doing Y will bring me X. Under these circumstances, I will probably decide to do Y. This decision is perfectly rational, given that I want X. And because most of our desires are instrumental, it follows that most of our desires are rational, taken in context. It is this fact, as much as anything, that gives rise to the common perception that our desires are rational.

But as we have seen, the desire that gives rise to instrumental desires might not itself be rational. In particular, my wanting X might not be rational: I might not have *decided* to want X; to the contrary, this desire might simply have popped into my head. In this case, my desire to do Y is a rational way to pursue a nonrational goal, and therefore my desire to do Y is itself in some sense nonrational. Suppose, for example, that I like burritos, and to get one, I drive to a restaurant. My desire to drive to the restaurant is perfectly rational, given that I like burritos. My liking burritos, on the other hand, cannot be rationally justified: I just like them, that's all. For this reason, my desire to drive to the restaurant cannot, in the last analysis, be rationally justified, meaning that despite appearances to the contrary, it is a nonrational desire.

Along these lines, Zajonc argues that many of our decisions are simply reflections of our likes and dislikes: "Quite often 'I decided in favor of X' is no more than 'I liked X.' Most of the time, information collected about alternatives serves us less for making a decision than for justifying it afterward. . . . We buy the cars we 'like,' choose the jobs and houses that we find 'attractive,' and then justify those choices by various reasons that might appear convincing to others."[34] But experiments performed by Zajonc and others suggest that our likes and dislikes are often formed subconsciously: "Preferences can be built up without participants' awareness of the sources of these preferences."[35] He concludes that our likes and dislikes not only can be formed in a nonrational manner but often are; as he succinctly puts it, "preferences need no inferences."[36] But if our likes are nonrational, so are the desires we form based on these likes.

To be sure, Zajonc is not the first person to recognize the subconscious and nonrational manner in which we form preferences. Nineteenth-century psychologist William Carpenter comments on the way "our feelings towards persons and objects may undergo most important changes, without our being in the least degree aware, until we have our attention directed to our own mental state, of the alteration which has taken place in them." Indeed, he points out that when we are falling in love with someone, we are often the last to know: "The existence of a mutual attachment . . . is often recognised by a by-stander (especially if the perception be sharpened by jealousy, which leads to an intuitive interpretation of many minute occurrences that would be without significance to an ordinary observer), before either of the parties has made the discovery." Carpenter also observes, with considerable insight, that our unconscious likes and dislikes can be stronger and more dangerous than our conscious likes and dislikes—more dangerous "because we cannot knowingly guard against them."[37]

Why do we embrace the ideal of conscious agency? Why, in other words, do we want our choices to have been conscious choices? In part because of social pressures. As Wegner points out, if you can't answer the question "What are you doing?" those around you are likely to think you are asleep, drugged, or crazy. In order to avoid having others think such things of us, we make up reasons for what we do. Indeed, we may even claim to have wanted to do things we couldn't possibly have wanted to do.[38]

But even if no one else were around to impress, we would embrace the ideal of conscious agency for the simple reason that we want to be free. We don't want our choice making to be an illusion, merely the reflection of deep brain processes of which we are not conscious and over which we have no control. Such choices, we fear, would not be meaningful. We are willing to go to great lengths to preserve, if not actual freedom, at least the feeling that we are free. One way to accomplish this is constantly to invent reasons why we are doing what we find ourselves doing: we are doing it because *we* want to, not because some deep brain process made us do it.

What really happens when we make a decision is something like this. We mull over the decision to be made. Then the magic moment comes: we make up our minds, we commit to a course of action. What transpires in that moment is a mystery. Before that moment we didn't want to do something; after that moment we do. The decision wasn't made at the conscious level. To the contrary, it sprang from our unconscious like a jack-in-the-box. And as soon as we become aware of what "we" have decided, our intellect takes credit for it: "Good idea. That must be what I want to do," it mutters.

In making decisions, we try to proceed in a rational manner, but the analytic process is often a sham. We might, for example, draw up a list of pros and cons. The problem with such lists is that we routinely cheat in constructing them. When the list isn't coming out "right," we rack our brains to come up with items to add to one side; when that doesn't work, we decide that the items on the "right" side, though fewer in number, should be given a greater weight. And if even that doesn't work, we simply throw the list away or conveniently misplace it. The list isn't so much an analytic technique for making a decision as it is a device for rationalizing a decision that deep down has already been made.

One of the things I teach my college students is decision theory—techniques for making decisions in a rational way. These techniques, I warn them, have their limits. For one thing, decision theory works only if you already know how desirable the various outcomes are. Decision theory can tell you how to increase your chances of getting whatever you desire, but it can't tell you what is desirable. In the words of philosopher

Michael Resnik, "Decision theory recognizes no distinction—either moral or rational—between the goals of killing oneself, being a sadist, making a million dollars, or being a missionary."[39]

Furthermore, decision theory is curiously circular: it takes decisions to use decision theory to make decisions. In his textbook on decision theory, for example, Resnik describes four different rules we can use in basic decision making.[40] But the rules themselves are inconsistent: if we use the so-called maximin rule to evaluate a decision table, decision theory will advise us to make a certain choice, but if we instead use the so-called maximax-regret rule to evaluate the same table, decision theory will advise us to choose otherwise. In other words, our decision about which rule to use will affect the decision that decision theory advises us to make, meaning that if we didn't already possess a capacity to make decisions without the aid of decision theory, we would have trouble applying it. Resnik admits as much: "To avoid an infinite regress of decision analyses any application of [decision] theory must be based ultimately on choices that are made without its benefit," and many of those choices will be made, he says, in our guts, not in our heads.[41]

Decision theory tends to work best for trivial decisions, such as when you are in a casino, trying to decide whether to play craps or roulette. For life's biggest decisions, such as whether to get married or have children, it is pretty much useless.

In daily life we experience the battle between reason and the emotions. We are taught to trust our reason and to distrust our emotions. We are cautioned that if we let our emotions get in the way of our decision making, we will make bad decisions. I accepted this advice—indeed, I worked hard at becoming the Rational Man—until I encountered the research of neurologist Antonio Damasio, who specializes in helping patients suffering from brain damage that incapacitates their emotions without simultaneously compromising their reasoning ability. His patients, in other words, are the earthly equivalent of the rational but emotionless Vulcans of *Star Trek* fame. The curious thing about Damasio's patients is that their lack of emotions, rather than improving their ability to make decisions, incapacitates it.

Damasio was trying to schedule an appointment with one such hyperrational patient and suggested two possible dates. The patient's behavior while trying to choose between the dates was, Damasio tells us, remarkable. He walked Damasio through a tedious cost-benefit analysis, taking into account other engagements he had, what the weather might be like on the dates in question, and so forth. The analysis went on for nearly half an hour before Damasio brought it to a halt by instructing the patient to come on the latter date. The patient instantly agreed. Says Damasio, "This behavior is a good example of the limits of pure reason. It is also a good example of the calamitous consequence of not having automated mechanisms of decision making."[42]

To better understand the predicament of someone who is rational but emotionless, consider computers. Give a computer a program to run, and it will use flawless logic to execute it. But unless you give a computer a program to run, it will just sit there. Computers need a motivating force before they will do anything, and it is the job of the programmer to provide this motivating force. Damasio's patient was like an unprogrammed computer. His reasoning ability was useless to him in the absence of a motivating force that told him what to do with it. He could form what we have called nonhedonic terminal desires, but as we have seen, such desires are generally feeble things.

Another Damasio patient, "Elliot," was a successful husband, father, and businessman until undergoing brain surgery on a tumor. The surgery damaged his frontal lobe and thereby affected his ability to carry through on plans. He would embark on a project only to lose sight of his goal in doing so. For example, asked to sort documents, he would go overboard: "He was likely, all of a sudden, to turn from the sorting task he had initiated to reading one of those papers carefully and intelligently, and to spend an entire day doing so. Or he might spend a whole afternoon deliberating on which principle of categorization should be applied."[43]

Although Elliot had a superior IQ, his emotional capacity had been seriously compromised. In Damasio's words, Elliot's predicament was *"to know but not to feel."*[44] We might think diminished emotional capacity would improve a person's ability to make choices: there would be fewer emotions to interfere with rational decision making. What Damasio found is that, to the contrary, emotional capacity is a key ingredient in decision making: "Real life has a way of forcing you into choices. If you do not succumb to the forcing, you can be just as undecided as Elliot." Indeed, writes Damasio, "As we are confronted by a task, a number of options open themselves in front of us and we must select our path correctly, time after time, if we are to keep on target. Elliot could no longer select the path."[45] Damasio concludes that "certain aspects of the process of emotion and feeling are indispensable for rationality. At their best, feelings point us in the proper direction, take us to the appropriate place in a decision-making space, where we may put the instruments of logic to good use."[46] Our emotional states "do not deliberate for us. They assist the deliberation by highlighting some options (either dangerous or favorable), and eliminating them rapidly from subsequent consideration."[47]

Even before the above psychological research was conducted, many thoughtful individuals reflected on how desires arose within them and their fellow humans, and concluded that the desire formation process was to a considerable extent nonrational and beyond our control. The research I have described vindicates many of their suspicions.

At the end of the fourth century, St. Augustine commented on how strange it is that our desires, something mental, should be marginally controllable by our minds: "The mind commands the body, and it obeys instantly; the mind commands itself, and is resisted. The mind commands the hand to be moved; and such readiness is there, that command is scarce distinct from obedience. Yet the mind is mind, the hand is body. The mind commands the mind, its own self, to will, and yet it doth not."[48]

In the seventeenth century, philosopher Benedict de Spinoza argued that "human beings think themselves to be free in so far as they are conscious of their volitions and of their appetite, and do not even dream of the causes by which they are led to appetition and to will, since they are ignorant of them."[49]

Philosopher David Hume was outspoken in his rejection of the rationality of desire. In the eighteenth century he wrote, "We speak not strictly and philosophically when we talk of the combat of passion and of reason. Reason is, and ought only to be, the slave of the passions, and can never pretend to any other office than to serve and obey them."[50] According to Hume, reason is capable of telling us that if we do X, Y will result. It is incapable of telling us, however, whether Y is worth obtaining, and therefore whether we ought to do X. It is only when reason is coupled with a value system—with a feeling that something is worth having—that reason can motivate behavior.

Hume claimed, famously, that we can't derive *ought* from *is*: no matter how many factual statements we pile up, they alone will not constitute a sufficient basis from which to deduce an ethical claim.[51] In particular, from the fact that a person will suffer if we shoot him and that his wife and children will also suffer, it does not follow that it is wrong for us to shoot him; instead, we need to couple these factual statements together with a value judgment, such as that it is wrong to cause others to suffer.

Hume could likewise have claimed that you can't derive *want* from *is*. It may be true that if I buy an expensive car I will win the admiration of my neighbors and experience pleasure driving it around. But unless we couple these factual statements together with some statement about what I want—that, for instance, I seek the admiration of my neighbors or I seek pleasure—it will not follow that I should want the car. Indeed, if, because of an ascetic lifestyle, I disdain the admiration of my neighbors and the pleasure that might be derived from driving the car, it would be foolish for me to want it.

As Hume puts it, "'Tis not contrary to reason to prefer the destruction of the whole world to the scratching of my finger. 'Tis not contrary to reason for me to choose my total ruin, to prevent the least uneasiness of . . . [a] person wholly unknown to me."[52] Thus, imagine a person who was perfectly rational but who had no instinct for self-survival—no gut-level feeling that he must do whatever it takes to ensure his continued existence. This person might realize that if he runs from an oncoming bear he will live and that if he stays put he will die. If he values his continued existence, the choice is a no-brainer: he ought to run. But if he lacks an instinct for survival and other "passions," the decision will be impossible to make. Being mauled by the bear will seem no better or worse than continued existence.

Moving on to the nineteenth century, we find yet other thinkers who discerned the nonrational nature of desire. Arthur Schopenhauer argued that the intellect doesn't rule the will. According to him, "the intellect gets to know the conclusions of the will only *a posteriori* and empirically."[53] Indeed, the operation of the will is a "secret workshop" into which the intellect cannot penetrate.[54] The intellect, he concludes, is a "mere tool in the service of the will."[55]

At the end of the nineteenth century, biologist Thomas H. Huxley questioned whether our will to do something is the cause of our action or is itself merely a causal consequence of deeper brain processes. According to Huxley, the volition, if they have any, of brute animals is "an emotion *indicative* of physical changes, not a cause of such changes." Indeed, "their volitions do not enter into the chain of causation of their actions at all." He makes similar claims of humans: "The soul stands to the body as a bell of a clock to the works, and consciousness answers to the sound which the bell gives out when struck." Furthermore, "the feeling we call volition is not the cause of a voluntary act, but the symbol of that state in the brain which is the immediate cause of that act."[56] According to Huxley, we are conscious automata.[57]

Shortly thereafter, psychiatrist Sigmund Freud argued that we are to a considerable extent ruled by unconscious desires. He also commented on "defensive rationalization," the mind's ability to justify its owner's behavior. A person, on being asked why he is behaving in a certain way, "instead of saying that he has no idea . . . feels compelled to invent some obviously unsatisfactory reason."[58]

Writing in 1921, philosopher Bertrand Russell had much to say about the extent to which our desires are beyond our control. Russell points out that we are often oblivious to or mistaken about our motives for acting. Indeed, Russell argues that "a man's actions and beliefs may be wholly dominated by a desire of which he is quite unconscious, and which he indignantly repudiates when it is suggested to him." According to Russell, "the discovery of our own motives can only be made by the same process by which we discover other people's, namely, the process of observing our actions and inferring the desire which could prompt them."[59] He adds that we are quite proficient at deceiving ourselves about our desires—that we even go so far as to develop entire systems of false beliefs to keep ourselves ignorant of what it is, at base, that we desire.[60]

The reasoning of Russell and the others may have been prescientific, but subsequent research suggests that their intuitions about how desires arise within us were correct.

The psychological research described in this chapter has important implications for anyone wishing to master desire. It suggests that when it comes to our desires, we are living in a world of illusion. Desires bubble up from deep within us. When they do, we don't acknowledge them for what they typically are—the mental baggage of a few billion years of evolution—

and deal with them accordingly. Instead, we try to justify them. We try to convince ourselves that we *should* want whatever it is we find ourselves wanting. We put our intellect in the service of our emotions.

We are like a vacation home owner who, regardless of who shows up at the door, suitcase in hand, welcomes the visitor and convinces himself that he must have invited the visitor— although in truth he has no memory of doing so. This home-owner ends up living a life controlled by these drop-in guests. Their comings and goings determine when he goes to bed and awakens. They determine how he spends his leisure time. And when he is not at leisure, he must work extra hard to cover the expenses associated with housing them. If this vacation home owner would only step back and analyze the situation—if he would develop some backbone and turn away uninvited guests, and choose very carefully which guests to invite, if he invited any at all—he would be much better off.

We, too, would do well to develop some backbone and become a gatekeeper with respect to our desires, admitting and acting on some of them but rejecting many of them. Then we could, to the extent that it is possible to do so, live the life of our choosing, rather than the life our evolutionary past is attempting to foist upon us.

In every man, be he ever so noble and dignified, there
is in the depths of his nature, a mob of low and vulgar
desires which constitute him an animal.

—Arthur Schopenhauer

# The Evolution of Desire


At one time, the universe was without desire. Then came
creatures—possibly here on earth, but more likely elsewhere
in the universe—that were capable of desire. How did these
creatures gain this ability?

The obvious answer to this question is that they gained the
ability to desire through a process of natural selection. Some
creatures, presumably as the result of mutation, gained a very
primitive ability to desire. The creatures that possessed this
ability had a greater chance of surviving and reproducing than
those creatures that lacked it, and therefore the former creatures flourished. Although this answer is correct as far as it
goes, I think the evolution of desire was more complicated and
rather more interesting than this. In particular, I think it likely
that at the same time as animals gained the ability to desire,
they were "programmed" with specific desires. More precisely,
they were programmed so that some things "felt good" and
were therefore intrinsically desirable, while other things "felt
bad" and were therefore intrinsically undesirable.

When we humans later came on the scene, we carried with us a few billion years' worth of evolutionary baggage. We possess a highly advanced ability to desire; indeed, thanks to our reasoning ability, we can form elaborate plans to get what we want. But because of our evolutionary past, we find ourselves wanting certain things. Having sex, eating ice cream, and winning the admiration of others all make us feel good, and so we want to do these things. It isn't that we want to want to do them; the problem is that doing them feels good, whether we want it to or not, and is therefore intrinsically desirable to us. If our evolutionary past had been different, what we find to be desirable would probably be different as well, and as a result we would tend to form different desires than we do.

If our goal, then, is to figure out why we want what we want, we would do well to take a look at our evolutionary past.

A species suited to its environment is more likely to survive and reproduce than one that isn't. The problem is that environments change, not just from millennium to millennium but from second to second. Consequently, in order to be suited to an environment a species must be suited to a changing environment. This in turn means that members of a species benefit from being able to detect changes in their environment and react in a way that increases their chance of surviving and reproducing in that environment.

Consider the beet. It does not react when bitten by a bug; it just sits there and takes it like a beet. But we should not let the beet's seeming passivity deceive us, for although the lowly beet does not react to attacks by bugs, it responds to other changes in its environment. For example, the guard cells of the beet's leaves open and close in response to light.

Other plants are more responsive than beets. Sunflowers are heliotropic: their leaves and flowers turn during the day so that they constantly face the sun. Pine trees, when their bark is invaded by bugs, "fight back": they exude sap that traps the bugs trying to burrow into them. And single-celled animals are even more responsive than this. When, for example, a paramecium runs into a large object, it reverses its direction and randomly rotates its body, behavior that typically puts distance between itself and whatever it ran into. It is also responsive to temperature, the pull of gravity, and sound waves.

In none of these cases, though, is the reaction to a changed environment the result of desire. The sunflower does not want to face the sun, the pine tree does not want to fight bugs, and the paramecium does not want to reverse its direction. Lacking a brain, they cannot desire anything. Rather, the behavior they exhibit is the result of automatic physiological responses that require zero brainpower. Indeed, these responses don't even require a nervous system. In a full-fledged case of desire, by way of contrast, a creature is able to form a mental representation of the thing it desires, compare the current state of affairs with the desired state, and initiate action to diminish the difference between these states of affairs.[1] Only a creature with considerable brainpower will have these abilities.

Life-forms possessing a nervous system are capable of reflexive responses to changes in their environment. Reflexive action is typically faster than the physiological responses described above. An animal that reflexively pulls away from something biting it is less likely to get eaten—and therefore more likely to survive and reproduce—than a beet that stays put or than a pine tree that slowly exudes sap.

Reflexive behavior mimics desire, but like automatic physiological responses, it doesn't involve true desire. We say that we shiver because we are cold, and this makes it sound as though we are in control. In fact, we don't choose to shiver. We can't make ourselves shiver if we aren't cold; nor can we, by an act of will, stop ourselves from shivering if we are cold (although we can, by tensing our muscles, momentarily suppress our shivers). Likewise, when we jerk our hand away from a hot stove, it isn't because we wanted to jerk it away; indeed, our hand's motion probably came as a surprise to us.

Although reflexive behavior represents an improvement on physiological responses such as those described above, this behavior has significant shortcomings. To understand the first shortcoming, consider the logic of reflexive behavior. It has the form "When stimulus S is present, do action A"—for example, "When pepper is up your nose, sneeze." This simplistic logic is sometimes counterproductive. Suppose that while hiding from a bear, you get pepper up your nose. Sneezing could have fatal consequences. Instead of being biologically wired to do action A whenever stimulus S is present, we would benefit from being wired in a logically more sophisticated manner: "When stimulus S is present, do action A *unless condition C obtains.*" Such wiring might cause us to sneeze when pepper is up our nose *unless a bear is nearby.*

A second shortcoming of reflexive behavior is that the logic behind it is binary and therefore does not allow a proportioned response to changes in our environment. Our sneezes are equally violent, no matter how much pepper is up our nose. Another shortcoming is that because they are not coordinated, our reflexes can give rise to contradictory actions. It is possible, for example, for the sneeze reflex (in response to pepper up the nose) and the hiccup reflex (in response to an irritation of the diaphragm) to be triggered at the same time. When this happens, a person will expel air forcefully with a sneeze at the same time as he is inhaling it with a hiccup. The resulting "sneeccup"—a cross between a sneeze and a hiccup—not only is quite unpleasant but in no way improves our chances of surviving and reproducing.

Another very significant shortcoming of reflexive behavior is that it is focused on the present and oblivious to the future. It is wonderful that we are biologically wired to jerk our hand reflexively away from a hot stove; it would be even better, though, to possess the ability to learn from one act of touching a hot stove so we will avoid hot stoves and hot things in general, and therefore won't have to rely on this reflex in the future. It is likewise wonderful that we shiver when we are cold; doing so warms us. It would be even better, though, for us to possess the foresight to build a hut in which to spend the winter. Then we wouldn't have to shiver to stay warm.

Despite these shortcomings, reflexive behavior has one big advantage: it is neurologically cheap, in the sense that the "wiring" required to implement it is minimal. If a creature is to move beyond purely reflexive behavior, its wiring must become vastly more complex. Instead of responding automatically to a stimulus, the way a store door opens when we step into its ultrasonic beam, a creature must be capable of weighing the options open to it in responding to a stimulus and then choosing among these options. And once it has chosen, it must feel motivated to act on that choice. Only then is a creature truly capable of desire.

That humans—and, I think, many other animals as well—gained the ability to desire indicates that the neurological cost associated with this ability, though high, can be outweighed by the benefits, in terms of an increased chance of surviving and reproducing, of being able to desire.

Chickens build nests and tend the eggs in them, despite never having built a nest before, never having tended eggs, and never having received instruction on how to build nests and tend eggs. Likewise, squirrels gather and bury nuts in the fall, even though they don't know—particularly if they are in their first year of life—that winter is coming and don't realize that these same nuts will be a valuable food source in the coming spring. What causes this instinctive behavior? What makes the hen sit on her eggs or the squirrel bury nuts?

One theory is that instinctive behavior is just a complex form of reflexive behavior. Thus, when the hen sees her eggs, her knees reflexively weaken and she plops herself down on them. I would like, however, to explore an alternative, rather more plausible—but nonetheless speculative—theory suggested by philosopher and psychologist William James. He proposes that instinctive behavior is triggered by the likes and dislikes of animals. (Charles Darwin[2] and Herbert Spencer[3] suggested similar theories of instinctive behavior, only they stated theirs in terms of pleasure and pain.) In particular, James suggests that the hen tends her eggs because she finds them "utterly fascinating and precious and never-to-be-too-much-sat-upon."[4] It not only feels good to sit on her eggs but feels bad not to sit: if we prevent her from sitting, she will feel anxious. Likewise, a squirrel buries nuts because he likes to bury them and dislikes being prevented from burying them. Because of these likes and dislikes, the squirrel finds himself in the grip of a nut-burying mania.

With instinctive behavior, I think, came the first true desires. Why does the hen sit on her eggs? Because she *wants* to, and the reason she wants to is because it feels good to do so and feels bad not to do so.

The claim that the hen wants to sit on her eggs because it feels good to do so presents us with a chicken-and-egg question: which came first, the hen's biologically wired likes and dislikes, or her ability to desire? Allow me to describe a thought experiment that can help us answer this question.

Suppose we get together a bunch of biological engineers and ask them to design a hen. The optimal hen, we explain, can survive and reproduce despite changes in her environment. Our engineers will presumably begin by figuring out a way for the hen to extract energy from her surroundings. Accordingly, they will design her to have certain organs in which various automatic biological processes take place. The resulting hen, though, will be unresponsive to her environment: she will resemble a plant more than an animal.

To make the hen responsive, the engineers will endow her with the ability to sense her environment and the ability to react to environmental stimuli. This can be accomplished without sense organs and muscles—think of the sunflower—but by endowing their hen with sense organs and muscles, the engineers can dramatically improve her ability to respond to changes in the world around her.

The ability to sense her environment and the ability to react to it will not be conducive to the hen's survival, though, unless these abilities are coordinated. To make such coordination possible, the engineers will first wire the hen with "nerves" that transmit data from the sense organs and transmit data to the muscles. They will then wire the hen with a "program" that processes this data—that tells the hen what to do in response to various environmental stimuli. The basic behavioral program will consist of a series of commands of the form "If stimulus S is present, do action A"—for example, if poked with a pin, wince. What the engineers will have produced, at this point, is a robotic hen that responds to the world in a purely reflexive fashion. It is, to borrow a phrase from ethologist Patrick Colgan, "a sitting sack of reflexes."[5] The hen would be better able to cope with changes in her environment than a beet but less able than real-world hens. She would also lack the ability to desire.

The biological engineers might refine their creation by adding even more commands to the hen's program as they think of new contingencies that might arise in her environment, but at some point they will realize that the process of adding commands has its limits. In wiring reflexive behavior into the hen, the engineers are forcing her to do things that are conducive to her survival. No matter how smart the engineers are, though, they can't foresee all the dangers to which the hen, in her changing environment, will be exposed. Also, it is naive to think that the "proper" response to a stimulus will always be the same. Under some circumstances, the best response to stimulus S might be action A; under other circumstances in which an animal is presented with stimulus S, doing A might result in instant death. Furthermore, reflexive behavior is focused on present stimuli; ideally, the hen will also be concerned with future events.

If the engineers want to achieve a quantum leap in their hen's ability to adapt to environmental changes, they will have to move beyond purely reflexive behavior. They will have to find another way to get the hen to do what is in her interests. They can look to the world around them for inspiration on how to accomplish this.

Consider human parents. The goal of caring parents is to get their child to do what is good for him and not to do what is bad for him. They have two ways to accomplish this. They can, to begin with, resort to force. To get their child to brush his teeth, for example, they can put a toothbrush in his hand and then force that hand to make brushing motions, perhaps while their other hand holds the child's mouth open. And to get their child to avoid eating the leaves of a toxic houseplant, they can forcibly remove the leaves from the child's mouth. It is clear that force works. It is also clear that parents must resort to force when dealing with very young children. But as children get older and their ability to communicate and reason improves, parents typically abandon force in favor of another technique for getting their child to do what is good for him and not to do what is bad for him: they give the child incentives to behave in a certain way.

They might, for example, tell their child that unless he brushes his teeth, he will lose television privileges, or that if he rides his bike without a helmet, he will lose bike-riding privileges. Parents who resort to incentives will still have to monitor their children's behavior, but the job of parenting will be far easier than if they relied solely on force. Another advantage of incentives is that by resorting to them, parents can harness a child's ingenuity. Parents can tell a child that unless he passes an upcoming spelling test, he can't sleep over at a friend's house; they can then sit back and let the child figure out how best to prepare for the test.

Parents aren't the only ones who resort to incentives to shape the behavior of others. Employers, teachers, coaches, spouses, college deans, and prison wardens all do it. Animal trainers also modify the behavior of animals through incentives: they reward certain behavior and punish other behavior, and an animal soon figures out how to get the reward and avoid the punishment.

Our engineers can learn from these examples and use incentives to get their hen to do what is good for her. They can, that is, wire an incentive system into their hen—wire her so she will be rewarded for doing things that are conducive to survival and reproduction, and punished for doing things that hurt her chances of surviving and reproducing. In doing this, they are in essence giving her the following instructions: "Go out into the world and use your intelligence to respond in the way that will best enable you to win the rewards and avoid the punishments we have wired into you."

In following this design strategy, the engineers will create not a *robotic* hen, whose behavior is purely reflexive, but an *incentivized* hen. (When, in what follows, I speak of incentives, I mean to include both positive and negative incentives.) Incentivized hens will be more difficult to design than robotic hens, but incentivization, if successful, will avoid the shortcomings, described above, of reflexive behavior. The incentivized hen, one supposes, will have a considerably greater chance of surviving and reproducing in a changing environment than a robotic hen does.

How might engineers go about creating an incentivized hen? First, they will wire her so that she is capable of being punished. Their hen already has a "nervous system" that carries data about her environment. The engineers could modify this nervous system so that when the hen physically feels something, the feeling can feel bad: thus, the hen not only will realize that she is being poked by a pin but will find the poking sensation to be painful. This will require development of a bundle of nerves that can interpret certain environmental stimuli as being painful. (Pain is presumably the archetypal bad feeling.) The engineers will also want to wire the hen so things other than pain feel bad, including anxiety (which, as we have seen, plays an important role in desire) and fear (which involves focused anxiety). Once the hen gains the ability to feel bad, the engineers will be able to punish her for, say, going too long without eating or for walking toward a fox.

An incentive system offering only punishments would be suboptimal, though. Punishments are good at getting the hen not to do something, but they are ineffective at getting her to do things. (The one exception: if there were only one thing the engineers wanted the hen to do, they could wire her so it felt bad for her to do anything other than that one thing; of course, our engineers will have many things they want the hen to do.) For this reason, the engineers will also want to be able to reward the hen for engaging in certain behavior. Conferring this ability on the hen will likely require developing another bundle of nerves—a pleasure center—that, when triggered, will generate a good feeling.

Once they have a hen to which things can feel bad and good, our engineers will want to associate bad or good feelings with various stimuli and behavior. More precisely, they will want to wire the hen so things that are conducive to survival and reproduction feel good and things that aren't feel bad. Thus, they will wire the hen so she will feel bad when she is burned, something pokes her, or she goes too long without eating. They will wire her so sitting on her eggs feels good. They will wire her so foods that are nourishing not only taste different from those that are toxic but taste better. Likewise, roosters will not only look different from foxes but will look better: the hen will find the sight of a fox to be terrifying and the sight of a rooster to be comforting. And in order to encourage certain social behavior, the engineers might wire the hen so that isolation from other chickens feels bad.

The engineers will also want to wire the hen so that things that feel good won't feel equally good, and things that feel bad won't feel equally bad. They will wire her so that the more essential something is to her survival, the better it feels to have it and the worse it feels to do without it. This way, when the hen is faced with the choice between, say, eating or drinking, she need only reflect on the intensity of her thirst and hunger pangs: she will choose to act on whichever of these bad feelings feels worse. And even though it would feel good to her to sit on her eggs, she will not do so if a fox is approaching: the bad feelings—fear and anxiety—triggered by the presence of the fox will far outweigh the good feelings she would experience on tending her nest.

To better understand the nature of built-in incentive systems, consider various experiments in which scientists have tampered with the wiring of these systems. In the late 1950s, James Olds implanted electrodes in the brains of rats and put them in boxes with levers that, if pressed, would cause current to flow to their brains. The levers were set so that the rats couldn't self-stimulate simply by sitting on a lever: after the lever had been pressed for half a second, the rat had to push it again to get more stimulation. Olds found that if electrodes were implanted in the region of the brain known as the interpeduncular nucleus, rats self-stimulated 7,000 times per hour. (The highest stimulation rate possible—the result of one lever-press every half second—is 7,200 per hour; when rats were put in a box in which stimulation was not forthcoming, they would, in their random movements around the cage, step on the lever only 25 times an hour.) The obvious (but not the only) explanation of these results is that the stimulation felt very good to the rats and thereby caused a radical change in their behavior.[6]

How long would rats keep up this behavior? Would they self-stimulate to the exclusion of every other activity? Indeed, would they stimulate themselves to death? Biopsychologist Elliot Valenstein did an experiment to find out. He set up an apparatus like that used by Olds but made the box more liveable, with plenty of food and water. Valenstein found that the experimental rat did not self-stimulate to the exclusion of everything else. It took breaks to eat, drink, groom, and explore its surroundings. It also stopped self-stimulating to sleep. Nevertheless, self-stimulation was its dominant activity. The rat would wake up in the morning, stretch, and then start depressing the lever. (The rat's behavior, in other words, resembled that of a teenage boy with a new video game.) During the twenty-one days the experiment went on, the rat self-stimulated 850,000 times, compared to the 3.6 million times that were theoretically possible. According to Valenstein, the experiment came to an end due to the exhaustion not of the rat but of the experimenters who had been observing it around the clock.[7]

In another experiment, scientists rewired the incentive system of an army mule.[8] They placed electrodes in its brain and a stimulation device on its back, and they mounted a solar cell so that as long as the mule walked toward the sun, its brain would be stimulated. When released, the mule walked toward the sun, first crossing a field and then going over a hill. At that point, they reversed the solar cell so the mule's brain would be stimulated if it walked away from the sun. They released the mule, and it walked back to its starting point. These artificially incentivized mules, scientists thought, could provide the army with a way to move supplies from one point to another on the battlefield.

So much for rats and mules; what about people? In one experiment, humans were allowed to self-stimulate the way Olds's rats did. One patient had an electrode implanted in his septum, an area near the hypothalamus. He self-stimulated 1,500 times in a single three-hour session. The stimulation didn't just feel good; it caused him to experience an orgasm.[9]

It is possible, even with currently existing technology, to rewire a human so things that used to feel bad feel good. When you poke a person's left index finger with a pin, it causes pain signals to be sent along a particular nerve. The brain detects these signals and causes a bad feeling. A (slightly mad) scientist could divert this nerve's signals to an electronic unit that, whenever it detected pain signals, would stimulate a pleasure center in the person's brain. Because of the change in the wiring of this person's incentive system, he might spend his days poking his left index finger with a pin, something he wouldn't have dreamed of doing before.

This same scientist could also rewire a person so things that used to feel good feel bad. We can, for example, imagine him rewiring a person so a full stomach, rather than feeling good, would make it feel as though he had an excruciating pain in his left index finger. (In this case, instead of diverting the pain signals in the nerve from the person's left index finger, the scientist would synthesize pain signals in that nerve whenever a stomach-fullness detector implanted in his abdomen was triggered.) On being rewired in this fashion, the test subject would probably lose much of his interest in recreational eating.

Back in Chapter 1, I described a case in which doctors inadvertently tampered with a person's built-in incentives. They were electrically stimulating the brain of a sixty-five-year-old woman in an attempt to relieve the symptoms of Parkinson's disease. When they turned on the current, she was immediately plunged into a profound depression. "I don't want to live anymore," she said. "I'm disgusted with life." Doctors observed seven of the nine criteria for depression in her: profound sadness, feelings of emptiness and worthlessness, markedly diminished interest and pleasure, agitation, fatigue, decreased concentration, inappropriate guilt, and a morbid interest in death. The induced depression did not last long enough for the other two criteria—weight change and sleep disorder—to be met. When doctors turned off the current, the woman returned to normal. Indeed, she even joked with the researchers. The round trip—from a normal state of mind to deep depression and back—took eight minutes.

Doctors were able, with the patient's permission—brave woman!—to reproduce this "synthetic depression" on other days. (In their tests doctors were careful to check the veracity of the woman's reports: if they told her they were applying the current when in fact they weren't, she didn't lapse into depression.) Researchers suspect that their stimulation of the woman's brain affected the functioning of her amygdala and limbic structures, thereby disrupting her built-in system of incentives. In the end, doctors were successful in relieving the symptoms of Parkinson's disease that the woman had been experiencing, and despite the unexpected turn her treatment took, her mental state appeared to be unharmed.

In another case dating back to the 1950s, brain stimulation had the opposite effect on a patient. Dr. Robert Heath stimulated the septal area of a depressed patient who had just attempted suicide. The effect was immediate: the patient started to smile. He described his mental state in the following terms: "I feel good. I don't know why, I just suddenly felt good."[10]

It is astonishing, as well as a bit scary, that something as fundamental as the will to live can be turned on or off with a tiny electric current applied to a certain part of the brain. It is also scary to see, when this "organic" will to live has been knocked out, how ineffectual the intellect is in its attempts to "prove" that life is worth living.

Above I asked a chicken-and-egg question: which came first, the ability to feel bad and good, or the ability to desire? I would like to propose that the logical, sensible way for animals to gain these abilities is simultaneously, or nearly so.

One could argue, to begin with, that the ability to desire and the ability to feel bad and good are logically connected. More precisely, one could argue that in the same way as it is logically impossible for a bachelor to be married, it is logically impossible for a creature to possess the ability to feel bad and good without also possessing the ability to desire. Things that feel good to a creature are intrinsically desirable to it: to say that something feels good to a creature means that in the absence of other factors, the creature would rather experience the feeling than not experience it. Likewise, things that feel bad to a creature are intrinsically undesirable to it. Things cannot be desirable or undesirable, though, to a creature that lacks the ability to desire. But if this is true, when the engineers endow their hen with the ability to feel bad and good, they must simultaneously endow her with the ability to desire.

(Although I think it is impossible for engineers to design a hen that has the ability to feel bad and good but not the ability to desire, it might be possible for them to do the opposite of this—to design a hen that has the ability to desire but not the ability to feel bad and good. The desires this hen would form, though, would be relatively unmotivated. They would be nonhedonic terminal desires, like my desire to click my tongue. Whatever desires this hen forms, she will form them "just because.")

Suppose, for the sake of argument, that the above line of thought is mistaken: suppose the ability to desire and the ability to feel bad and good are *not* logically connected. There is nevertheless reason to think that animals possessing one of these abilities will contingently possess—that is, possess as a matter of fact rather than as a matter of logical necessity—the other ability as well. To see why I say this, let us return to the design challenge presented to our biological engineers. Suppose it is possible for them to wire the hen to have the ability to feel bad and good without thereby wiring her to have the ability to desire, or conversely. Would the engineers want to endow the hen with one of these abilities but not the other? Clearly not.

Consider, to begin with, a hen that had the ability to feel bad and good but not the ability to desire. This hen not only *wouldn't* want to avoid things that feel bad or want to make them stop, she *couldn't* want it. Suppose, for example, that a predator came up and started gnawing on the hen's leg. "That feels really bad," she would think, but, lacking the ability to desire, she would not feel motivated to do something to make the pain end. Such a hen would not be long for this world. Our biological engineers would realize as much and would see no point in endowing their hen with the ability to feel bad and good without also endowing her with the ability to desire. Gaining the ability to feel bad and good would require a fair amount of brainpower, and the brain is a resource-hungry organ. Only a wasteful, thoughtless engineer would wire a hen to be able to feel bad and good without also wiring her so she felt motivated to obtain the things that felt good and avoid the things that felt bad.

Conversely, consider a hen that had the ability to desire but not the ability to feel bad and good. A hen that has the ability both to desire and to feel bad and good can be guided in forming desires: she can be rewarded (with good feelings) for wanting things that are conducive to survival and reproduction, and punished (with bad feelings) for wanting things that aren't. The desires formed by a hen to which nothing felt good or bad could not be similarly guided. She would pay no price for wanting something that could result in her being mutilated; nor would she be rewarded for eating. One supposes that in the absence of rewards and punishments, her desires would be formed in a random fashion. One also supposes that she would therefore not be long for this world. Once again, our engineers will realize this and conclude that it is rather foolish, from a design point of view, to go to all the trouble of endowing a hen with the ability to desire unless you also endow her with the ability to feel bad and good.

So which came first, the ability to feel bad and good, or the ability to desire? Because it would be evolutionarily extravagant for animals to gain one of these abilities without gaining the other, there is reason to think that animals gained these abilities simultaneously, or nearly so.

Now suppose the engineers test their incentivized hen: they place her in front of her nest to see how she responds. Because she has been incentivized, it would feel good to sit on her eggs in the nest. The problem is that she is at present too stupid to figure out what she has to do to obtain this good feeling— namely, walk over to her nest and plunk down on her eggs. As a result, she will just stand there.

The point in incentivizing the hen was so she could use her ingenuity to get things that feel good and avoid things that feel bad. But the hen, at this point in the design process, has zero ingenuity. The engineers will want to remedy this shortcoming. They will want her to be smart enough to figure out what she needs to do to earn the rewards and avoid the punishments they have wired into her. In particular, they will want to endow her with the ability to remember past experiences and generalize from them.

Suppose, then, that the engineers add memory and basic reasoning ability to their hen. This smarter hen, as she randomly explores her world, will discover the things that feel bad and good, and will remember them. If we subsequently place her in front of her nest, she will realize that she has (at least) two options open to her: either she can continue to stand there or she can walk over and sit on her nest. She will recall that in the past, sitting on her nest felt good, and she will infer that perhaps this time sitting on it will feel good—or at any rate will feel better than continuing to stand there. She will likewise realize that eating will make hunger pangs go away, that drinking will make thirst go away, that seeking out other chickens will make unpleasant feelings of isolation go away, and so forth.

More generally, the engineers will want to endow their hen with decision-making ability: she will be smart enough to realize the various actions open to her, weigh the consequences of each of these actions with regard to her feelings, and choose an action accordingly; and on making this choice, she will feel motivated to act. To ensure that she does feel motivated, the engineers can wire her so that once she realizes, intellectually, what she needs to do to feel good, she will feel anxious until she does it. They can wire her, in other words, so that she is subject to the anxiety transfer process described in Chapter 4.

The hen designed by our biological engineers would at this point pretty much resemble a standard hen. She would have a good chance of being able to survive and reproduce. And if the engineers coded their design into the hen's genes, her offspring would probably also survive and reproduce.

Suppose our biological engineers, not content with having designed a standard hen, decide to press on and come up with a design for a superhen—one whose chances of surviving and reproducing are considerably greater than those of a standard hen. The most obvious way to accomplish this would be to enhance the hen's reasoning ability. The hen could then form long chains of desire. Instead of simply responding to current environmental stimuli, she could plan for the future: she could lay out various possible courses of action and, based on her past experience, choose the one that would maximize the future pleasure and minimize the future pain she would experience. Instead of waiting for the fox to appear in front of her before reacting to it, she might take steps to detect its coming or to prevent it from gaining entry to the hen house. The standard hen described above had the ability to choose, from a list of possible actions, the action that had the best consequences for how she would feel. The superhen would also have the ability to add items to the list, and because she has this ability, she would increase her chances of surviving in the future.

The ability to form long chains of desire is pointless, though, unless the superhen also feels motivated to ascend the chains she forms. Our engineers could motivate her by extending the anxiety transfer process described above. As new links were added to chains of desire, anxiety would flow down to them, and the hen would be as anxious to fulfill the tenth link in a chain as to fulfill the first. They could also wire her so that if she failed to fulfill the tenth link in a chain of desire, her level of anxiety would spike upward: she would experience an unpleasant sense of frustration, despite the fact that fulfilling this tenth link is not itself intrinsically desirable and is only remotely connected with getting what she really wants—namely, fulfillment of the top link of the chain. And they could wire her so that, after failing to fulfill the tenth link, she would obsess over the failure and find other ways to ascend her chain of desire.

The engineers could also introduce rewards for successfully ascending a long chain of desire. They could wire the superhen so that she experiences a pleasurable feeling of accomplishment on fulfilling each link in a chain and an intensely pleasurable feeling—the rush of success—on finally fulfilling the top link. By wiring the superhen so that she feels good if she ascends a chain of desire and feels bad if she doesn't, they give her a powerful motivation to ascend any chains of desire she might form.

Once the superhen gains the ability to form long chains of desire and is rewarded for ascending the chains she forms, a new phenomenon will arise. Because it feels good to ascend a chain of desire and feels euphorically wonderful to reach the top link of it, she has an incentive to form chains of desire that end in things that in no way contribute to her chances of surviving and reproducing—indeed, that end in things that themselves don't even feel good. Thus, a hen that has experienced the rush of success might start embarking on seemingly foolish ventures, such as climbing to the top of the henhouse "because it is there."

And in much the same way as the superhen might "misuse" her ability to feel the rush of success, she might "misuse" her ability to make choices. She might, in particular, use her choice-making ability to form what I have called nonhedonic terminal desires. In Chapter 3, I described one such desire—my desire to click my tongue. I clicked it not because I thought doing so would make me feel good or let me avoid feeling bad; to the contrary, I clicked it for no particular reason. I clicked it because I could. Our superhen might likewise form a nonhedonic terminal desire to cluck, not because clucking will make her feel good, but "just because."

At this stage of development, the superhen will resemble a human in the manner in which she forms desires.

The above story about how biological engineers might design a chicken capable of desiring is, I hope, both entertaining and enlightening, but we must be careful not to read too much into it. Things are much more complicated than my story makes them out to be. I talk, for example, about the engineers wiring the hen so things can feel bad and good to her. Although people have thought about what it would take to wire machines to feel bad or good—there may be advantages, for example, to building robots that can experience emotions[11]—no one has come close to building a machine capable of feeling bad or good.

Furthermore, we should not make the mistake of thinking that the above story about how engineers might design an incentivized hen counts as evidence about how evolution designed chickens and other animals capable of desire. It is far easier to talk about the questions that arise in designing an animal, which is what I am doing above, than it is to determine how an animal actually came into existence by means of evolutionary processes: as cybernetician and neuroanatomist Valentino Braitenberg likes to remind us, "analysis is more difficult than invention."[12]

Indeed, we can be certain evolution *didn't* design chickens in the manner described above, since we know that evolution doesn't design things at all. It doesn't spend time puzzling about the issues involved in chicken design. It doesn't scribble plans on the backs of envelopes. It doesn't avoid certain designs as being wasteful and foolish. (In fact, evolution is perfectly capable of suboptimal designs. Consider, for example, the "inside-out" design of the human retina, with blood vessels and nerves being placed above the photoreceptors, where they interfere with the passage of light. This placement also increases the chance of a detached retina.)[13] What evolution does—to the extent that it "does" anything at all—is allow for random variations on a design theme. Those variations that are well suited to their environment will be replicated and will thereby become more common; those that aren't won't.

Above I argued that the "logical, sensible way" for animals to gain the ability to feel bad and good and the ability to desire was to gain these abilities "simultaneously, or nearly so." From this, though, it doesn't follow that this is how animals *in fact* gained these abilities. There is, after all, no guarantee that evolutionary processes will be either logical or sensible.

I will leave it to others to speculate, if they wish, about the exact steps by which purely reflexive animals came to be incentivized, but it presumably happened something like this.

At some point in the past, animals gained nervous systems that enabled them to respond reflexively to external stimuli. With the passage of time, these nervous systems became more complex, and with greater complexity came increased logical ability, the ability to remember, and the ability to feel good and bad. This combination of abilities gave rise to the world's first incentivized animals. They were also, I think, the first creatures capable of desire. This might have happened—on earth, at any rate—two hundred million to three hundred million years ago, when animals' brains developed limbic systems.

In some of these incentivized animals, the things that felt good happened to be things that were conducive to survival and reproduction; in others, they were not. The former animals were more likely to survive and reproduce than the latter. With the passage of time, incentivized animals—and in particular those that were incentivized to want what was good for them—became commonplace.

Some of our evolutionary ancestors, having gained the ability to desire and the reasoning skills this ability required, went on to become fully rational. The important thing to realize, though, is that they developed this improved reasoning ability not so they could transcend their built-in system of incentives but so they could more effectively earn its rewards and avoid its punishments, and thereby survive and reproduce. Indeed, in modern humans, our intellect typically functions as an adjunct to our emotions. Our intellect can rebel against the built-in incentive system: we can wish sex didn't feel so good or that we never got hungry. Most of the time, though, our intellect doesn't rebel; instead, it spends its days in the service of the incentive system, patiently devising strategies by which to gain things that feel good and avoid things that feel bad.

In the Rig Veda—a sacred Hindu text written in perhaps 1500 B.C.—we are told that the universe began not with light, as the Old Testament claims, but with desire.[14] What an extraordinarily beautiful way for a universe to begin!

If we look instead to science, though, we find that desire was a relative latecomer to our universe. Indeed, it was the last of the three great "miracles" in cosmic history. The first miracle was the creation of the universe itself: that there should be something rather than nothing is miraculous. The second miracle was that some of the inanimate matter formed by the first miracle came to life. And the third great miracle was that some of those living things gained the ability to be motivated, to seek, and even to hope.

Before this last miracle, the universe was filled with activity, none of which was purposeful. Atoms spun, and light beams whizzed through space. Flowers opened and closed, single-celled animals replicated, and sponges fed. None of this activity, though, had a point. And yet somehow, in the midst of all this pointless activity, there arose collections of atoms capable of forming goals and striving toward them. At last, there was meaning in the universe—not meaning in the cosmic sense, perhaps, but meaning nonetheless.

If I am ordering a meal in a restaurant I may be free to choose whatever I like from among the alternatives on the menu. But I am not free to choose *what I like* shall be. I cannot say to myself: "Up to this point in my life I have always detested spinach, but just for today I am going to like it." . . . What I am in the mood for, and what I like or detest, are not at my command.

—Brian Magee

# The Biological Incentive System

We humans are incentivized. All of us have implanted within us a biological incentive system—let us refer to it as a BIS (rhymes with *his*). We have the BIS we do because our evolutionary ancestors who had it had a better chance of surviving and reproducing than those who didn't. Why does sex feel good? Because if it had felt bad to someone—if sex, rather than leading to an orgasm, resulted in intense pain—it is unlikely that he would reproduce and therefore unlikely that he would go on to become anyone's evolutionary ancestor. Why does getting burned feel bad? Because if someone had enjoyed getting burned—if burns, rather than being intensely painful, triggered orgasms—he would be unlikely to survive: he would soon succumb to self-inflicted burn injuries and would therefore be unlikely to reproduce, which in turn means he would be unlikely to become anyone's evolutionary ancestor.

To better understand the nature of incentive systems, consider the situation at a workplace. A midlevel manager might be responsible for developing a schedule of incentives that tells what employee activities will be rewarded and punished and what the rewards and punishments will be. She might produce a document that says, for example, that salespeople who meet their sales quota will get a free dinner at a local restaurant and salespeople caught stealing office supplies will be fired. She will give the schedule of incentives to a sales manager, who will inform salespeople of its existence, and reward and punish them in accordance with it.

For an incentive system to be effective, its rewards must be things that employees find desirable and its punishments things they find undesirable. It would be foolish, for example, to reward salespeople who meet their sales quotas with a reduction in pay and to punish salespeople caught stealing office supplies with a free trip to a vacation spot. This in turn means that an effective incentive system will take into account the desires of those subject to it. (It also means that it is impossible, through the use of an incentive system, to influence the behavior of creatures incapable of desire.)

An effective schedule of incentives will also be consistent: it shouldn't both punish and reward a single action, nor should it punish employees for doing things (such as talking to clients) that necessarily precede activities it rewards (such as making sales). A system's schedule of incentives should also be stable. If a company makes significant changes in its schedule of incentives daily or even monthly, employees will have trouble keeping track of exactly what the incentives are. An incentive system with a schedule of incentives that is inconsistent or unstable won't really count as a *system,* and its effect on people's behavior will be unpredictable.

Furthermore, to be effective an incentive system has to dispense the rewards promised and mete out the punishments threatened by its schedule of incentives. If a system lacks an enforcement mechanism, it will have little effect on people's behavior; to them, the schedule of incentives will be just a sheet of paper. (Indeed, in any workplace, employees are very good at figuring out which company policies are enforced and which aren't, and ignoring the latter policies.) Finally, for an incentive system to be maximally effective, people need to be aware of its existence. It is for this reason that companies publish their schedule of incentives, perhaps as part of an employee handbook.

To better understand the advantages of publicizing an incentive system, suppose two companies have the same schedule of incentives and are equally adept at enforcing it, meaning that they reward and punish employee behavior in the same way. For example, they both treat employees who meet their sales quota to a free dinner, and they both fire employees caught stealing office supplies. Suppose, however, that whereas the first company makes public its schedule of incentives, the second company keeps its schedule a secret.

In the first company, new hires not only are presented with the corporate schedule of incentives but are asked to sign a document stating that they have read and understood it. In the second company, by way of contrast, employees are never shown or told about the schedule of incentives but are nevertheless rewarded and punished in accordance with it. Thus, a salesman for this second company who has met his sales quota might be surprised to find a coupon for a free dinner in his mailbox and more surprised still when no one will tell him why he received it. This salesman might likewise be surprised to watch as a fellow salesman (who had a reputation for taking home office supplies) is fired without any explanation being given for his dismissal. On the basis of such events, the salesman will conclude that his company has an incentive system.

The second company's covert incentive system will shape employee behavior, but it will do so far less effectively than the first company's overt incentive system. In the second company, employees won't know that the corporate incentive system rewards or punishes a certain type of behavior until someone engages in that behavior and is subsequently rewarded or punished. Even then, employees might draw the wrong conclusion about the exact behavior for which they are being rewarded or punished: the salesman who gets the free-dinner coupons might mistakenly think they are a reward not for meeting his sales quota but for having kept his desk tidy. Most companies understand full well the advantages of an overt incentive system. Having gone to the trouble of coming up with a schedule of incentives, they do what they can to make employees cognizant of those incentives.

Having said this, I should add that in the real world, companies typically have both published and unpublished schedules of incentives. Nowhere in a company's published schedule of incentives, for example, will it say that if you yawn or belch while the boss is talking to you, you will be punished for doing so, but you nevertheless probably will. Most employees realize that their company's unwritten schedule of incentives is as important as its written schedule, and they spend considerable time and effort figuring out the details of the unwritten schedule.

Like an incentive system at a workplace, our BIS has a schedule of incentives that dictates the behavior for which we will be rewarded or punished and what those rewards and punishments will be. This schedule of incentives is written into our wiring. Like any good incentive system, it is both consistent and stable. Furthermore, our BIS rigorously enforces its schedule of incentives: it rewards us for engaging in some behaviors and punishes us for engaging in other behaviors.

In saying that our BIS rewards or punishes our behaviors, I do not mean to suggest that it rewards or punishes every single action of ours. Under normal circumstances, for example, my BIS doesn't care whether I click my tongue: it will neither reward nor punish me for doing so. (An exception would be if my tongue is injured; then my BIS will care.) In this respect, our BIS again resembles the incentive system one might find at a workplace. Your boss might reward you for filling in a form and punish you for failing to fill it in but be utterly indifferent about whether the pen you use to fill it in has blue or black ink.

Our BIS, we should note, has two ways of rewarding and punishing us. First and most obviously, it can mete out *physical* rewards and punishments. If we haven't eaten, it will cause us to experience hunger pangs, and if a mosquito bites us, it will cause us to experience an unpleasant itch. If, on experiencing hunger pangs, we eat, our BIS will again punish us if we try to consume a poison hemlock plant; it will taste unpleasantly bitter. But if we consume a ripe banana instead, it will reward us with a pleasant taste, and if we eat enough bananas, our BIS will reward us with a physically pleasant sensation of fullness. Likewise, if we have sex, our BIS will reward us with intensely pleasurable physical sensations.

Our BIS can also mete out *mental* rewards and punishments. It does this by causing us to experience emotions—also known as feelings. Some of these emotions feel good; others feel bad. If, for example, I win first place in a competition, my BIS will reward me with a feeling of triumph, but if I instead come in last in that same competition, my BIS will punish me with a feeling of humiliation. Among the feel-good emotions our BIS can reward us with are feelings of joy, pride, happiness, and tranquility; among the feel-bad emotions our BIS can punish us with are feelings of shame, regret, loneliness, embarrassment, anxiety, frustration, and fear.

Our BIS happens to be a covert incentive system. We can't read the schedule of incentives of our BIS for the simple reason that it isn't written in words; rather, it is written into our wiring. We find out the rewards and punishments it has to offer through a process of trial and error. We stick our finger into a flame, and it hurts; we conclude that our BIS punishes us for getting burned. It is, to be sure, an inefficient way to administer an incentive system, but it is apparently efficient enough to have allowed our species to flourish.

By the time we are preadolescents, we have a pretty good idea of the rewards and punishments our BIS holds in store for us, but even then, surprises are possible. A person's first orgasm, for example, is generally an astonishing event: who would have thought you would be rewarded so intensely for doing *that*? Likewise, the first person who harvested sap from opium poppies and smoked it must have been surprised by the rewards that awaited him.

It is, as we have seen, inefficient for corporate schedules of incentives to be unstable. If a schedule of incentives changes daily or even monthly, employees will have a hard time keeping track of which incentives are currently in force, and their behavior won't be changed in a systematic fashion. Too much stability in a schedule of incentives can also be problematic, though. Suppose, for example, a telephone manufacturing company goes decades without changing its schedule of incentives. As a result, the company continues to reward employees for trying to sell dial telephones, even though technological change means the company won't profit from the sale of these phones. In this case, a schedule of incentives that used to promote corporate profitability no longer does. Most companies recognize this danger and periodically update their schedule of incentives to reflect changes in their business environment.

Another thing to realize about incentive systems is that even if a company keeps its schedule of incentives current, clever employees will figure out ways to "game" the system—ways, that is, to gain the rewards the system has to offer without behaving in a manner that benefits the company. These employees might, for example, forge documents in order to make it look as though they have met their sales quota when in fact they haven't. The rewards the company showers on these employees will be counterproductive. Companies will therefore want to be on the lookout for "gamers" and perhaps modify their incentive systems to prevent them from being manipulated by employees.

Our BIS is supposed to reward us for behavior that increases our chances of surviving and reproducing and punish us for behavior that reduces our chances. But our BIS rewards us for gorging ourselves with sweet, fattening foods—they taste so good!—even though doing so increases the chance that we will die prematurely. Likewise, our BIS rewards us intensely for snorting cocaine even though doing so can detract from our ability to survive and reproduce. How come?

Sweet, fattening foods taste good because our ancestors who enjoyed the taste of such foods were more likely—living, as they did, in a time when starvation was an ever-present risk—to survive and reproduce. Consequently, it made perfect sense for their BIS to reward them for eating it. The problem is that the dietary environment has changed. For many people today, the principal dietary risk is not starvation but diseases brought on by overconsumption of sweet, fattening foods. Our BIS has not been modified to keep up with these dietary changes. In other words, our BIS is like the telephone company that is still rewarding its salespeople for trying to sell dial telephones.

And when a human gets high on cocaine, he is "gaming" his BIS: he is tricking it into giving him a reward—a feeling of euphoria—that he hasn't earned. His evolutionary ancestors, by way of contrast, had to accomplish a significant goal, such as rising to the position of alpha male within their band, to experience the same feeling of euphoria. In other words, a cocaine user is like a salesman who earns the reward for meeting his sales quota not by making sales but by submitting forged documents.

It should be clear from these examples that our BIS is flawed. If we worked for a company with a flawed incentive system, we could quit and find employment elsewhere. We cannot similarly escape our BIS. Like it or not, we are stuck with it and its flaws for life. I will have more to say about our predicament—being forced to live under a flawed incentive system—in the next chapter.

In much the same way as a salesman's workdays are shaped by the system of incentives at his place of work, our days are shaped by our BIS, which acts like a goad to drive us along in our daily routine. We awaken, but as we lie in bed we notice that our bladder is full—or rather, that our BIS is punishing us for going so long without urinating. We get up and walk toward the bathroom. On the way, we stub our toe, and our BIS punishes our awkwardness by making us experience intense pain. Not long after we climb back into bed, we find ourselves worrying about our car's water pump. It has been making a tick-tick noise for weeks, but we have neglected to have a mechanic look at it. By causing feelings of anxiety within us, our BIS is punishing us for this neglect.

We push this worry out of our mind, only to realize that we are hungry—that our BIS is punishing us for having let our blood sugar level fall so low. We go down for breakfast, and as we decide what to eat, we recall that our BIS will reward us for eating sweet, fattening foods. Consequently, we treat ourselves to a breakfast of bacon, eggs, and pancakes with butter and maple syrup. Over breakfast, while reading the newspaper, we come across a flattering article about ourselves. We feel a little rush of delight, as our BIS rewards us for having gained social status. We eat until our feeling of hunger is replaced by a pleasant feeling of fullness, a reward from our BIS for having taken advantage of the food resources available to us. We have been up for only an hour, but in that time our BIS has been quite active.

Because our BIS is so active, we are oblivious to its presence within us. We have been exposed to its system of punishments and rewards for so long—since birth or quite possibly even before birth—that we take it for granted that some behavior on our part will be punished and other behavior will be rewarded. We are like slaves who, because we have been slaves all our lives, don't think to ask what gives our master the right to order us about. Indeed, we can't even conceive of what freedom would be like.

Notice that if our BIS had a different schedule of incentives, our behavior would have been different. Suppose, for example, that the full bladder that drove us from bed, rather than feeling bad, felt satisfying, the way a full stomach feels satisfying. We would not, under these circumstances, have felt compelled to get out of bed—or if we did get out of bed, it would be to drink water, not to urinate. Likewise, suppose that maple syrup, rather than tasting sweet, tasted bitter. We would then be unlikely to drown our pancakes in syrup.

Even more radically, notice that if we lacked a BIS altogether—if our behavior were neither rewarded nor punished by our wiring—there is no telling how we would act on waking up. Indeed, without a BIS to motivate us, we might just lie there in bed, like a person in a deep depression.

The schedule of incentives of our BIS is determined by our wiring—by how our neurons are configured and by what hormones and neurotransmitters are present within us. Change our neuronal wiring or body chemistry, and you change what feels bad or good to us. For example, deprive us of the neurotransmitter serotonin, and our ability to feel good will be impaired; indeed, we will slip into depression. Deprive a male of testosterone, and gazing at a beautiful woman won't be as pleasurable as it once was.

Although our genes are the dominant factor in determining our BIS, other factors are also at work. Indeed, even though we have the same genetic makeup throughout our lives, our BIS changes with the passage of time. Some of these changes are "preprogrammed." For example, our genetic makeup dictates that we go through puberty at a certain age. During puberty, our hormones change, which in turn changes our BIS; as a result, what feels, tastes, looks, and smells good to us changes as well. Other changes to our BIS are not preprogrammed in this manner but depend on our life experience. Suppose, for example, we are thrown from a horse. Unless (folk wisdom would have us believe) we remount immediately, our BIS will be permanently altered: we will develop a fear of horses, and as a result, something that used to feel good to us—riding horses—will henceforth feel bad.

Sometimes what feels bad to us changes not because of a change in our BIS but because of a change in our body. Suppose, for example, we sprain our ankle. Although our BIS formerly rewarded us with an endorphin high for jogging, it now punishes us for even trying to walk. In this case, unlike when we fell from the horse, it isn't our BIS that changed, it is our body. Notice, after all, that even before the sprain, our BIS would have punished us for wrenching the ligaments in our ankle. By way of contrast, before we fell from a horse, our BIS would not have punished us for getting on one; after our fall, it will. The fall reprogrammed our BIS.

To better understand how our BIS is affected by our life experiences, consider food preferences. Foods taste and smell the way they do because of our biological wiring, and the tastes and smells in question are good or bad because of our BIS. It is no accident that toxic things tend to taste bitter: our evolutionary ancestors whose BISes were wired so that plants containing toxins were unpleasantly bitter were less likely to ingest them—and more likely to survive—than our ancestors who weren't wired in this manner. Likewise, it is no accident that things that are good for us (or, more precisely, would have been good for our evolutionary ancestors), such as ripe fruit, tend to taste pleasantly sweet.

The food preferences generated by our BIS are not fixed. Indeed, consider the manner in which babies form food preferences. Although they may be averse to eating things that taste bitter or spicy, babies are remarkable for their gastronomic promiscuity. They try to eat almost anything they encounter, a fact that keeps parents on their toes, making sure houseplants and toxic chemicals are out of reach. By the time they are toddlers, though, most children's food preferences collapse radically, and they become some of the world's pickiest eaters.

There is presumably an evolutionary explanation for this. It is important for newborns to find a wide variety of foods to be palatable, since people living in different places will have different diets. It is also important for children to stick to the diet their parents introduce them to, since this will probably be one of the most nutritious diets possible, given their circumstances. Babies who are wired to be open to a wide range of tastes at birth and picky eaters a few years later—liking only foods to which they have been repeatedly exposed—are therefore most likely to survive childhood.

It is possible for our food preferences to change in a matter of minutes, as the result of subtle changes in our internal state. Psychologist Michel Cabanac did an experiment in which fasting subjects were asked to smell orange syrup. They found it pleasant-smelling until they ingested a glucose solution. Within fifteen minutes the orange syrup no longer smelled good, and after an hour it smelled very unpleasant.[1]

We are also biologically wired to develop a dislike for foods that make us feel sick. These dislikes can be irrational but are nevertheless compelling. Along these lines, psychologist Robert

Ornstein tells the (presumably autobiographical) story of a psychologist who has filet mignon with béarnaise sauce—one of his favorite dishes—for dinner, goes to the opera with his wife, and then becomes violently ill. As a result of this series of events, he develops an aversion not to opera, not to his wife, and not even to the person who gave him the flu that he knows to be the cause of his illness, but to filet mignon with béarnaise sauce. Says Ornstein, "The tendency to make a connection between nausea and prior food taste is so strongly prepared in us that it defies reason."[2]

The food preferences of rats can likewise be altered as the result of becoming nauseated after eating something. Experimenters let rats taste saccharin and then injected them with lithium salt, which apparently makes them feel nauseated. The rats thereafter avoided saccharin. Significantly, when experimenters let rats taste saccharin and then administered an electric shock, the rats didn't likewise develop an aversion to saccharin.[3] In this case, a feeling of nausea was capable of reprogramming their BIS, but a shock was not.

We have little control over our food preferences. A person who likes the taste of beef may think it is a food preference of his own choosing, but chances are he likes it because he was raised to like it: if he had spent his childhood in India and been raised in a Hindu family, he would probably, as an adult, be nauseated by the taste of beef. Conversely, the person who dislikes the taste of beef might dislike it not by choice but because of an accident like the one that befell Robert Ornstein.

One problem with purely reflexive behavior, as we have seen, is that it doesn't allow flexibility in our response to environmental stimuli. Incentivized behavior, by way of contrast, allows us to respond flexibly to our environment: we get to choose what our response to a stimulus will be. Thus, despite having a BIS, we have considerable discretion in determining what to eat. We can pick among all the things that, because of how our BIS is wired, taste good. We can also choose to eat something that, again because of how our BIS is wired, tastes bad. We might do this to please a host, to win a bet, or, if we are in desperate circumstances and there is nothing else to eat, to stay alive.

The above examples demonstrate that our BIS, besides allowing us to respond flexibly to stimuli, is itself flexible in the sense that its schedule of incentives—the rewards promised and punishments threatened by it—can change. Think again about our food preferences. Although our BIS determines these preferences, it is flexible in the manner in which it does so. First, our BIS is programmed so that our food preferences, rather than being fixed at birth, depend upon the foods we are exposed to as infants. And once these tastes have been programmed, they can be temporarily reprogrammed by our ingesting, say, glucose and permanently reprogrammed if we get sick after eating a food. If having a BIS, because of the flexibility it allows, is advantageous, having a flexible BIS—one whose rewards and punishments can be reprogrammed—is better still.

The first incentivized animals presumably had BISes that were fixed for life. Then came new, improved BISes that could change depending on an animal's age. Early in life they would offer one set of rewards and punishments; later they would offer another set. Then came, one supposes, BISes that could be altered by an animal's life experience. An animal might be indifferent to another species of animal until a member of that species attacked it. The attack would reprogram the animal's BIS so that in the future, if approached by a member of the attacking species, it would experience fear.

Having a reprogrammable BIS, it should be noted, allows a primitive kind of learning to take place. If an animal attacks another animal and the attacked animal has sufficient mental ability, it can remember the attack and generalize from it. On the basis of its memories and generalizations, it can, when it confronts a similar animal in the future, decide that the prudent thing to do is flee. Suppose, however, that an animal has limited ability to remember things or generalize. If the attacked animal has a reprogrammable BIS, its BIS can be altered by the attack so that the attacked animal will feel fear whenever it sees an animal that looks like the attacker. It might not "remember" the previous attack and therefore might not know why it feels fear, but it will nevertheless respond to the presence of the other animal by fleeing. In a sense, the animal will have learned from being attacked.

By determining what feels good and what feels bad to us, our BIS has considerable influence over what desires we form: we tend to want things that feel good and want to avoid things that feel bad. These desires are reflected in our behavior. The path of least resistance is to behave in a manner that earns the rewards offered by our BIS and avoids the punishments threatened by it.

Indeed, similarities in people's behavior can often be traced to similarities in the incentive systems to which they are subject. If we visit a marine boot camp, we quickly notice that the soldiers all dress alike and end sentences with "sir." This is no accident; it is a direct consequence of the incentive system imposed on them by their drill instructor. If we leave boot camp and head for a nearby fast-food restaurant, we will notice that although the restaurant employees behave in a similar manner—they dress alike and end each encounter with the question "Do you want fries with that?"—they behave quite differently from the soldiers. The restaurant employees behave alike because of the incentive system imposed on them by the restaurant, and they behave differently from the soldiers because their incentive system is different from the one imposed on the soldiers.

As we have seen, our genetic makeup has a considerable influence on our BIS. Because humans have similar genetic makeups, they have similar BISes and therefore tend to behave in a similar manner. A soldier and a restaurant employee may behave differently in certain respects, but in most respects they behave alike; for example, they will both tend to enjoy sweet foods, alcohol, praise, and sex, and they will both dislike bitter or rotten food, sprained ankles, insults, and isolation from other people.

During the twentieth century, social scientists largely abandoned the notion of a human nature. I would argue, though, that humans, because we have similar BISes, do have a nature. Indeed, someone who understands the rewards and punishments offered by human BISes—or as we used to say, someone who has a good understanding of human nature—will be in a good position to predict what people will do under various circumstances. I would also argue that it is in large part because human BISes are different from horse or cow BISes (because of our different wiring, a consequence of our different genetic makeup) that human nature differs from equine nature, which in turn differs from bovine nature.

I would even go so far as to say that among humans, male nature differs from female nature. Because men's hormones, and perhaps their brain structure as well, differ from women's, men's BISes differ from women's; consequently, what feels good to a man might not feel good—or feel *as* good—to a woman, and conversely. Because people tend to do what feels good and avoid doing what feels bad, men tend to behave differently than women. It is because of differences in their BISes, I would argue, that (most) men are sexually attracted to women and (most) women are sexually attracted to men. I also think differences in BISes are to a considerable extent responsible for various gender differences, including differences in the way boys and girls play.

At this point, some might take me to task for ignoring the environmental component of human behavior: it isn't just their BISes that makes men and women behave the way they do; their upbringing also has a major impact. I entirely agree with this claim. For one thing, because we have BISes, we routinely take the environment into account when deciding how to behave. Whether our BIS rewards or punishes us, after all, is to a considerable extent determined by how we interact with our environment. Thus, on a cold day our BIS might reward us for standing *in front of* a roaring fire but punish us for standing *in* that same fire. I also agree that past interactions with our environment can affect our current behavior. This can happen, as we have seen, when we fall off a horse or get sick after eating a certain food.

Why do little girls tend to play with dolls? Why do little boys, instead of playing with dolls, tend to play games that involve pretend acts of violence? They do so, I would argue, in large part because of the rewards offered by their BIS. For (most) girls, it feels good to engage in nurturing behavior, and so they play with dolls; for (most) boys, it doesn't feel good—or doesn't feel *as* good—to engage in nurturing behavior, and so they don't. I also think, though, that there is an environmental component in the behavior of boys and girls. In particular, besides rewarding her for engaging in nurturing behavior, a girl's BIS also rewards her for gaining the approval of other people. Consequently, if the people around her approve of her playing with dolls, it will feel doubly good for her to do so: she will be rewarded both for engaging in nurturing behavior and for gaining the praise of others.

When a girl is praised for playing with dolls, an *external* incentive system is superimposed over the *internal* incentive system that I call her BIS. If the same girl had been exposed to a different external incentive system—suppose, for example, that her parents beat her rather than praised her for playing with dolls—her behavior would have been affected in a different manner. The reward she got (from her BIS) for engaging in nurturing behavior would have been overwhelmed by the punishment she got (from her parents) for engaging in this same behavior, and consequently it would, on balance, feel bad for her to play with dolls, so she would refrain from doing so—at least while her parents were around to enforce their external incentive system. If the beatings were bad enough, they could result in a reprogramming of her BIS. In this case, even if she was rescued from her abusive parents, playing with dolls would no longer feel good.

That external incentive systems can shape our behavior is undeniable. But the thing to keep in mind when considering these systems is that *they are effective only if they take account of and exploit a person's (or creature's) BIS.* Suppose a girl had a very unusual BIS, one that made beatings feel good. Her behavior would not be altered by the external incentive system just described. Indeed, if a creature lacked a BIS and therefore nothing felt good or bad to it, external incentive systems could have no impact on its behavior.

We can debate whether girls' BISes are "naturally" programmed to reward them for engaging in nurturing behavior. (I think they are, but many feminists will disagree.) We can also debate whether girls are harmed by having parents who allow or encourage them to play with dolls. (I think they aren't, but again, many feminists will disagree.) What is undebatable, though, is that whether a girl plays with dolls is determined, to a considerable extent, by whether it feels good or bad for her to do so; that how it feels to her depends to a large extent on her BIS; and that when external incentive systems affect how it feels to her, they do so by exploiting the girl's BIS.

Although humans, because their BISes are similar, share a nature, differences in individual BISes will cause differences in the long-term behavioral tendencies of individuals—will cause, in other words, personality differences.

Why do we behave as we do? Why are we extroverts rather than introverts? Why are we inquisitive rather than incurious? Why are we nurturers rather than competitors? What determines the component traits of our personality? To a considerable extent, *we* don't determine them; our BIS determines them for us. Being sensible people, we want to feel good and avoid feeling bad. We have personalities because we tend to take the path of least resistance with respect to our BIS. If our BIS rewards us for gaining the attention of other people, we are likely to be extroverted, but if our BIS makes us feel awkward and pained when we deal with other people, we are likely to be shy. If our BIS rewards us with a feeling of satisfaction when we learn new things, we are likely to be inquisitive, but if no such feeling is forthcoming, we are likely to be indifferent to the acquisition of knowledge. If our BIS rewards us with a feeling of accomplishment when we help others, we are likely to become nurturers, but if our BIS rewards us with a feeling of triumph when we defeat other people, we are likely to become competitors.

We saw earlier that our BIS can change with the passage of time. Some changes are preprogrammed and others are the result of life experiences. When our BIS changes, our personality can change as well. The onset of puberty, for example, alters our BIS by changing the hormones present within us, and by altering our BIS, it changes our personality: a child who was sweet at age four might be a pouty teenager at age fourteen. Life experiences can also affect our BIS and thereby change our personality. Children who are abused, for example, end up with personalities that are different than if they hadn't been abused.

It is likewise possible for illness to rewire our BIS and thereby alter our personality. The onset of schizophrenia in a young adult, for example, can cause a radical change in her personality, and the onset of Alzheimer's in an elderly person can expunge whatever personality she might have had. Less tragically, neurologist Oliver Sacks tells of a ninety-year-old woman who had always been shy but who in her late eighties started to giggle, tell jokes, and flirt. Friends noticed and were concerned. It turned out that the woman had neurosyphilis, which had reemerged after lying dormant for seventy years. The disease was easily treatable, but the woman wasn't sure she wanted to be treated: she liked being an extrovert. The solution was simple: giving the woman penicillin would prevent further brain damage but would not reverse the damage that had already been done.[4] Sacks also describes a woman who in a short period of time transformed from a reserved research chemist into an impulsive and facetious punster, full of quips and wisecracks. The cause of this personality change was a huge carcinoma in her brain.[5]

Notice that this woman did not choose to become a punster; nor, for that matter, does the sweet four-year-old choose to transmogrify into an obnoxious teenager. Our personality is largely beyond our control, for the simple reason that the BIS responsible for our personality is largely beyond our control. The inquisitive person does not choose to be inquisitive: it feels good to her to learn new things, and so she does. Nor does the shy person choose to be shy. Indeed, the shy person might wish he were more expansive, but he is powerless, by a mere act of will, to change the fact that he feels uncomfortable during social interactions. He cannot simply wake up one morning and decide that he is no longer going to be shy, no more than he can wake up and decide that he is no longer going to get hungry when he doesn't eat.

In saying this, I am not suggesting that it is impossible for us to act contrary to our personalities. We clearly can; it's just that it requires substantial effort to do so. The shy person can *act* as if he weren't shy. He can go to a bar, approach strange women, and participate in karaoke, but his BIS will be punishing him all the while and offering him very few rewards, so the effort will probably exhaust him. Likewise, the extrovert can spend Saturday night reading quietly in a library, but he will probably be miserable doing so.

In a sense, then, we are trapped within our personality. Most people realize this and accept the personality they are stuck with. They do as much with that personality as they can: it is what they have to work with—or work around.

Besides determining our personality, our BIS is also responsible, I think, for those short-term distortions of our personality that we call moods. Moods are presumably caused by subtle changes in our brain chemistry, which in turn affect what feels good and bad to us. Drink some alcohol, for example, and your brain chemistry is temporarily altered, triggering a mood. In some people this alcohol-induced mood is good; in others it is bad.

Suppose that when we are in the grip of a mood, someone comments on the fact. Our first inclination will probably be to dismiss their suggestion; to agree with it, after all, is to admit that our current behavior is in some sense involuntary, and this is something most people are reluctant to do. Internally, though, we might recognize the truth of what they say. What is interesting, in such cases, is how hard it is for us, once we recognize that we are in a mood, to neutralize it. If a mood is good, we won't want to neutralize it; if it is bad, we will find that it takes genuine effort to cheer up—or if not to cheer up, at least to act cheerful. When we are in a bad mood, it isn't that we have to be snappish with other people. It's just that it feels strangely satisfying to be snappish, and not at all rewarding to be nice. The path of least resistance, and therefore the path taken by most people in a bad mood, is to behave snappishly.

Before going any further in my discussion of the BIS, allow me to clarify one thing: although I think our BIS shapes our behavior in many important ways, I am *not* saying our behavior is programmed, the way a computer's behavior is. Computers respond to the world in an utterly reflexive fashion. When presented with a stimulus, they don't get to choose how they respond; to the contrary, they must do exactly what their program tells them to do.

Some of our behavior—more precisely, our reflexive behavior—is programmed in this manner. When we hear a loud, unexpected noise, for example, we are startled. We have no choice in the matter. In particular, we don't have the luxury of considering what our response to the noise should be. Most of our behavior, though, is not programmed in this manner. Suppose a doctor is about to give us an injection. We can't choose whether the injection will be painful; because we have the BIS we do, it will hurt. We do get to choose, however, what our response to the pain will be: we can remain still as the needle enters our skin, or we can pull away.

Although our BIS gives us incentives to behave in some ways and not to behave in others, we retain the ability to ignore these incentives. Our BIS will, for example, reward us with an orgasm if we have sex, but we can choose to remain celibate— if, that is, we can deal with the feelings of lust that our BIS will inflict on us when we refrain from sexual activity. And our BIS will punish us with hunger pangs if we miss a meal, but we can choose to skip lunch. We can, in other words, buck our biological incentive system.

The same is true of nonbiological incentive systems. Workplace incentive systems, for example, are in some sense coercive, but nevertheless the people subject to them retain their freedom. Employees can buck their company's incentive system, although doing so will set back their career prospects. Likewise, soldiers in boot camp don't have to end each sentence with "sir." They can use "fathead" instead. It will cost them dearly to do so, but they *can* do it.

If we choose to buck our BIS, we are in a sense misusing our ability to choose. It is not at all uncommon for us to misuse our evolutionary legacy in this manner. Consider our ability to hear: we evolved this ability so we could detect predators, but we instead use it to listen to music. We evolved a nose so we could better smell our food; besides using it for this purpose, we use it to hold up our eyeglasses, a use that evolution utterly failed to anticipate. There is nothing wrong with this kind of misuse. Indeed, in Part Three of this book, I will suggest that it is by consciously misusing our ability to choose— by choosing to ignore certain of the rewards and punishments of our BIS—that we can, to the extent possible, confer meaning on our life.

Psychologists debate whether human behavior is "hardwired." In one sense of the word *hardwired,* it indisputably is. Most of our "wiring" is in the form of neurons that can be seen through a microscope. The rest of our wiring is in the form of chemicals, including neurotransmitters and hormones, that cannot be seen but can nevertheless be detected. Our behavior is determined by what happens in this wiring.

The connection between wiring and behavior is best studied in simple animals. Consider the roundworm *Caenorhabditis elegans,* whose nervous system has only 302 neurons. Scientists have used it to demonstrate the connection between neural wiring and behavior. They have, for example, used microscope-guided lasers to see how destruction of a single neuron affects a worm's behavior.[6] The neural wiring of humans, of course, is far more complex than that of the roundworm, but all human behavior can nevertheless be explained in terms of how we are wired. Indeed, to the extent that the environment shapes our behavior, it does so by affecting our wiring. If we knew enough about our neural wiring (we probably never will), we could accurately predict how humans would respond to various stimuli and the choices they would make under various circumstances. Indeed, someone who knew enough about our neural wiring could even predict whether and how we would respond to the incentives offered by our BIS.

Someone might at this point object that if the choices we make are determined by our wiring, then they aren't really choices at all. It may *feel as though* we are making choices, but this is just an illusion: a "choice" that we *have to make,* because of our wiring or otherwise, isn't a genuine choice.

I will not attempt to answer here the age-old question of whether humans have free will. Suffice it to say that I am attracted to philosopher David Hume's suggestion that, contrary to popular opinion, the claim that our choices are causally determined is compatible with the claim that we have free will. For Hume, a choice is made freely if, when we make it, we feel that we have alternatives open to us and can choose among them. Even though our wiring determines the choices we make, those choices are free as long as they are preceded by an appropriate choice-making process.

I am convinced that the choices we make are causally determined. The laws of physics don't stop at our skulls. What happens inside our heads is as much subject to these laws as what happens inside a computer, and what happens inside our heads determines the choices we make. At the same time, it is clear that we have the ability to "make choices"; indeed, it is an ability that we exercise almost nonstop while awake. It is also clear that the process we go through in making a choice is different from the process computers go through when they "make choices."

The whole point to having a BIS, as we have seen, is that it allows us to move beyond programmed, reflexive behavior and the limits thereof. This is why the engineers described in the previous chapter endowed their hen with reasoning ability; otherwise, she could not consider the possible actions open to her and *choose* one to act upon. At a more advanced level of incentivization, a creature will have not only the ability to choose from a list of possible actions but the ability to think up additional actions to add to the list.

Like computers, humans are hardwired, but unlike computers, we are incentivized. Incentivization requires the ability to make choices, even though this ability is in a sense illusory. We respond to stimuli not in a reflexive manner but by laying out possible responses and choosing among them. In deciding which choice to make, we are guided by whether our BIS will reward or punish us for making a particular choice, and we will typically be concerned not only with immediate rewards and punishments but with how we will be rewarded and punished in the long term. We might, for example, make a choice that involves some pain now (such as getting a flu shot) but lessens our chance of experiencing considerable pain (brought on by a bout of the flu) in the future.

Gaining the ability to choose came as part of gaining the ability to desire: purely reflexive animals don't need to make choices. And gaining the ability to desire probably came as part of a package deal: animals that gained this ability were also implanted with a biological incentive system that made some things desirable and other things undesirable. In other words, the ability to choose came with strings attached: yes, we can choose what we desire, but we are "programmed" to think some things are more desirable than others. Thus, we are in a sense coerced into making some choices rather than others.

It is as if we made a bargain with an Evolutionary Creator. He was willing to grant us (by means of a process of natural selection) the ability to desire, but only if we agreed to let him implant within us an incentive system that would guide our desires in a way that would let him accomplish his goal of having us survive and reproduce. In fact, though, we didn't enter into any bargain; instead, this package deal was forced on us. And if the Evolutionary Creator had asked if we agreed to the bargain, what could we have said? We certainly couldn't have said that we preferred some other deal since, lacking the ability to desire, we couldn't prefer anything.

When Adam and Eve gained knowledge of good and evil, it precipitated, some would have us believe, the fall of man. They noticed, for the first time, each other's nakedness. As punishment, God declared that henceforth Eve would experience pain on giving birth and Adam would have to work for his bread. They were driven out of the Garden of Eden, and we, their descendants, have inherited their fallen condition.

Something like this happened, I would like to suggest, when animals gained the ability to desire. With this ability came disturbing emotions and the possibility of pain and suffering. Furthermore, when desires arose within animals—to eat or to have sex—they felt compelled to work to fulfill these desires. And because the ability to desire was genetically hardwired into them, their condition was transmitted to their progeny. We humans continue to pay a price for our ancestors having gained the ability to desire.

# PART THREE

# DEALING WITH OUR DESIRES

Every man bears the whole stamp of the human
condition.

—Michel de Montaigne

# EIGHT

# The Human Condition

We are forced, as we have seen, to live under a system of
incentives. That system—I call it our biological incentive system, or BIS for short—is wired into us. Because of it, some
things, such as having sex, feel good to us and other things,
such as getting burned, feel bad. We retain the ability to resist
our BIS: we can, for example, act contrary to its incentives and
deliberately burn ourselves, and we can refrain from having
sex. Such resistance comes at a price, though. It takes willpower
to refuse the rewards dangled before us by our BIS and even
more willpower to submit voluntarily to its punishments.

Our BIS was imposed upon us without our consent. This
might be tolerable if the force responsible for the imposition
were benevolent and had our interests in mind when devising
our BIS's schedule of incentives. It would be tolerable, in particular, if this force did all it could to ensure that we had happy,
meaningful lives. But this is not the case. The force in question—
namely, the process of natural selection—cares little about
whether we are happy and cares even less about whether we
feel that our lives are meaningful. What it cares about is that

we survive and reproduce. As long as our feelings of unhappiness and futility do not lessen our chances of surviving and reproducing—as long as, despite these feelings, we take the steps necessary to stay alive and have sex—the process of natural selection is indifferent to them.

Indeed, thanks to our evolutionary past, we are wired to feel dissatisfied with our circumstances, whatever they may be. An early human who was happy with what he had—who spent his days lazing on the savannas of Africa thinking about how good life is—was far less likely to survive and reproduce than his neighbor who spent every waking moment trying to improve his situation. We, the evolutionary descendants of these humans, have inherited this predisposition toward dissatisfaction: we have a BIS that, regardless of what we have, will make us itch for more.

This, in a nutshell, is the human condition: because we have a BIS, we are forced to live under an incentive system that we did not devise, that we cannot escape, and whose incentives not only aren't calculated to induce us to have happy, meaningful lives but will, if we respond to them, keep us in a state of dissatisfaction.

Actually, it is an overstatement to say we are forced to live under the system of incentives that is wired into us. We can, after all, fiddle with the wiring of our BIS. In particular, we can alter our brain chemistry and thereby alter our BIS. A drink of alcohol can change what feels good and bad to us for a few hours. Drugs such as Prozac alter the levels of neurotransmitters in people's brains and thereby alter their BIS. Tranquilizers interfere with the BIS's ability to punish us with unpleasant feelings of anxiety. We can also alter the operation of our BIS by suppressing our production of hormones. A male whose sexual impulses are out of control can use a drug such as Depo-Provera. His BIS, which formerly badgered him to have sex, will now grow strangely silent on the topic.

As medicine advances, it might someday be possible for us, through a combination of drugs and surgery, to safely, effectively, and permanently alter our BIS. We would be able to specify in detail what our BIS will and won't reward us for—what, in other words, will feel good and feel bad. The possibility of altering our BIS gives rise to an interesting hypothetical question: if we had it in our power to redesign our BIS, how should we use this power?

It might initially be suggested that we modify our BIS by removing our ability to feel bad and enhancing our ability to feel good. Why not experience the rush of success on getting out of bed each morning? Why not experience an orgasm every time we inhale? (Imagine it: with each exhalation, a low moan of ecstasy.) Or why not experience continual orgasmic pleasure?

This might sound like a wonderful idea, but we need to keep in mind that our current BIS rewards behavior that increases our chances (or more correctly, increased our evolutionary ancestors' chances) of surviving and reproducing, and it punishes behavior that lessens our chances. Therefore, altering our BIS will affect our ability to survive and reproduce. Suppose, then, that we transform our current BIS into a feel-good BIS. Someone wired to experience continual orgasmic pleasure would probably just lie there in ecstasy, feeling no need to eat, drink, or even breathe, and he would soon perish.

This brings us to another radical proposal: instead of altering our BIS, why not eliminate it altogether? Humans subject to the rewards and punishments of a BIS are not truly free.

The BIS is an invisible tyrant who uses coercion to make us do his bidding. By eliminating our BIS, we can overthrow this tyrant and live the life of our choosing.

This suggestion sounds attractive—to free humanity by eliminating the BIS—but further thought reveals the drawbacks of a BIS-less existence. As we saw in Chapter 4, our desires have two sources, our emotions and our intellect. Our emotions are good at forming what I called hedonic terminal desires: they push us to seek what feels good and avoid what feels bad. Our intellect spends most of its time forming instrumental desires, fulfillment of which will lead to fulfillment of the desires formed by the emotions. Without a BIS, though, nothing would feel good or bad, and our emotions would dry up as a source of desire. In the absence of hedonic terminal desires generated by the emotions, our intellect would find itself without much to do. All we would be left with is the nonhedonic terminal desires formed by our intellect, such as my desire to click my tongue. But as we saw, these desires are generally feeble things.

Imagine, then, our BIS-less self. Would we want to eat? There would be no reward (pleasant tastes and a pleasant sensation of fullness) for doing so, and no punishment (hunger pangs) for fasting. Would we want to reproduce? Sexual activity would feel neither good nor bad, and it wouldn't end in an orgasm. Nor would we take delight in our offspring. We might think that, being sensible people, we would take steps to ensure that we survive and reproduce, but why survive and reproduce? What motivation do we have? Why go on living in a world in which living has no rewards? Our BIS-less self, one suspects, would resemble a depressed person: we would spend our days lying in bed. Or maybe our BIS-less self would resemble an intellectual antihero in a bleak Russian novel: we would get out of bed only to wonder what was the point in living.

We may not like having a BIS forced upon us by nature. We may not like having to deal with a BIS. We may not like the way our BIS prompts us to do things that, although conducive to our surviving and reproducing, are not conducive to our happiness. But life without a BIS is arguably even worse than life with one.

Instead of contemplating ways to change our BIS, let's get practical and think about how best to live with our current BIS.

We have three options in dealing with our BIS. We can become hedonists: we can take our BIS as a fact of life and spend our days assiduously seeking its pleasures and avoiding its punishments. Or we can become ascetics and struggle against our BIS. If something feels good, we can refrain from doing it, and if something feels bad, we can welcome it with open arms. Finally, we can take the middle path between hedonism and asceticism. We can superimpose our own plan for living over that set by our BIS. Sometimes living in accordance with our plan will earn us the rewards of our BIS. When this happens, we will gladly accept them. Other times, living in accordance with our plan will mean forgoing the rewards offered by our BIS or, even worse, falling victim to its punishments. We will willingly pay this price, knowing that there is no way to avoid it, if our goal is to have the most meaningful life possible, given the existence of our BIS.

This third option, by the way, is the one recommended by Buddha, not that he thought in terms of a BIS. Buddha enjoyed a hedonistic existence in his father's palace but found it unrewarding. He left the palace and practiced rigorous asceticism, "patiently torturing himself and suppressing the wants of nature."[1] After six years of this, Buddha recognized the futility of fighting his BIS at every turn and abandoned asceticism in favor of what he called the middle path.

To practice asceticism, we need to master our desires completely; that is the only way we can consistently ignore the rewards our BIS has to offer. To practice hedonism, we don't need to master our desires at all; we need only listen to our BIS and do its bidding. To follow the middle path, by way of contrast, we need to attain considerable but not complete mastery over our desires. In following the middle path, our job will be harder than that of the hedonist but easier than that of the ascetic.

If we are to gain a degree of mastery over our desires, it is important for us to understand the workings of desire. If this book has done its job, the reader has already attained this understanding. But what quickly becomes clear is that this understanding alone will not enable us to master desire. Indeed, an understanding of desire can initially be a source of considerable frustration.

When I taught a college course on desire, one student expressed this frustration in the following terms: "Okay, you've convinced me. I have a head full of desires I didn't choose. I am held captive by my evolutionary past. I would be better off if I could master my desires. Admitting this is easy; doing it is the hard part."

I share this woman's predicament. Thanks to my research, I have grown acutely aware of the process by which desires form within me. I know what it is about my evolutionary past that caused me to form a particular desire, and I can even speculate about what took place in my brain when I formed it. All this knowledge does not prevent me, however, from forming desires I find to be undesirable. Indeed, it makes it that much more irritating when they arise. A stranger insults me. I am angry and want to put this person in his place, even though I know I will never encounter him again. "This is stupid," I tell myself, and yet the anger persists. A day later I am still thinking about what I should have said to this person. "This is really, really stupid," I tell myself, yet annoying thoughts continue to plague me.

What the abovementioned student sought, what I seek, and what a reader hoping to follow the middle path successfully will likewise seek is advice on how to master desire. Let us, therefore, turn our attention in the next four chapters to some of the advice that has been given over the millennia and across cultures on how we can gain a happy and meaningful life by controlling our desires. In the first two of these chapters I describe religious advice, in the third I describe philosophical advice, and in the fourth I consider what can best be described as eccentric advice: the people offering this advice were not doing so within a religious framework or a system of philosophy, but their advice is worth examining nevertheless.

In describing advice on dealing with desire, one unavoidably encounters problems of interpretation. When I talk, for example, about *the* Buddhist advice with respect to desire, I am speaking loosely. There are lots of interpretations of Buddhism, and they differ on the details of Buddha's teachings with respect to desire. (And when it comes to Zen Buddhism, the question is not *which* interpretation is correct but *whether any* interpretation is—whether Zen Buddhism can be put into words at all.) Likewise, when I speak of the Stoic philosopher Epictetus's advice with respect to desire, I am in fact speaking of my interpretation of his advice; different students of Stoicism will find different messages in his work. I do not pretend to be giving the final, authoritative word in any of the areas I consider.

> Satisfy the necessities of life like the butterfly that
> sips the flower, without destroying its fragrance or
> its texture.
>
> —Buddha

<br>

NINE

# Religious Advice

Almost all religions require adherents to curb their desires, and almost all religions offer advice on how desire can be curbed. They might recommend a certain lifestyle as being less likely to give rise to unwholesome desires, or they might encourage adherents to pray or meditate in order to overcome these desires.

Those who join a religion are typically motivated by desire. Some join because they want to make their time on earth more pleasant. They might seek spiritual solace, want to be socially accepted by their neighbors, or dream of having a church wedding. Others join because they want their afterlife to be more enjoyable: they prefer the infinite bliss of heaven to the unspeakable suffering of hell. (The desire to spend an eternity in heaven, by the way, is one more manifestation of human insatiability. For most people, a lifetime of earthly satisfaction simply isn't enough; they instead seek an infinite period of infinite satisfaction, although it is far from clear, as we shall see, whether even heaven would satisfy them.)

My goal in this and the following chapter is not to endorse any particular religion and the advice it gives with respect to desire. I will not, for example, argue that Christianity is the one true religion—or that it is not. Nor will I argue that Christianity has a better solution to the problem of desire than, say, Buddhism. (Some argue that Buddhism is a "way of liberation" rather than a religion, but for purposes of this discussion, it is convenient to group it with religions.) My goal is instead to explore the range of religious advice that has been given with respect to desire.

I have described Siddhartha's crisis of desire. He renounced a lavish lifestyle and set out in search of something more satisfying. After leaving his palace, he visited two sages, hoping thereby to gain enlightenment, but they did not have what he was looking for. Siddhartha then went to live with five ascetics and spent six years practicing the most rigorously ascetic life possible. He systematically deprived himself of the pleasures life had to offer. He not only fasted but worked his way down to eating only one grain of hemp per day. In the end, his body resembled a withered branch, and yet he found that renouncing worldly pleasures did not extinguish desire or lead to the enlightenment he sought. He left the ascetics and began his solitary wanderings.

Sometime later, while he was sitting under a bodhi tree, enlightenment struck: "Surely if living creatures saw the results of all their evil deeds, they would turn away from them in disgust. But selfhood blinds them, and they cling to their obnoxious desires. They crave pleasure for themselves and they cause pain to others; when death destroys their individuality, they find no peace; their thirst for existence abides and their selfhood reappears in new births. Thus they continue to move in the coil and can find no escape from the hell of their own making. And how empty are their pleasures, how vain are their endeavors! Hollow like the plantain-tree and without contents like the bubble. The world is full of evil and sorrow, because it is full of lust."[1] The best way to end the evil and sorrow of the world is therefore to overcome desire. On realizing this, Siddhartha became Buddha, the Enlightened One.

Buddha's insight is generally stated in the form of the Four Noble Truths. The first Noble Truth is that life is full of suffering—and not just physical suffering but an even more significant element of psychological suffering. Buddhist scholar Bhikkhu Bodhi describes it as a feeling that our lives are not satisfactory—a feeling that "hovers at the edge of our awareness as a vague unlocalized sense that things are never quite perfect, never fully adequate to our expectations of what they should be."[2] The second Noble Truth is that this suffering is caused by desire and ignorance. Because we desire, we feel dissatisfied and are thereby led to feel envy, hatred, and anger; because of our ignorance, we fail to see that our desire is the cause of our grief. The third Noble Truth is that by overcoming desire and gaining wisdom we can overcome suffering. The question is, how can we gain wisdom? It isn't enough simply to be informed of the source of our suffering: the pleasures to be derived from fulfilling our desires are so intense that they will make us soon forget any lessons we have learned. Instead we must devise a strategy for dealing with desire. This strategy is laid out in Buddha's fourth Noble Truth, which tells us, according to Bodhi, that the best way to deal with desire is to follow the Noble Eightfold Path.

As we have seen, Buddha tried and rejected hedonism and asceticism; he instead advises us to follow what he calls the middle path. "The [Perfect One] does not seek salvation in austerities, but neither does he for that reason indulge in worldly pleasures, nor live in abundance. The [Perfect One] has found the middle path. . . . There are two extremes . . . which the man who has given up the world ought not to follow—the habitual practice, on the one hand, of self-indulgence which is unworthy, vain and fit only for the worldly-minded—and the habitual practice, on the other hand, of self-mortification, which is painful, useless and unprofitable."[3] He defends his rejection of asceticism by arguing that for someone "to satisfy the necessities of life is not evil. To keep the body in good health is a duty, for otherwise we shall not be able to trim the lamp of wisdom, and keep our minds strong and clear."[4]

This piece of advice raises a new concern. If we acknowledge our desires, don't we increase our chance of succumbing to them? Isn't the advice that we follow the middle path akin to advising an alcoholic not to give up alcohol altogether but to cut back to a six-pack of beer a day? Isn't it likely that in following this advice, he will be led once again into an uncontrollable form of alcoholism? Buddha realizes the dangers inherent in acknowledging our desires. He therefore provides us with a program for living—the Noble Eightfold Path—that he thinks will let us selectively satisfy our desires without succumbing to them.

It is easy to state the components of the Noble Eightfold Path: right view, intention, speech, action, livelihood, effort, mindfulness, and concentration. Exactly what is involved in following the Eightfold Path, however, is open to interpretation.

According to Bodhi, right view involves the correct understanding of the Four Noble Truths.[5] Right intention involves, in part, a renunciation of desire: "The way of the world is the way of desire, and the unenlightened who follow this way flow with the current of desire, seeking happiness by pursuing the objects in which they imagine they will find fulfilment."[6] According to Buddha, though, the world is mistaken on this point: "The pull of desire is to be resisted and eventually abandoned," and the reason we should overcome our desires is not because they are morally evil but because we will suffer until we overcome them.[7] How can we overcome desire? Not, says Bodhi, by repressing our desires but by "changing our perspective on them so that they no longer bind us. When we understand the nature of desire, when we investigate it closely with keen attention, desire falls away by itself, without need for struggle."[8] Once we understand desire, he says, "attachments are shed like the leaves of a tree, naturally and spontaneously."[9]

Right speech, action, and livelihood, Bodhi explains, are prescribed as aids to mental purification. Right speech includes not telling lies or saying things intended to cause pain to others, right action includes not stealing or engaging in sexual misconduct, and right livelihood includes not killing animals or selling intoxicants.

Right effort is the attempt to keep our minds free of unwholesome thoughts, including, most prominently, the "five hindrances": sensual desire, ill will, dullness and drowsiness, restlessness and worry, and doubt. How are we to banish unwholesome thoughts? Through the use of various psychological techniques. One of these involves driving out an unwholesome thought with the opposite (and therefore wholesome) thought. If you are experiencing an attack of greed, force yourself to think of generous acts. Since contrary thoughts cannot occupy a mind at the same time, the unwholesome thought will be driven out.[10]

To better understand this thought substitution process, consider the following metaphor, suggested by Bodhi. In timber-frame construction, houses are held together not with nails but with wooden pegs. Sometimes a peg will rot in a timber, thereby threatening the integrity of the house. The obvious solution is to remove the old peg and, after it is out, put in a new peg; the problem is that as soon as the old peg is removed, the timber might fall and take the rest of the house with it. The less obvious but manifestly elegant solution is to use a new peg to drive out the old peg. In similar manner, we can use a new thought to drive out an old, unwholesome thought.[11]

Suppose we find ourselves plagued by sexual desires. We can try to suppress them, but our efforts will probably fail. Suppression, Bodhi points out, "does not resolve the problem but only pushes it below the surface, where it continues to thrive."[12] Buddhists have therefore developed techniques for dealing with unwholesome sexual thoughts. A Buddhist plagued by such thoughts might meditate on the human body and in the process dwell on its repulsive nature: don't think about her full breasts and flaxen hair; think instead about her lungs, excrement, phlegm, pus, spittle, or any of the twenty-seven other body parts toward which Buddhist texts encourage us to direct our attention. According to Bodhi, this meditation demonstrates that although a body may look beautiful, this beauty is a mirage: the component parts of the body are anything but beautiful. (The aim of this meditation, Bodhi reminds us, "is not to produce aversion and disgust but detachment, to extinguish the fire of lust by removing its fuel.") And if this doesn't end our unwholesome thoughts, we can perform a "cemetery meditation" and picture the human body in the various stages of decomposition.[13]

Two components of the Eightfold Path remain—right mindfulness and right concentration. Right mindfulness involves a sort of attentiveness or awareness of what is going on within us and around us. We take note of the world as it comes without continuously trying to interpret it. Right mindfulness therefore involves *not* doing certain things—not thinking, judging, associating, planning, imagining, or wishing. The idea is that these are activities that either involve or give rise to desire. Right concentration involves focused, balanced thinking, which can be developed through the practice of meditation. And meditation does take practice, for our mind, Buddha says, is like a fish flopping around on dry land: it cannot stay fixed on one idea for any length of time but is soon distracted by other ideas.[14] Foremost among these distractions are the desires that spontaneously appear in our heads. One thing we gain by practicing meditation is insight into the manner in which desires arise within us. This insight, Buddhists claim, makes it easier for us to master our desires.

To follow the Eightfold Path, then, is to adopt a certain lifestyle. The claim isn't that those who adopt this lifestyle will instantly be transformed—will instantly master their desires. Rather, the claim is that if they continue to follow the Eightfold Path for years or decades, they will slowly be transformed. This is one of the most significant insights of Buddhism: there is no instant cure for unwanted desire. To the contrary, overcoming desire is a long, slow process, and those participating in it will periodically experience setbacks. Buddhism not only anticipates these setbacks but provides its adherents with techniques for dealing with them.

Another notable feature of the Eightfold Path is its practical, worldly nature: a person can follow the Eightfold Path without becoming a Buddhist monk. Consider the story of Anathapindika, a man of "unmeasured wealth." He visited Buddha and explained his circumstances: "My life is full of work, and having acquired great wealth, I am surrounded with cares. Yet I enjoy my work, and apply myself to it with all diligence. Many people are in my employ and depend upon the success of my enterprises." His question for Buddha: "Must I give up my wealth, my home, and my business enterprises, and, like thyself, go into homelessness in order to attain the bliss of a religious life?" Buddha's reply: "The bliss of a religious life is attainable by every one who walks in the noble eightfold path. He that cleaves to wealth had better cast it away than allow his heart to be poisoned by it; but he who does not cleave to wealth, and possessing riches, uses them rightly, will be a blessing unto his fellows. It is not life and wealth and power that enslave men, but the cleaving to life and wealth and power."[15]

And what is the reward for successfully following the Eightfold Path? Tranquility.

Zen Buddhism represents a fusion of Buddhism and Taoism. For this reason, it contains elements of Indian, Chinese, and Japanese culture. Zen Buddhists supplement the Buddhist lifestyle with certain techniques, the practice of which, they believe, increases their chance of gaining enlightenment.

The problem with writing about Zen, and Taoism as well, is their ineffability. Zen masters have a profound distrust for language and think the truths of Zen cannot be expressed in words. Ask a Zen master to explain the meaning of Buddhism, and he might respond by striking you with a stick.[16] Indeed, if someone tells you the inner meaning of Zen, chances are he is an imposter, since in Zen, as in Taoism, "One who knows does not speak; one who speaks does not know."[17] Adding to the confusion, there are different forms of Zen. In one, a teacher might cut a cat in half to illustrate a point; in another, such an act would be inconceivable.[18] Even Christian mystics such as St. John of the Cross—more on him in a moment—are accessible compared to the Zen masters.

To understand Zen, one must study it, and studying it isn't easy. The typical student of Zen, for example, will practice zazen, a meditation in which he sits perfectly still with as empty a mind as possible, for hours and hours. If he drifts off while sitting there, his Zen master might thwack him with a stick and yell at him to wake up. While not practicing zazen, he might take in a Zen lecture in which his Zen master announces, "Mountains are mountains. Mountains are not mountains. Mountains are mountains."[19] And throughout it all, as a background activity, the student of Zen might attempt to "solve" a koan, such as "What is the sound of one hand clapping?" or "What is your original face before you were born?" There is no one solution to these puzzles. Rather, you "pass" the koan when the master thinks you truly understand the question— at which point you are given another koan to solve. (In some Zen schools, monks spend thirty years solving fifty koans.) Zen is in some profound sense illogical—or maybe extralogical, outside the scope of logic, would be a better way to put it. To understand Zen, you must live it.

This brings us to an important paradox of desire. In most of life, the way to get something is consciously to make it our goal and then work hard to get it. But if our goal is to free ourselves from the grip of desire, this technique will not work. In the process of desiring intensely not to desire, we create a new desire for ourselves, and this takes us, if anything, further from our goal of overcoming desire. (There is a story about a Zen student who goes to a temple and asks how long it will take him to gain enlightenment if he joins the community. "Ten years," says the Zen master. "Well, how about if I really work and double my effort?" "Twenty years," comes the reply.)[20] This suggests that we need to use a radically different technique if we wish to overcome desire.

Zen practice is supposed to allow us to overcome desire without desiring that we overcome it. Zen encourages us to do something not obviously connected with overcoming desire in the belief that while we are engaged in this other practice—while we are both distracted and gaining insight, as it were—we will have the moment of enlightenment that allows us to master desire without consciously wishing to master it. According to one Zen master, "Gaining enlightenment is an accident. Spiritual practice simply makes us accident-prone."[21] For this reason, Zen practice might involve spending our days solving koans or practicing zazen. It might also involve doing our ordinary work, playing the flute, doing archery, or performing the tea ceremony. What it does not involve is consciously seeking enlightenment.

Because Zen Buddhists don't directly seek enlightenment, it is possible for them to experience enlightenment spontaneously, without having undergone Zen training. Furthermore, undergoing Zen training by no means guarantees that they will experience enlightenment. Consider, by way of illustration, the story of Hui-neng, an illiterate peasant who went to a monastery hoping to become a monk but, because of his low social status, was instead put to work in the kitchen. The patriarch of the monastery nevertheless became aware of Hui-neng's enlightened state, and when it came time to appoint a successor, he chose this kitchen helper over the monks. (He also advised Hui-neng to hide in the mountains for a while, since the monks would be none too happy about his being selected.)[22]

What Zen Buddhists "seek" (apparently) is a moment of enlightenment, a moment at which the futility of desire becomes deeply, instinctively clear. This moment is called *tun wu* in Chinese and *satori* in Japanese. Alan Watts describes it as a moment "when it is clearly understood that all one's intentional acts—desires, ideals, stratagems—are in vain." It is a moment in which a person "sees that his grasp upon the world is his strangle-hold about his own neck, the hold which is depriving him of the very life he so longs to attain. And there is no way out, no way of letting go, which he can take by effort, by a decision of the will." It is a moment at which our "consciousness of the inescapable trap in which we are at once the trapper and the trapped reaches a breaking point. One might almost say that it 'matures' or 'ripens.' . . . In this moment all sense of constraint drops away, and the cocoon which the silkworm spun around himself opens to let him go forth winged as a moth. . . . Contrivances, ideals, ambitions, and self-propitiations are no longer necessary, since it is now possible to live spontaneously without trying to be spontaneous."[23]

The moment of enlightenment can come when you least expect it. Sometimes its coming is wonderfully poetic: one midsummer night in 1420, a twenty-six-year-old monk named Ikkyū was sitting in a boat on Lake Biwa, and the caw of a crow triggered his moment of enlightenment. People have also gained enlightenment by listening to the sound of softly falling snow,[24] while cleaning up after breakfast,[25] by being knocked unconscious,[26] and by getting struck by lightning.[27] (In this last case, the person was literally enlightened.)

Sometimes the moment of enlightenment is horrific. According to one Zen story, the monk Shen-kuang sat in meditation outside the cave of Bodhidharma, hoping he would offer Shen-kuang instruction, but Bodhidharma kept refusing. Snow came, and still Shen-kuang sat meditating. Finally, in an act of desperation, Shen-kuang cut off his left arm and gave it to Bodhidharma, who finally took notice of him. He asked what Shen-kuang wanted.

"Peace of mind," he replied.

"Bring out your mind here before me, and I will pacify it," said Bodhidharma.

"But when I seek my own mind, I cannot find it," replied Shen-kuang.

To which Bodhidharma replied: "There! I have pacified your mind!"

This triggered Shen-kuang's moment of awakening. It was also, according to Alan Watts, possibly the first instance of the use of questions and answers as a teaching method in Zen.[28]

The enlightened person is spared much of the anxiety of decision making. He is able to make decisions, as Watts describes it, "without a second thought."[29] Life becomes simple; actions lose their affectation. Here is how Watts describes an enlightened existence: "I feel myself in a new world in which, however, it is obvious that I have always been living. As soon as I recognize that my voluntary and purposeful action happens spontaneously 'by itself,' just like breathing, hearing, and feeling, I am no longer caught in the contradiction of trying to be spontaneous." This new world has "an extraordinary transparency or freedom from barriers," and its inhabitant—the enlightened individual—comes to feel like "the empty space in which everything is happening."[30]

Enlightenment allows for undesiring choice: "Much of Zen training," says Watts, "consists in confronting the student with dilemmas which he is expected to handle without stopping to deliberate and 'choose.'" The goal of the Zen Buddhist is to replace conscious thought with spontaneous functioning and, having made a "choice," to embark on it wholeheartedly.[31]

Another reward of enlightenment is the ability to live in the moment. For most people, this ability does not come naturally, inasmuch as we are biologically wired to spend the current moment thinking about future moments. (Early humans who spent the moment calmly contemplating the now in Zen-like fashion were much less likely to survive and reproduce than those who spent the moment thinking about that lion over yonder and worrying about where their next meal was coming from.) Zen enlightenment is supposed to confer on us an unnatural ability to spend moments *in* moments.

For most people, *now* represents an infinitesimal slice in the infinity of time. To an enlightened person, now—the current moment—is all we can know or experience. We are stuck in the present moment, in an eternal now. The past and future are known only by inference. Because the enlightened person has the ability to stay in the moment, he can experience beauty and wonder during even the most commonplace moments. The unenlightened person cannot.

When, for example, an unenlightened person is stuck in traffic, he will likely sit there in a distracted state of mind. He might experience anxiety about being stuck—and of course it is pointless anxiety, since there is nothing he can do to get unstuck. He might think about the things he must do when he gets to his office and about how good it will feel to get home that evening. The enlightened person, in the same situation, might instead contemplate the sky. It is not only blue but a beautiful blue that changes from hour to hour, and it is typically populated with clouds of varying shape, color, and texture. And if the sky is overcast with leaden clouds, he might instead contemplate the smoke drifting up from the tailpipes of the cars in front of him—the way it swirls and then dissolves into nothingness. If it is raining, he might study the way the raindrops on his windshield merge and the irregular paths they take as they trickle down. Indeed, he might even contemplate the glass of his windshield: how miraculous that a substance can block the wind but transmit light! The enlightened individual will become a master of inconspicuous consumption, as compared to the conspicuous consumption in which most of us revel. While the drivers around him are experiencing boredom and anxiety, the enlightened driver might experience bliss.

Some, on hearing this description of enlightenment, will ridicule the person who can find pleasure gazing at the smoke drifting up from the tailpipes of the cars blocking his way. Such a person is at best childlike and at worst a fool. They will pity him. But who is more to be pitied, the person who is almost incapable of satisfaction and must therefore spend unsatisfying days in pursuit of a moment or two of satisfaction, or the person who can find satisfaction in the most ordinary moments and whose days are therefore filled with satisfying moments? If what we are interested in is satisfaction, it is the former person who is to be pitied; but as I shall argue in the final chapter of this book, most of us aren't interested in satisfaction. We are instead interested in "success," which not only is different from satisfaction but is to a considerable extent incompatible with it.

What is it like to gain enlightenment? Different Zen schools offer different answers to this question. Some schools hold that a person can be enlightened only once; others hold that a person can be enlightened repeatedly. Some schools hold that only one degree of enlightenment is possible—namely, perfect enlightenment; others hold that some enlightenments are more significant than others. Some schools even reject the idea of a moment of enlightenment and instead claim that enlightenment can come gradually.

Curiously, on gaining enlightenment, some individuals have celebrated by obtaining a certificate of enlightenment. There is, to be sure, something un-Zen-like about someone who has achieved enlightenment caring about the possession of a certificate that attests to the fact. True enlightenment, one imagines, should free someone of the need for certificates.

If a person has gained enlightenment, will it be obvious to the rest of us? Will he spend his days sitting there with a Buddha-like glow? Apparently not. Ikkyū, whose enlightenment was triggered by a cawing crow, liked to meditate in the day and carouse in town at night. Enlightenment does not appear to have diminished his desire for sex and strong drink; indeed, he writes of "wandering about for years in brothels and wine shops."[32] Zen master Ryōkan (1758–1831) also had a taste for strong drink and writes of drifting off peacefully, drunk and happy, on a paddy bank. He also enjoyed playing hide-and-seek with children. His enlightenment didn't spare him, though, from emotional anguish: Ryōkan writes of shedding tears of loneliness.[33]

Writer Natalie Goldberg practiced Zen for many years under a Zen master who was, she tells us, shockingly ordinary. He was married and liked to watch television. He not only liked to eat at chain restaurants but ate meat, despite having taken a vow to help all beings. He bought and drank cheap wine by the gallon box.[34] After his death, Goldberg was stunned to learn that her Zen master was not master of his own desires: he had been sleeping with his Zen students.[35] Goldberg also tells of another Zen master who used to arrive at lectures two hours late. Those who waited patiently for him assumed that in making them wait, he was teaching them an important Zen lesson. She later discovered that a more likely reason for his lateness was alcoholism.[36] In conclusion, it might be difficult to tell, just by looking at the desires to which people are subject and the extent to which they submit to them, who is enlightened and who is not.

These cases, by the way, should not be taken as a refutation of Zen—as evidence that it does not in fact help us master our desires. It might be that the Zen masters described above never actually achieved enlightenment. Or it could be that they did achieve enlightenment and that their subsequent enjoyment of the world was free from the constraints of desire: their drunkenness or lechery might have been spontaneous and "without second thought." (Indeed, Ikkyū thought it made as much sense to practice Zen enjoying sex and sake as to practice it meditating in forests and mountains.)[37] It could also be that the enlightenment of the above Zen masters, while not enabling them to master desire completely, enabled them to master it to the extent humanly possible. This last conjecture, if true, would be a testament to the power of desire.

Writer and meditation teacher Jack Kornfield has investigated what happens to people after they gain enlightenment. What he discovered is that enlightened people still have to do their laundry and take out the trash. They have to deal with the envy of those around them. They have to deal with divorce, depression, and the death of loved ones. They even have to deal, if they are parents, with surly teenage offspring. (Kornfield writes of a Zen master whose teenage son stayed out all night; when the worried father confronted him the next morning, the son responded with sarcasm: "You're a Zen master, and look how attached you are.")[38] What makes enlightened people different is that when they deal with life's difficulties, they do so with insight, gained during their enlightenment.

The world's great religions—Christianity, Judaism, Islam, Buddhism, and Hinduism—all recognize the importance of desire in human affairs. The first three of these—Christianity, Judaism, and Islam—take the Old Testament to contain God's word. The Old Testament begins, of course, with a cautionary tale about desire and its consequences: Eve had no apparent desire to eat from the tree of knowledge until the serpent awakened— or should we say created?—a desire within her. (Although the Koran repeats the story of Adam and Eve, in its version it was Adam who was tempted by Satan.)

Part of what it means to be a good Christian is to control certain of your desires. Four of the seven deadly sins (envy, gluttony, lust, and greed) directly involve desire, and the remaining three (sloth, wrath, and pride) can do so indirectly: one presumably becomes wrathful, for example, because one wants things to be different than they are. The Tenth Commandment explicitly calls on us to curb our desires: "Thou shalt not covet thy neighbor's house, thou shalt not covet thy neighbor's wife, nor his manservant, nor his maidservant, nor his ox, nor his ass, nor anything that is thy neighbor's." It is significant that covetousness makes God's short list of prohibited activities—that this crime of desire merits mention alongside crimes such as murder and theft. (Then again, if we can overcome our covetousness, we will be less likely to commit such crimes.)

In Christianity, the goal is not to extinguish desire but to overcome certain sinful desires. For example, a Christian can desire sex within marriage but not outside of marriage. How are Christians to overcome their undesirable desires? Largely by means of prayer. For example, a Christian who detected in herself a desire to embark on an extramarital fling might pray for strength in dealing with this temptation.

Not all Christian prayers, to be sure, are directed at overcoming desires; indeed, some are directed at satisfying them. The prayers in question might have an altruistic object: a Christian might pray for world peace or that an ailing friend recover. Prayers can also be selfish: a Christian might pray that his favorite team win the Super Bowl or that he win the lottery.

Prayers of thanks form another important subgroup of Christian prayer. When, for example, people say grace at a meal, they offer thanks for the food they are about to eat. If such prayers are done sincerely and with understanding, they can prevent people from taking for granted the things they already have. This in turn can increase their satisfaction with life as it is and thereby subdue their tendency to form new desires.

Let us focus our attention on Christian prayers that deal with unwanted desires. To the extent that these prayers work—to the extent that we can, by praying, rid ourselves of unwanted desires—*how* do they work? What, in other words, is the mechanism by which prayer can extinguish desire? There are two mechanisms to which a Christian might point. Some argue that prayer works by triggering divine intervention: God removes the offending desire from the person offering the prayer. He plucks it out of her mind, the way He might pluck a tumor out of her brain. Other Christians argue that prayer works by triggering psychological processes that extinguish the unwanted desire: it isn't God who removes the desire, it's the Christian. Most Christians will add that the psychological processes in question work because the person praying believes in God: there is an important difference between an atheist who many times a day says to herself, "I wish I could overcome my lustful tendencies," and a Christian who says to herself, "Lord, please help me overcome my lustful tendencies." Invoking a higher power turns a wishful thought into a prayer, and it is likely that prayers are more efficacious than wishful thoughts. Indeed, prayers can help a believer master her desires, even if it turns out that the God to whom she directs these prayers doesn't exist.

According to the sixteenth-century theologian John Calvin, for a prayer to be genuine, the person offering it must—figuratively and possibly literally as well—prostrate himself before God. He "must divest himself of all vain-glorious thoughts, lay aside all idea of worth; in short, discard all self-confidence, humbly giving God the whole glory, lest by arrogating anything, however little, to himself, vain pride cause him to turn away his face."[39] To pray, then, is to admit your own powerlessness. (If it were within your power to obtain the thing prayed for, you wouldn't need to pray for it.) The act of supplication, like the act of begging, is a humbling experience. Humility is important, Calvin would argue, if we are to keep our desires in check.

For more insight into the psychological impact of belief in a higher power, consider alcohol and drug addictions. They are notoriously difficult to overcome. One of the most successful ways to deal with them is through a twelve-step program, and of the twelve steps, the most important is arguably that an addict believe in the existence of a higher power who can help him overcome his addiction. The people at Alcoholics Anonymous don't argue that a higher power in fact exists. They simply point out that unless you believe one exists and can help you with your addiction, you are unlikely to overcome it. It is the belief in a higher power that tips the odds in your favor, psychologically speaking.

Prayer isn't the only technique by which Christians attempt to master their desires. Christians who belong to the Catholic Church, for example, also make use of confession. One of the things a person might confess to is a sinful desire. The theory is that by revealing such desires to a trusted confidant, you increase your chances of extinguishing the desire in question. Again, the technique is based on psychological insights.

Besides offering techniques for overcoming unwholesome desires, Christianity provides people with an incentive for overcoming them: if they do, they increase their chance of making it into heaven.

The concept of heaven was important to early Christians. They watched pagans enjoy comfortable, pleasure-filled lives while they—despised, hounded, brutalized, and often martyred—lived wretched lives. The mere fact that God approved of their lifestyle wasn't much consolation. They wanted God to reward their behavior. They wanted, in the end, to come out ahead of the pagans. Otherwise, why be a Christian?

Christianity could have held that mastering one's desires, in conformance with God's will, was its own reward. Such a doctrine, however, would not have rung true with the early Christians. So instead of a reward on earth, Christianity promised a reward in heaven. It may have been true that while on earth, early Christians were frustrated individuals who saw many of their basic desires go unfulfilled. But by curbing their desires while on earth, they could gain entry into heaven, where their desires would be wonderfully satisfied. The existence of heaven allowed Christians to comprehend their martyrdom. Yes, their earthly life was miserable. Yes, their lives were often cut short. Yes, they sacrificed in ways that the pagans around them didn't have to. But in the long run, Christians would come out ahead.

In Christian heaven, people's earthly fates are reversed: the poor are rich, and the rich are poor. Consider Lazarus, who lay at a rich man's door covered with sores. According to the Bible, when Lazarus died, he went to heaven; when the rich man died, he went to hell. When the rich man cried out for pity, Abraham in heaven replied, "Remember . . . that all the good things fell to you while you were alive, and all the bad to Lazarus; now he has his consolation here and it is you who are in agony."[40]

Given that heaven is the Christian reward for proper behavior while on earth, what sort of reward will it be? The Bible makes it clear that heaven is where God lives—where his throne is and where he answers and occasionally thunders from. It assures us that if we are righteous, we will go to heaven: "How blest are those who have suffered persecution for the cause of right; the kingdom of Heaven is theirs."[41] And the Bible tells us that any sensible person will want to go to heaven: "How blest you are, when you suffer insults and persecution and every kind of calumny for my sake. Accept it with gladness and exultation, for you have a rich reward in heaven."[42] It says next to nothing, though, about what heaven is like and consequently why someone will want to go there.

The prophet Ezekiel claimed to have seen God in heaven. He reports that God was on a sapphire in the shape of a throne. He had a human form but looked like "brass glowing like fire in a furnace from the waist upwards." Below his waist was what looked like "fire with encircling radiance." He summarizes: "Like a rainbow in the clouds on a rainy day was the sight of that encircling radiance; it was like the appearance of the glory of the Lord."[43] The Book of Revelation also offers a description of heaven.[44] There was a throne, and on it sat "one whose appearance was like the gleam of jasper and cornelian; and round the throne was a rainbow, bright as an emerald." Before this throne were seven flaming torches, and around it were twenty-four elders wearing white robes and golden crowns and sitting on twenty-four thrones. Before this collection of thrones stretched what seemed to be a sea of glass. These descriptions are clearly intended to impress, and impress they do. Who wouldn't like to see such a place? And yet, one fears, it would be like seeing the pyramids or Niagara Falls: after contemplating them for a few hours, one would grow bored. The novelty would wear off, and one would start longing for a new spectacle. Of course, in heaven, there would be no other spectacle available to you. It would be that one spectacle *for eternity*. Some reward!

Some early Christians were not impressed by this image of heaven and instead came up with the concept of a heaven on earth. St. Irenaeus, born sometime in the first half of the second century, describes a heaven in which people can enjoy the material blessings they might have been deprived of while on earth. His heaven is basically an earth without frustrations. Those who enter this heaven will retain their earthly bodies. Women will have all the children they want. The climate will be ideal. There will be wine and grain in abundance. People will no longer need to work to eat, since the Lord will supply them with delicacies. There will be no enemies. Wild animals will be subject to human rule. No one will die. On the real earth, righteous people often fail to get what they want; in Irenaeus's heaven on earth, the desires of the righteous will be satisfied. Irenaeus apparently thought that the material desires of people were satiable, so that if they got what they wanted, they would be happy.

The Church subsequently rejected and ultimately outlawed the notion of a heaven on earth and more generally the notion of a heaven in which people could satisfy earthly desires. They offered instead an unearthly heaven in which, instead of enjoying all the bread and wine they could consume, people spent their days in blissful contemplation of God. Around A.D. 400, St. Augustine offered one such vision of heaven. He had experienced mystical raptures in which he seemed to have direct access to God. Wouldn't it be wonderful, he thought, if the delight of these raptures could be eternal? And this, he decided, is what people would experience in heaven.

Initially Augustine thought the residents of heaven would not have bodies. They would instead exist as souls and would spend all their time contemplating God. In doing this, they would find perfect happiness; in particular, they would never tire of seeing Him: "He shall be the end of our desires who shall be seen without end, loved without cloy, praised without weariness."[45] (For Augustine, then, the desire to look on God is simultaneously satisfying and insatiable.)

Augustine later modified these views and said that in heaven it would be possible for us to encounter, in a spiritual way, our family and friends. In particular, we would have bodies we could use to communicate with them. Our heavenly bodies would have been repaired: if we were sick on earth, we would not likewise be sick for an eternity in heaven. (One exception: scarred martyrs got to keep their scars in heaven, apparently as a kind of badge of honor.) We could eat and drink, but for pleasure, not because we were hungry or thirsty. At the same time, there would, in Augustine's scheme of things, be no lust in heaven, and to ensure that our heavenly selves didn't experience lust, our resurrected bodies would not be anatomically correct.[46]

Other Christians have come up with other visions of heaven. What these visions have in common is that residing in heaven will be a rewarding experience—although different visions of heaven offer different rewards—and that it will be you who enjoys the reward—although different visions have different notions of exactly what your heavenly self will be. In summary, Christianity involves a battle not against desire in general but against certain desires. The reward for winning this battle is that certain other desires will be satisfied, to the greatest extent possible and for an eternity.

St. John of the Cross (1542–1591) was an important exception to the above generalizations about Christianity. He thought one of the primary goals of any Christian should be to overcome desire: "Deny your desires and you will find what your heart longs for."[47] Furthermore, although he believed in heaven, he mentions it infrequently. Instead, he emphasizes the benefits to people *here on earth* of overcoming their desires. For one thing, they will find tranquility; for another—and more importantly—they will achieve a union with God while still alive. Let us now examine some of the advice John offered on how to overcome our desires.

John counsels those seeking divine union—beginners and proficients alike—to mortify their appetites, and to achieve mortification, he advises us to cleanse our soul of desires, attachments, and ambitions.[48] "To reach satisfaction in all, desire satisfaction in nothing," he tells us; "To come to possess all, desire the possession of nothing."[49] He adds that God will reward the soul that is "naked of desires and whims."[50]

John advises us not to rejoice in temporal prosperity. To the contrary, we should give away what we possess, even though we may need it. We must also submit ourselves to the will of a higher power: "Although you perform many works, if you do not deny your will and submit yourself, losing all solicitude about yourself and your affairs, you will not make progress."[51]

John realizes how much of our lives is devoted to winning the admiration of other people; he also realizes how damaging their admiration can be. He advises us to make every effort to stop caring about what others think of us. He also suggests that rather than taking steps to enhance our self-esteem, we take steps to deflate whatever self-esteem we may possess. We should, for example, keep our good works a secret—we should not even seek that God knows of what we do. When we find ourselves in a competitive situation, we should lose and let others win. We should not complain about others, nor should we seek their approval. Indeed, says John, we should "consider it the mercy of God" that someone occasionally praises us, for we deserve none.[52] We should act, speak, and think with self-contempt, and we should desire that others treat us with contempt. John's summary advice about our relations with other people is uncompromising: "Live as though only God and yourself were in this world, so that your heart may not be detained by anything human."[53]

If we are to overcome desire, John advises, we should pay as much attention to trifling desires as to seemingly more consequential ones. Thus, we must try to overcome the desire to chat with other people and any attachment we might have to our clothing, to a book, or to the way our food is prepared. He argues that these seemingly trivial desires can be as harmful as consequential ones: "It makes little difference whether a bird is tied by a thin thread or by a cord. Even if it is tied by thread, the bird will be held bound as surely as if it were tied by cord."[54] He offers the following admonishment: "We have witnessed many persons . . . fall from happiness and stability in their spiritual exercises and end up losing everything merely because they began to indulge in some slight attachment to conversation and friendship under the appearance of good."[55]

In order to overcome your desires, says John, you should "have habitual desire to imitate Christ in all your deeds by bringing [your] life into conformity with his." In keeping with this desire, you should "endeavor to be inclined always: not to the easiest, but to the most difficult; not to the most delightful, but to the most distasteful; not to the most gratifying, but to the less pleasant; not to what means rest for you, but to hard work; not to the consoling, but to the unconsoling; not to the most, but to the least; not to the highest and most precious, but to the lowest and most despised; not to wanting something, but to wanting nothing."[56] This sounds like asceticism, pure and simple, but we should remember that John's ultimate goal in all this sacrifice is not to vanquish desire but to fulfill his desire to achieve union with God.

The Islamic take on desire resembles, in many respects, that of Christianity. Like Christians, Muslims are enjoined to struggle against certain desires. (The Muslim list of prohibited desires, however, is different from the Christian list: Muslim men, for example, can desire a second wife, while Christian men shouldn't. Christian men can desire pork; Muslim men shouldn't.) Like Christians, Muslims pray to overcome these forbidden desires. And like Christians, Muslims who win the battle against unwholesome desires are rewarded with heaven.

Christians, as we have seen, toyed with but ultimately rejected the idea of an earthly heaven. The Muslims appear to have embraced it. According to the Koran, heaven—where the righteous go after death—is a garden. More precisely, it is a garden of bliss—having "many varieties of trees, . . . two springs flowing full . . . and every type of fruit." The fruit will be "hanging low within easy reach." Those in heaven will "recline on couches above carpets, the linings of which will be of thick brocade." The couches will be "inwrought with gold and jewels." Those on the couches will be "waited on by ageless youths, carrying goblets and ewers and cups filled out of a flowing spring, neither causing headache nor inebriating." They will be able to enjoy "such fruits as they choose, and the flesh of birds as they may desire." For companions they will have "maidens with lovely black eyes, pure as pearls well guarded."[57] What is being described sounds like the perfect oasis—the desert-dwelling nomad's dream come true. In other words, Islam, like Christianity, is not about overcoming desire; it is about overcoming certain desires so that we can satisfy other desires—in heaven, if not on earth.

There is no Buddhist heaven. When I began my research, I seized on this fact as evidence that Buddhism's take on desire was fundamentally different from that of Christianity and Islam. Buddhism, I thought, is about overcoming desire, and the reward for doing so is a better, more tranquil earthly existence. Christianity and Islam, on the other hand, seek not to overcome desire but to maximize fulfillment of our desires. If we suppress certain desires today, we will be compensated by having other desires satisfied in the future—if not during our earthly existence, then during our afterlife.

Further research, however, suggests that the difference between Buddhism's take on desire and that of Christianity and Islam is not as great as I had thought. For one thing, practicing Christianity or Islam can improve our earthly existence by allowing us at least to curb our desires, if not to extinguish them. Furthermore, although Buddhists don't believe in a heaven like that of Christianity or Islam, they do believe in an afterlife. They believe, after all, in reincarnation. The realm one currently inhabits is the result of choices made in past lives, and the realm one will inhabit in the next life is determined in part by the choices one makes in this life. According to the doctrine of karma, one can improve one's future lives—it is better, Buddhists think, to come back as a human than as a cockroach—by making proper choices in this life. Indeed, make the right choices and you improve your chances of not being reincarnated, of escaping from the cycle of death and rebirth. For Buddhists, then, the ultimate point in curbing desires is not to extinguish them but to maximize the extent to which our desires are satisfied. In this respect, Buddhism has something in common with Christianity and Islam.

> How good we have it! The outside world has no idea
> what they are missing.
>
> —An Amish couple, quoted by Donald Kraybill

# Religious Advice
# Continued: Protestant Sects

It is misleading to talk about *the* Protestant take on desire. There are lots of Protestant sects, and these sects generally have subsects and sub-subsects. One of the things that distinguishes the various sects is their take on desire, with different sects labeling different desires as being unwholesome. Thus, while most Protestant sects see nothing wrong with adherents wanting to dance, some Southern Baptist sects regard this desire as unwholesome. In some sects—for example, the Old Order Amish—the list of proscribed desires is quite long, while in others—for example, the Unitarians—it is quite short. And while the various sects agree on the power of prayer to help adherents overcome unwholesome desires and agree that heaven is our reward for successfully overcoming them, they differ with respect to other desire-control techniques. Some sects, for example, resort to community pressure to help followers keep their desires in check; others argue that we should not judge our neighbors.

In this chapter, I will examine the treatment of desire by various Protestant sects, beginning with the Amish. (When I say "Amish" I mean Old Order Amish; many of the remarks that follow do not apply to more "progressive" Amish sects.) Even though there are only a hundred thousand or so Amish in America, they are of particular interest in any examination of desire because their battle against it is unusually thoughtful and unusually visible.

The Amish are different. They dress differently, speak a different language (when among themselves), and drive around in buggies. A common reaction is that the Amish are simply strange, that they are religious fanatics, or that they are fighting against progress. A bit of research, however, indicates that what makes the Amish different is in large part their strategy for dealing with desire.

The behavior of the Amish is circumscribed by a largely unwritten set of rules known as the *Ordnung*. It allows the Amish to ride in cars but not to drive them, to use tractors in their barns but not their fields, and to use in-line skates but not bicycles. According to the *Ordnung*, the Amish cannot have a freezer in their own home but can have one in the home of a non-Amish neighbor. They can use calculators but not computers.

The basic principle of Amish life is *Gelassenheit*, submission to a higher authority. The higher authority in question includes both God and the Amish community. If you are Amish, your neighbors will have considerable say over how you live your life. The Amish are notable for their self-denial and self-sacrifice—for the extent to which they conform their own desires to the will of God and to the wishes of their neighbors.

As sociologist Donald B. Kraybill notes, while non-Amish Americans are busy finding themselves, the Amish are working hard to lose themselves.[1] The Amish are not rugged individualists; they are rugged communalists—rugged since they are willing to put up with the ridicule of the outside world in order to live up to their communal ideals.

Many people assume that the primary goal of the Amish is to remain in the nineteenth century. This assumption is incorrect. What the Amish seek is a certain way of life. They think many of the conveniences of modern living—most of which came along in the twentieth century—put that way of life in jeopardy. In particular, they think that if what one values is a strong sense of community, many of the technological breakthroughs of the last century are to be looked upon as curses, not blessings.

The Amish do not shun technology; they accept it selectively. They adopt technologies they think will strengthen the community and shun technologies they think will weaken it. In the words of Kraybill, "The Amish are suspicious that beneath the glitter of modernity lurks a divisive force that in time might fragment and obliterate their close-knit community." He adds that this fear isn't idle, inasmuch as social separation is one major consequence of industrialization.[2]

The thing to realize about technological breakthroughs is that it is possible to live without them. In fact, for most of the history of mankind, people *did* live without them. When a new technology comes along, it will, if we adopt it, change our lives, but will it change them for the better? The Amish feel that many of the changes made possible by technological breakthroughs are changes for the worse. In particular, they argue that having telephones, computers, and dishwashers in homes doesn't improve people's lives, if what they seek is a strong sense of community and strong family relations.

If we point out to the Amish that dishwashers are labor-saving devices, they will ask what we are saving the labor for. Are we saving it so we have more free time? If so, what will we do with the free time in question? Enjoy our leisure? The Amish regard leisure as a significant obstacle to happiness, since it is when we have nothing to do that unwholesome desires are most likely to arise within us. Idle hands, the Amish will remind us, are the Devil's workshop. As a result, the Amish are not interested in saving labor; instead, they are interested in expanding labor to fill the time available. (Because the Amish work so hard and refuse to spend their money on every new consumer gadget that comes along, they often become quite wealthy. There are even Amish millionaires.)

If we ask the Amish why they refuse to use electricity from power lines—they don't object to using electricity drawn from batteries or, in some cases, from on-site generators—they will reply that relying on the outside world for electricity lessens their self-sufficiency. To the Amish, self-sufficiency is more important than the convenience of power from external sources. And having said this, we should qualify the kind of self-sufficiency the Amish seek: they have no problem at all relying on other members of their community to help them fulfill their needs; what they object to is having to rely on people outside their community.

Of course, in relying on batteries and generators, the Amish *are* relying on people outside their community to supply them with power. The batteries they use are produced outside, as is the fuel consumed by their generators. Then again, if all external sources of power suddenly dried up—if power lines went dead, battery makers stopped manufacturing batteries, and oil companies stopped selling fuel—one supposes that the Amish, accustomed only to batteries and on-site generators, would fare better than the rest of us.

One of the primary concerns of the Amish is to keep their social desires in check. Most of us seek personal aggrandizement. We want others to notice, respect, or admire us. We might even want others to envy us. These social desires, to a considerable extent, rule our lives. They determine where we live, how we live, and how hard we work to maintain our chosen lifestyle. The Amish are just the opposite. They don't dress to impress, they dress to conform. The last thing you want to do, if you are Amish, is dress in a way that calls attention to yourself—that makes it look as though you think you are different from the rest of the people or—horrors!—better than the rest. Likewise, Amish buggies look the same because no one wants a buggy that stands out. Non-Amish Americans work hard to keep up with the Joneses; the Amish, on the other hand, work to keep *down* with the Joneses.

When the Amish express pride—when they seem to be getting full of themselves—their neighbors are quick to criticize them and put them back in their place. To avoid this, the Amish go to great lengths to preserve an image of humility. If an Amishman writes an article for a newspaper, he might not sign it, and if he wins an award, he might ask that newspapers not print his name when they report the award.

Being a minister confers considerable prestige on an Amishman. This raises the possibility that people will "campaign" for the job or will behave in a prideful fashion on attaining it.

To avoid this evil, Amish ministers are chosen by lot and on being chosen are expected to live even more humbly than their neighbors: ordinary Amishmen might have windshields on their buggies, but Amish ministers might not allow themselves this luxury.

By trying to blend in rather than stand out, the Amish pre-empt a whole range of social desires that might otherwise cause them grief. People who try to outshine their neighbors are engaged in a curious kind of social competition. If they lose, they feel pangs of envy; if they win, they typically do so at considerable financial cost and run the risk of becoming targets of their neighbors' envy. A thoughtful person will think twice about engaging in a competition in which, no matter whether you win or lose, you are worse off. According to Kraybill, it is because the Amish are thoughtful that they refuse to compete socially with their neighbors: "Amish attempts to harness selfishness, pride, and power are not based on the premise that the material world or pleasure itself is evil. . . . Evil, the Amish believe, is found in human desires for self-exaltation, not in the material world itself."[3]

The social conformity of the Amish has other benefits. For example, Amish standards of dress free them from having to spend time, effort, and money struggling to keep up with fashion. Wouldn't it be nice to get up in the morning and not have to worry about which outfit to wear? Amish conformity, Kraybill observes, "frees them from incessant choice."[4]

Because they mistrust external influences that can undermine their communities, the Amish shun various technologies. Many television programs scoff at religion and family values, and the commercials shown during these programs are poorly disguised attempts at tricking people into wanting goods and services they don't really need. Given Amish values, it would be foolish for them to pay for the privilege of exposing themselves to these influences, and so they forgo television. The telephone is objectionable to the Amish not only because it allows them to communicate with—and be influenced by—the outside world but because it changes communications within the Amish community: telephone conversations displace face-to-face conversations. (Actually, it is home phones to which the Amish object; they generally allow phones to be used for business purposes.) The car makes it much easier for people to travel to non-Amish regions and thereby to be exposed to non-Amish influences, and for this reason, the Amish object to ownership of cars.

Amish prohibitions may in some sense be arbitrary, but it does not follow from this that they are unreasonable. Consider, for example, the Amish rule that farmers can use tractors in their barns—primarily to power farm equipment—but not in the fields, which is the obvious place to use them. The Amish offer the following rationale for this prohibition. Suppose farmers were allowed to use their tractors in the field. Before long, they would take them off the farm. They might drive to town to pick up heavy loads that would be difficult to carry in the buggy. And while they were in town, they might save a trip and pick up groceries. After that, they might take the tractor into town just to get groceries. But if you can take a tractor into town, why not take a car instead? And if you can take a car into town, why can't you take it to distant places? Allowing tractors in the field, the Amish argue, would put them at the top of a slippery slope that ends in the use of a car for travel to distant places—and thus weakens the community. The Amish use a similar slippery-slope argument to justify their prohibition against wiring houses for electricity. If electricity is available, it will seem foolish not to put it to work in lights, microwave ovens, and televisions—all of which, the Amish argue, weaken the fabric of Amish life.

Slippery-slope arguments such as those just given are suspect: there is no logical reason, after all, why someone poised at the top of a slippery slope cannot remain there indefinitely. The Amish will agree with this observation but go on to point out that what greases slippery slopes is not logic but human psychology. While it is true that people *can* remain indefinitely at the top of a slippery slope, most people *don't* remain there. They take one seemingly innocent step, and before they know it they are picking themselves up at the bottom of the slope.

Amish apprehension with respect to slippery slopes is borne out by their experience with splinter groups. When the telephone came along at the beginning of the twentieth century, some of the Amish started using it. Amish bishops, fearing the consequences of adopting this new technology, prohibited telephonic communication. One group decided they could not abide by this prohibition. In 1910 they split off to form their own church, and from there they proceeded to slide down the slippery slope, adopting first tractors and electric lights, then cars. (The Amish appear to harbor a suppressed desire to own a car; in the words of one Amishman, "The first thing people do when they leave the Amish church is get a car.")[5]

Anyone who wishes to deal with desire must adopt semiarbitrary rules for living. Indeed, if we look at our own lives, we can discover any number of self-imposed, semi-arbitrary rules. With respect to alcohol, we might forbid ourselves to drink alone, to drink before sunset, to drink hard liquor, or to drink wine costing more than a certain amount per bottle. With respect to credit cards, we might forbid ourselves to let a balance carry over at the end of the month, triggering finance charges. Or we might forbid ourselves to use credit cards, or limit ourselves to a certain number of cards or a certain credit limit. With respect to entertainment, we might refuse to have a television in our house, for fear of how its presence will affect our lives, or we might have a television but refuse to get cable. It is, to be sure, difficult to justify the exact place at which we draw the line with respect to our behavior, but slippery-slope reasoning can be invoked to show the importance of drawing *some* line—even an arbitrary one—in order to prevent a gradual deterioration of our lifestyle.

Adopting semiarbitrary rules for living is also an important way to fight human insatiability. In the words of Schopenhauer, "*Limitation always makes for happiness.* We are happy in proportion as our range of vision, our sphere of work, our points of contact with the world, are restricted and circumscribed."[6] If you fail to restrain yourself, you will always want more and will thereby put yourself on the satisfaction treadmill. By placing arbitrary limits on your use of, say, credit, you are acknowledging your own potential insatiability with respect to it; you are announcing to yourself that in this case at least, you had better learn to be satisfied with a limited amount of credit, because more is not forthcoming.

One important Amish insight into desire is that self-set and self-enforced limits on our behavior are fragile things. It is for this reason that the Amish let their community set and enforce behavioral limits. When the Amish break the rules of the *Ordnung*, they might be asked to make a public confession of their error, possibly on their knees and before their neighbors. (Catholicism also relies on confession to get its adherents to behave in conformity with church dictates, but the confession in question is to a confessor, who will keep their sins a secret.) If no confession is forthcoming, the Amish transgressor might be excommunicated.

Amish excommunication has real teeth. It is hard for the Amish, having been raised Amish, simply to abandon their community for life in "the World." They will have trouble fitting in. And if they remain in their community despite having been excommunicated, they will be subjected to shunning. The Amish can talk to shunned individuals but cannot shake hands with them. They can give something to shunned individuals but cannot accept anything from them. (Thus, a shunned woman may not hand her baby directly to her mother; instead the child must be passed on by an intermediary.) If a shunned person goes to the wedding of a relative, he or she might be seated at a separate table. In the words of one Amishman, a shunned person comes to feel like a goat or a piece of dirt.[7] Shunning is a potent social force, powerful enough to make all but a handful of the Amish keep their desires within the limits prescribed by the *Ordnung*.

Of course, shunning can work only if a person cares about what members of his community think of him and only if he has a sense of shame. For many of their non-Amish neighbors, then, shunning would be utterly ineffective. Consider, in particular, those individuals who, when they lose a battle with desire, don't feel a sense of shame but instead go on a television talk show to boast to all the world of their failure.

It is instructive to contrast the harnessing of social forces by the Amish with the repudiation of these same forces by many modern Westerners. When these last individuals join a religion, they don't submit to its authority and strive to conform their behavior to the church's dictates; instead they campaign to change the church's dictates to bring them into conformity with their chosen lifestyle. And for a growing number of people, even this minimal interference with their lifestyle is intolerable: instead of joining a church, they create their own personal religion, combining, perhaps, equal parts of Judaism, Methodism, and Christian Science, with a dash of Buddhism thrown in to lighten the mix. Since they created the religion, they are their own authority, meaning that if they don't punish themselves for their transgressions, no one will. The danger is that this personal religion will do nothing at all to help them curb their desires, for the simple reason that they will never punish themselves.

Suppose a neighbor, on observing their lifestyle, is critical of these individuals. Indeed, suppose the whole community condemns the lifestyle choices they make within the framework of their personal religion. Those being criticized are unlikely, under these circumstances, to pay heed to their neighbors' condemnation. They are unlikely even to feel shame. Instead, they will probably accuse those who condemn them of an even worse offense than their own alleged misdeeds: they will accuse them of being judgmental.

Many people want absolute freedom to pursue the objects of their desires. They want other people not just to tolerate this pursuit but to endorse it. What they fail to realize is that by putting no bounds at all on their desires, they are unlikely ever to gain satisfaction. Indeed, it is entirely possible that the Amishman, faced with humiliation if he puts a telephone in his living room, has a better shot at lasting happiness than the person who spends his days striving to fulfill whatever desires enter his head, regardless of what his God or his neighbors think.

Joining a religion can do a number of things for us. It can help us fit in with our neighbors, give us the option of a church wedding, or make us more acceptable as a political candidate. It might even help us get into heaven. But one of the most important things joining a religion can do is enable us to transform ourselves by helping us master our desires. In doing this, it increases our chance of having a happy, meaningful life. Yet, sadly, all too many of those who claim adherence to a religion refuse to let this transformation take place.

The Amish celebrate a rite of passage—they call it *rumspringa,* which literally means "running around"—that sheds light on human desire. Amish children are raised with *Gelassenheit* in mind: from their earliest days, they are taught the importance of submission to the will of God and their community. Consequently, as adolescents they are extremely well behaved. When they turn sixteen, though, discipline is relaxed. In the old days, *rumspringa* involved a degree of mingling between young men and young women. It also involved mild protests against authority: in the 1950s and 1960s, Amish youth might have cut their hair shorter than their elders, and in the 1970s and 1980s, they might have grown it longer.

By the 1990s, though, *rumspringa* had become a decidedly worldly affair. Amish teens started dressing like non-Amish teens. They also partied like them, at dances with kegs of beer and live bands playing electric guitars. They installed (battery-powered) CD players in their buggies. If they had rich and indulgent parents, they might even acquire a sporty automobile.

What these Amish teens are doing, of course, is swapping one sort of conformity for another, but this thought probably doesn't occur to them.

By the late 1990s, *rumspringa* had become, for some Amish youth, an exercise in excess. They experimented with drugs, and in 1998, two Amish teens were arrested for selling cocaine for—irony of ironies!—the Pagans motorcycle gang. They were sentenced to twelve months in prison, a sentence many of the Amish found too lenient.[8]

At the end of *rumspringa*—which usually happens when they are between ages nineteen and twenty-two—Amish youth must make a choice. They can either join the church—the Amish, like all Anabaptist sects, believe in adult baptism—in which case they will have to give up the pleasures of the World, or they can continue to enjoy these pleasures but must forgo the benefits of community life and cannot marry within the Amish faith. What is striking is that 90 percent of Amish youth, faced with this choice, give up the World's pleasures for the rather more austere pleasures offered by an Amish lifestyle. Perhaps it is because they recognize that keeping their desires within community-set limits will ultimately lead to more happiness than attempting to fulfill whatever desire might pop into their head, or perhaps it is because—the non-Amish cynic might suggest—they have been so brainwashed during their first sixteen years of life that they cannot conceive of an alternative existence.

The Amish allow this period of youthful hedonism for two reasons. The first stems from their theological beliefs. Because they believe in adult baptism, a person's decision to join the church must be free and informed. If their children were never allowed to explore alternatives to the Amish lifestyle, their decision to join the church would be neither free nor informed.

The second reason is practical. For Amish communities to survive, it is important that their members be like-minded individuals who understand the importance of submitting to the will of the community. If the Amish forced their more individualistic offspring to join the community, they would be planting the seeds of future disharmony.

*Rumspringa,* by the way, tells us something about child development. Non-Amish parents watch as their sweet and loving child turns, sometime in his teens, into someone surly, rebellious, and unpleasant. They might wonder whether their child would have done this if they had been stricter—if they had raised him with a firm hand and eliminated all corrupting influences. The Amish experience shows that even if you raise your child with a firm hand and carefully control his environment, he will still rebel against your authority.

The Hutterites are another Old Order group. Whereas the Amish live mostly in Pennsylvania, Ohio, Indiana, and surrounding states, the Hutterites live in Montana, South Dakota, and the provinces of Alberta, Saskatchewan, and Manitoba. The Hutterites are more than a century older than the Amish but came to North America more than a century later.

To the casual observer, the Hutterites resemble the Amish. They are alike in being visibly different from the World's people and in wanting to live apart from them. Both groups take steps to block outside influences. (The Hutterites justify a ban on television by pointing out that "TV brings destruction, and Hollywood is the sewer pipe of the world.")[9] Farming is the primary occupation of both the Hutterites and the Amish. The Hutterites also agree with the Amish on the importance of fighting pride and self-will, and surrendering yourself to a higher authority. Finally, the religious views of the Hutterites resemble those of the Amish, but this is what one would expect, given that both groups trace their roots back to the Anabaptists.

Despite these similarities, the Hutterites and the Amish differ in certain respects. For one thing, the Hutterites are more comfortable with technology than are the Amish. On their farms, the Hutterites own and use trucks, vans, and tractors without a second thought. In their homes, they take full advantage of remotely supplied electricity. In their kitchens, they use electric ovens and freezers, although not automatic dishwashers. (The ban on dishwashers appears to be an example of male leaders drawing semiarbitrary lines.)

The biggest difference, though, between the Hutterites and the Amish—the difference most worth examining in our exploration of desire—is their views on private property. The Amish allow it. They own their homes, their farms, their buggies. Thanks to the acquisition of property, an Amishman may become, as we have seen, not just wealthy but a millionaire. The Hutterites, on the other hand, do not allow private property, aside from clothing and a few personal possessions. They live in communal housing. Each Hutterite colony has a cluster of apartment buildings that circle communal dining facilities and a church building. They don't work for pay. Some communities give members a cash allowance with which to acquire private property, but it is minimal—under $10 per month. If you leave the Hutterite community, you leave with only the clothes on your back and a few personal items. (When you are baptized, you have to relinquish all claims to colony property.) It is estimated, by the way, that only 5 percent of Hutterites choose to leave the community.

Private property gives rise to desires—the desire to own what others have, the feelings of envy that go with this desire, and the unquenchable desire, however much one might own, to own even more. Ban private property and you put an end to one of the principal causes of human strife and personal dissatisfaction. It is not surprising that the Hutterites believe this; what is perhaps surprising is that the other Old Order sects, who are willing to go to extreme lengths to guard against unwholesome desires, would stop short of banning private property.

The battle against private property is difficult since, in the words of one seventeenth-century Hutterite leader, "men hang on to property like caterpillars to a cabbage leaf."[10] To make their prohibition of private property work, Hutterites teach their children to share. And because they live in such close quarters, it is very difficult for anyone to violate the prohibition: spies are all around. Those caught accumulating property might be required to confess in public. Other punishments might involve public humiliation, such as having to eat alone or sleep in the kindergarten building. Their ban on private property seems to be working: the Hutterites are arguably the oldest and most successful communal group in North America.

Why would Hutterites submit to this intrusion into their lives? For them, life in a Hutterite colony offers a double reward. The first comes on earth, where they enjoy a profound sense of community and are free of many of the worries of modern living. In particular, they don't have to worry about climbing a career ladder or projecting an image of success, and they don't have to worry about their retirement. The second reward will come in heaven; indeed, they view their colonies as the vestibule of heaven.

Although the Hutterites gave up private property, they, like the Amish, allow sexual relationships within marriage. But doesn't the possibility of "sexually owning" another person give rise to desires even more unwholesome than the possibility of owning things? Why not, besides giving up private property, give up sex? Why not enforce communal celibacy?

Some religious groups—the Catholic Church, for example—require that *some* members (its priests) be celibate. The Shakers are remarkable for requiring that *all* members be celibate. The Shakers, whose official name is United Society of Believers in Christ's Second Appearing, trace their roots back to the Camisards of France, who came into existence as a result of the Revocation of the Edict of Nantes in 1685. The Shakers came to the United States in 1774.

The Shakers resembled the Hutterites in a number of respects. Like the Hutterites, they were not afraid of progress: the circular saw and washing machine are among the inventions credited to the Shakers. And like the Hutterites, they abolished private property: in Shaker communities, land and buildings were communally owned. But unlike the Hutterites, they did not tolerate sexual relationships between members. The Shakers thought celibacy improved a person's chances of achieving salvation. It also fostered a strong sense of community, something quite important to the Shakers.

Most religions have a dual growth strategy: they gain members by conversion and, since they require adherents to raise their children in the religion, by procreation. The Hutterites and Shakers are exceptions to this strategy. Hutterites do not proselytize, nor do they greet would-be converts with open arms. They are, however, superlative procreators: in the twentieth century, their high reproductive rates—ten children per family was typical in the first half of the century—made them perhaps the fastest-growing religious group on the planet. The Shakers, on the other hand, grew solely by conversion. Unmarried individuals came to join, as did families. (When a married couple joined, they were expected to forgo further sexual relations, as well as any special attachment to each other.) The Shakers also took in and raised orphaned children, many of whom chose, on maturing, to live the Shaker life.

Notwithstanding this obstacle to their growth, the Shakers did quite well for themselves. From the handful of members who came to America at the end of the eighteenth century, the Shakers grew to number six thousand at the peak of their popularity, in the decade before the Civil War. Today, few Shakers are left. Their decline is arguably due more to social changes than to their celibate ways.

What is celibacy? Historically, to be celibate simply meant to be unmarried. These days, a celibate person is one who abstains from sexual intercourse, either inside or outside of marriage. And for people in some religious orders, celibacy involves more than abstaining from sexual intercourse; they also abstain from masturbation.

Being celibate isn't easy: we are, after all, biologically wired so that sexual desires arise within us. What we need, if we wish to be celibate, is a strategy for preventing these desires. One such strategy involves removing sources of sexual stimulation from our environment. We can accomplish this by living alone, but solitude is oppressive. Alternatively, we can live in a single-sex community, but even then, the presence of other people can give rise to sexual thoughts. For this reason, monasteries take steps to prevent monks from inadvertently arousing other monks. In the monastery at Tabennisi, for example, Pachomius instructed monks to keep their knees covered when sitting, to keep their posteriors covered when bending over, and not to remove thorns from each other's feet.[11]

If a community mingles the sexes, as the Shakers did, even greater care must be taken to prevent men and women from triggering sexual feelings in each other. For this reason, the Millennial Laws of the Shakers forbade men and women to be alone together, work together, converse in private, write to each other, pass each other on the stairs, try on the clothes of members of the opposite sex, shake hands, or even blink at each other. Women could not mend a man's clothes while he was wearing them. Women were also enjoined not to sit "crosslegged nor in any awkward posture" at Shaker meetings.[12]

Those whose celibacy is motivated by religion commonly resort to prayer in their battle against sexual temptation. In the words of one nun, quoted by author and poet Kathleen Norris, who has spent a considerable amount of time living in convents and monasteries with people who have taken vows of celibacy, "One needs a deep prayer life to maintain a celibate life. It is only through prayer that the hard choices get made, over time, only prayer that can give me the self-transcendence that celibacy requires."[13] And of course, for those living in convents and monasteries, the knowledge that the rules of the order forbid sexual activities and that they will experience humiliation if they are caught engaging in such activities gives them another incentive to stay true to their vows of celibacy. According to Norris, by the way, although the nuns she interviewed were expected to remain celibate, they were given little advice on how, exactly, they could maintain their celibacy. As one sister explained: "We were pretty much left on our own to work it out, because sexual matters simply were not discussed."[14]

Another technique for maintaining celibacy is to cultivate a deep hatred for members of the opposite sex. This technique appears to have been common among monks in the first millennium, although most modern monks, rather than being woman-haters, have developed, through their celibacy, an appreciation of women that arguably surpasses that of men whose relationships with women are partially motivated by sex.

Even if it is possible to give up sex, why do so? This is the big question for modern minds. Why refuse to take advantage of an opportunity for pleasure?

Before answering this question, it is worth pointing out that most people routinely refuse to take advantage of opportunities for pleasure. Most people, for example, refuse to use cocaine or heroin, even though they know it would be intensely pleasurable to do so. And even in the realm of sex, most of us are "selectively celibate": we sometimes pass up opportunities for sexual intercourse. We might refuse to have sex with prostitutes or to have premarital sex. If we are in a stable relationship, we might refuse to be unfaithful to our partner. Rare is the person who takes advantage of *every* sexual opportunity that comes along. The reason for this is simple: the pleasures associated with sex, like the pleasures associated with drug use, come at a price. We are selectively celibate because we realize that sometimes the price associated with having sex isn't worth paying. What makes true celibates special is their belief that the price is *never* worth paying. They think that in leading a sexual existence, we lose more than we gain.

What is the price of sexuality? According to the Shakers, sexuality decreases your chances of salvation, a very high price to pay. The Shakers also thought that those who enjoy a sexual existence pay an earthly price. For one thing, a strong sense of community is possible only when people regard the community as their family, and this cannot happen when those in a community regard some members as being closer or more connected than other members. (As Norris observes, "Monastic people are celibate for a very practical reason: the kind of community life to which they aspire can't be sustained if people are pairing off.")[15]

Even if we are not interested in getting into heaven or fostering a strong sense of community, we pay a price for our sexuality. When we experience lust, we are distracted from whatever we might have been doing, and falling in love can fill our heads with intrusive thoughts and thereby impair our ability to concentrate. Our sexuality consumes much of our energy—diverts it from other, "nobler" tasks.

Celibates hope that by suppressing—or, better still, extinguishing—their sexual desires, they will regain their focus and be able to spend their days doing what they think needs to be done, not what their evolutionary programming tells them to do. Celibates have a much better chance of staying on task than sexual beings and will have more energy to achieve whatever tasks they set for themselves. Thus, the celibates Norris spoke to tried to "sublimate their sexual energies toward another purpose than sexual intercourse and procreation."[16]

Sexual beings pay another price in their human relationships. Their sexuality taints relationships with members of the opposite sex—or, if they are homosexual, with members of their own sex. Sexual beings tend to classify the people they meet according to their desirability as sexual partners. A man at a party might break off a conversation with an intelligent but homely woman in order to cross the room and converse with a woman who, though strikingly attractive, hasn't had a thought in weeks. A woman might refuse the friendship of a man because she suspects that what he is really after is sex—or might refuse his friendship because she fears that it will lessen her chances of being sexually attractive to some other man. The social relationships of celibates are not similarly tainted. Celibates appreciate people not as potential sex partners but as human beings.

To interact socially with a celibate can be a refreshing and eye-opening experience. According to Norris, "The attractiveness of the celibate is that he or she can make us feel appreciated, enlarged, no matter who we are. . . . The thoughtful way in which they converse, listening and responding with complete attention, seems always a marvel." They "listen without possessiveness, without imposing themselves."[17] Norris describes an obese and homely college student who, during a conversation with young monks, was astonished that they paid as much attention to what she said as to what her pretty roommate had to say.

Celibates routinely experience a kind of love that the rest of us rarely do. Celibate love isn't exclusive: celibates don't let their love for one person detract from their love for another. Nor is their love possessive: they aren't trying to use or take advantage of the object of their love; to the contrary, they are trying to help him or her. In the words of one nun, "To be celibate . . . means first of all being a loving person in a way that frees you to serve others. Otherwise celibacy has no point."[18]

Celibate love resembles the love that parents have for their children. Parental love is generally neither exclusive (the love parents have for one child doesn't lessen the love they have for another) nor possessive (good parents seek not to exploit their children but to help them flourish). Those who have experienced parental love know what a wonderful thing it is. Imagine being able to experience this same kind of love not just toward a few children but toward everyone around you.

Sexual beings like to think that they are free and that celibates are repressed. Celibates take the opposite view of things. "When mature celibates talk about the value of celibacy," says Norris, "'freedom' is a word they commonly use. Freedom to keep their energies focused on ministry and communal living, freedom to love many people without being unfaithful to any of them." According to one sister, a healthy celibacy "means not focusing on 'what I gave up,' but on what being freed by what I gave up has allowed me to do in terms of service to the church and other people."[19]

The Oneida Community was founded by John Humphrey Noyes at Oneida, New York, in 1848 and was subsequently led by him. Noyes had visited a Shaker community before founding Oneida and was attracted by their way of life. Indeed, he wrote, "If I believed in a Shaker heaven I would be a Shaker now."[20] His Oneida Community resembled Shaker communities in some respects: private property was abolished, and selfish interests were to be sacrificed for the good of the community. And like the Shakers, his primary motivation in founding a community was religious. (Noyes practiced Perfectionism, a religion that has been described as "a breakaway from New England Congregationalism.")[21] He also agreed with the Shakers that sexual desires cause people to pair off and form family units, much to the detriment of the community, and that these desires had to be dealt with if a community was to be strong.

Noyes thought the best way to lessen the destructive power of sexual desires was not to suppress them, as the celibate Shakers did, but to satisfy them. His reasoning: "Forbid sexual intercourse altogether and you attain the same results, so far as shutting off the jealousies and strifes of exclusiveness is concerned, as we attain by making sexual intercourse free. In this matter the Shakers show their shrewdness. But they sacrifice the vitality of society, in securing its peace."[22]

Within the Oneida Community, free love reigned. No one was married to anyone—rather, every man was married to every woman. People routinely switched sexual partners. When it looked as though an exclusive relationship—a community-threatening "special love"—was forming between two people, they were subjected to "mutual criticism," in which community members would berate them and tell them to mend their ways. If an individual was unrepentant, his or her sexual privileges might be suspended or limited. In one case, the special love experienced by one couple proved intractable. They were told that if they wanted to stay in the community, they had to have children outside their relationship. They obeyed.[23]

Noyes thought allowing sexual relations would have the effect of devaluing them. If one has sex frequently and with enough different people, sex loses its emotional impact; it becomes the emotional equivalent of a handshake. Indeed, Noyes thought there was no reason, religious or otherwise, to treat sexual intercourse as different from a handshake. According to him, "The outward act of sexual connection is as innocent and comely as any other act."[24] Likewise, he argued that "in a holy community, there is no more reason why sexual intercourse should be restricted by law, than why eating and drinking should be—and there is as little occasion for shame in the one case as in the other."[25]

One naturally wonders whether, in a time before effective contraception, the Oneida experiment was a formula for never-ending pregnancy. Although Noyes had no objection to sexual intercourse, he thought it improper for a man to ejaculate into a woman. Doing this, he suggested, was the moral equivalent of firing "a gun at one's best friend merely for the sake of unloading it."[26] He also disapproved of coitus interruptus, which he said was wasteful. What he advocated was "male continence"—what historian Lawrence Foster has called "celibate intercourse"[27]—in which the man doesn't ejaculate, either during intercourse or after withdrawal.[28] Women past menopause taught new members the technique. (The community sometimes allowed intercourse for reproductive purposes, in which case the ban on ejaculation was obviously waived, but only when a man and woman had gotten permission from the community or been asked by it to engage in reproductive sex.)

Celibate intercourse appears to have been an effective means of birth control, and it presumably made sex more enjoyable for women. But whether it prevented romantic attachments is debatable. Noyes himself seems to have experienced an ongoing special love for community member Mary Cragin.

The Oneida Community lasted nearly thirty-two years and at its peak had 250 members. It was ultimately abandoned in part because of internal tensions and in part because of external pressures: one imagines that nineteenth-century Americans wouldn't welcome the presence of a community devoted to free love.

If Noyes were alive today, he would probably marvel at the extent to which his notions on the proper way to deal with sexual desire have triumphed. In America and much of the world, the "sex hang-up" that so troubled people in the 1960s has been conquered. Sex has gone from being a very special activity, to be engaged in with one special person under special circumstances, to something that is engaged in casually, the way one might go bowling. On college campuses, for example, many students take pride not in their grades or their capacity for hard work but in their extravagant sexual lifestyles. They like to think that unlike their parents—and certainly unlike their great-grandparents—they are free.

A case can be made, though, that it was their great-grandparents who were free: they controlled their sexual desires rather than being controlled by them. Conversely, their sexually liberated descendants are doing precisely what their evolutionary programming prompts them to do: have sex when the opportunity arises. Rather than being free, they have allowed themselves to become enslaved by their loins. Indeed, so deeply enslaved are they that some of them make their lack of sexual restraint—their ability to obey without hesitation the dictates of their evolutionary programming—a central part of their personal identity. They resemble slaves who, because their enslavement is so complete, feel proud to labor for their master.

Because of their success in overcoming the "sex hang-up"—because, that is, of their lack of sexual self-restraint—many young women become pregnant out of wedlock. In doing so, they often make a muddle of their lives: rather than being able to live the life of their choosing, they must try to balance single-parenthood with going to school and working at a minimum-wage job that they probably dislike. The fathers of their children likewise have to juggle school and a job that will let them make child-support payments. The lives of their offspring are similarly muddled, but this is another story.

Sometimes teenagers go out of their way to become pregnant. They have seen parenthood transform others, and seek a similar transformation of themselves. What they don't realize is that this transformation, when it takes place, happens because a woman is willing to sacrifice for her child. The sacrifices in question are possible because the woman has gained a degree of mastery over her desires: what she wants for herself simply isn't that important anymore. And because she has been transformed, her sacrifices won't really seem like sacrifices. When a young woman gets pregnant but refuses to sacrifice for her child, the transformation cannot take place. Rather than finding motherhood to be an incredibly rewarding and enriching experience, she probably finds it to be endlessly annoying.

To the sexually liberated individuals I have been describing, celibacy is a nonstarter: to them, the disadvantages of sexual self-restraint clearly outweigh the advantages. But when they were children, these individuals were all celibate, and life nevertheless had much to offer them. And as they grow old, many of them will again, as a result of natural processes, drift into celibacy. Some will lament the decline of their sexuality, but to those seeking to master desire, it will come as a godsend. The Greek dramatist Sophocles, when he had grown old, was asked whether, despite his years, he could still make love to a woman. His reply: "I am very glad to have escaped from this, like a slave who has escaped from a mad and cruel master."[29] Today's sexually liberated individuals, although they fail to realize it, proudly wear the chains of this same master.

Barley porridge, or a crust of barley bread, and water
do not make a very cheerful diet, but nothing gives
one keener pleasure than the ability to derive pleasure
even from that.

—Seneca

# ELEVEN

# Philosophical Advice

Philosophical advice regarding the problem of desire differs
from religious advice in two important respects: the advice must
deliver benefits to us here and now, not in an afterlife or in
some future reincarnation, and it must employ reason rather
than prayer or meditation to provide those benefits.

In my discussion of philosophical advice, I will focus my
attention on three Hellenistic philosophies—Stoicism, Epicu-
reanism, and Skepticism—that flourished two thousand years
ago. Indeed, I will have almost nothing to say about twentieth-
century philosophies and philosophers. Why ignore modern
philosophy? Because most modern philosophers are horrified
by the thought of giving people advice on how to live better
lives. They prefer to spend their days dealing with theoretical
disputes, the resolution of which (assuming they are someday
resolved—most philosophical disputes never are) will make
absolutely no difference in the life of anyone who isn't a pro-
fessional philosopher. Most modern philosophers simply have
no use for "philosophies of life."

For the Hellenistic philosophers, by way of contrast, the primary reason for doing philosophy is so we can live better lives. Epicurus (341–270 B.C.) argued that "vain is the word of a philosopher which does not heal any suffering of man."[1] Stoic philosopher Seneca (3 B.C.– A.D. 65) offered similar sentiments: "A person who goes to a philosopher should carry away with him something or other of value every day; he should return home a sounder man or at least more capable of becoming one."[2] And what is the proper goal of philosophy? According to Seneca, "Philosophy . . . takes as her aim the state of happiness."[3]

The first thing to realize about the Stoics is that they were not stoical, in the lowercase-*s* sense of the word. According to the dictionary, a stoic is someone "seemingly indifferent to or un-affected by joy, grief, pleasure, or pain." This definition might lead us to conclude that the Stoics were emotional zombies. A bit of research, however, indicates that uppercase-*S* Stoics were anything but zombies. Among the Stoics we find Posidonius of Rhodes, who is described as being "versatile and learned, a historian and a traveller, a man of scientific interests who cal-culated the circumference of the earth and proved the connec-tion between the tides and the phases of the moon."[4] We find Cato the Younger, who valiantly opposed the dictatorship of Julius Caesar. We find Seneca, who was one of the most re-markable people of his time or any time: he deserves a place in the history books not just for his philosophical writings but for acting as primary advisor to the emperor Nero, for his skill and success as a dramatist, and for his financial acumen—he was a first-century equivalent of a modern investment banker. We also find Marcus Aurelius (121–180), who, besides being the last great Stoic philosopher, was not just an emperor of Rome but was arguably one of the greatest.

The Stoic philosophers agreed that the key to having a good life is to master desire. Thus, Marcus Aurelius counsels us to "resist the murmurs of the flesh"[5] and not to "indulge in dreams of having what you have not."[6] More generally, he advises us to "erase fancy; curb impulse; quench desire."[7] And what is our reward for mastering desire? Tranquility.

It is important to realize that the tranquility sought by the Stoics is not at all like that provided by tranquilizers. Here is how Seneca characterizes tranquility: "What we [Stoics] are seeking . . . is how the mind may always pursue a steady and favourable course, may be well-disposed towards itself, and may view its conditions with joy, and suffer no interruption of this joy, but may abide in a peaceful state, being never uplifted nor ever cast down."[8]

This passage, besides explaining what the Stoics mean by tranquility, demonstrates that the Stoics are not impassive. A lowercase-*s* stoic might be indifferent to joy, but an uppercase-*S* Stoic will welcome it. Indeed, according to Seneca, a man who successfully embodies Stoic principles—a so-called Stoic sage—"must, whether he wills or not, necessarily be attended by constant cheerfulness and a joy that is deep and issues from deep within, since he finds delight in his own resources, and desires no joys greater than his inner joys."[9] (Seneca adds that compared to these joys, the pleasures offered by "the wretched body" are "paltry and trivial and fleeting.")[10] More generally, the Stoics are not out to banish the emotions; they are out to reduce, to the extent possible, negative emotions, such as feelings of anger or grief, that will disrupt our tranquility. They value positive emotions, with feelings of joy being at the top of their list.

The advice that we master desire and thereby gain tranquility is doubtless good advice, but it leaves us with the question of how, exactly, we are to master desire. The Stoics don't advocate that we meditate to gain mastery over our desires, as a Zen Buddhist might, or pray for the strength to master our desires, as a Christian might. Instead they argue that if we pay close attention to and think carefully about our desires, we can gain the upper hand on our undesirable desires. As a result, the Stoics became keen observers of desire. Their advice on how to master desire is based on these observations.

Thus, we find Stoic philosopher Epictetus (50–138) observing that if we wish to preserve our tranquility, we need to keep in mind that "some things are up to us and some things are not."[11] Among the things up to us are our opinions, impulses, desires, and aversions; among the things we can't control—or have at best partial control over—are our physical circumstances and our reputation. The key insight of Epictetus is that it makes no sense to fret about the things that aren't up to us. Doing so is a waste of time and energy, and this kind of fretting is a recipe for a life filled with disappointment.[12] You will be much happier, Epictetus argues, if you spend your time and energy concerning yourself with those aspects of life you can control. Stated differently, you should play only those games you are sure to win, for then you can be invincible.[13]

Wanting only what is in our power to obtain and retain, besides preserving our tranquility, provides us with the maximum possible freedom. "A person's master," says Epictetus, "is someone who has power over what he does or does not want, either to obtain it or take it away. Whoever wants to be free, therefore, let him not want or avoid anything that is up to others. Otherwise he will necessarily be a slave."[14]

Epictetus realizes that because we cannot control much of what goes on around us, life will occasionally deal us a blow.

We might get sick. Loved ones might die. Others might falsely accuse us of crimes. Our property might get stolen or destroyed. Epictetus's strategy for coping with these blows is to convince ourselves that these misfortunes were fated to happen, that they could not have been avoided. A fatalistic attitude, Epictetus thinks, takes away much of the sting of these blows. "Do not seek to have events happen as you want them to," he declares, "but instead want them to happen as they do happen, and your life will go well."[15] (The advice that we fatalistically accept the blows the world deals us sounds strange to modern ears, but when Epictetus offered this advice, people took it for granted that they had fates.)

Seneca thinks that one important step in overcoming our insatiability is to distinguish between natural and unnatural desires: "Natural desires are limited; those which spring from false opinions have nowhere to stop, for falsity has no point of termination."[16] Our desire for water when we are thirsty, then, is a natural desire: if we are thirsty and drink, our thirst will be quenched. Our desire for wealth, on the other hand, is unnatural, since no matter how much wealth we gain, we will want more. Seneca advises us to think twice before acting to satisfy an unnatural desire.

Suppressing our undesirable desires will take effort, but Seneca advises us to balance this effort against the effort that would be required to fulfill them. Consider, for example, our sexual desires. Fighting these desires won't be fun, but capitulating to them can make us miserable, for as Seneca observes, "chastity comes with time to spare, lechery has never a moment." More generally, he reminds us that "every virtue . . . is easy to guard, whereas vice costs a lot to cultivate."[17]

If tranquility is our goal, then anger is clearly our enemy. Indeed, if we cannot curb our anger, we are likely to be miserable, since there is so much in this imperfect world to be angry about. Here is Seneca's description of the life that awaits the man who cannot control his anger: "You will be angry with one person after another, with slaves and then freedmen, with your parents and then your children, with acquaintances and then with people unknown to you; everywhere you will find occasion for anger—unless the mind steps in to intercede. . . . What a waste of precious time on a bad business!"[18]

How can we control our anger? In his essay *On Anger* (*De Ira*), Seneca offers a number of techniques. We find, for example, the timeworn advice to count to ten before acting on our anger. (His actual words are "The greatest remedy for anger is delay.")[19] We also find, however, advice similar to the Buddhist "thought substitution" process described in Chapter 9: "We should turn all [anger's] indications into their opposites: the face should be relaxed, the voice gentler, the pace slower. Little by little, the externals will be matched by an inner formation."[20]

In Chapter 2, we explored the profound effect that other people have on us. Our desire to win their admiration can cause us much anxiety and thereby disrupt our tranquility. Epictetus's advice regarding our relations with other people is straightforward: "Pay no attention to whatever anyone says about you, since that falls outside what is yours."[21] If you instead spend your days worrying about what other people think, you will forfeit your freedom: "If it ever happens that you turn outward to want to please another person, certainly you have lost your plan of life."[22]

Other people can also disturb our tranquility by insulting us. Epictetus therefore offers advice for dealing with insults: you need to realize, he says, that when someone insults you, what irritates you is not the insult itself—it is merely words—but your mental reaction to the insult.[23] If you think, "I have been grievously insulted," you will feel the sting of the insult, but if you instead think, "The person who just tried to insult me is of no consequence. He is like a child or a barking dog. It would be foolish for me to take his words to heart," you will neutralize the insult. In other words, whenever you feel insulted by others, you have only yourself to blame.

But if we ignore the insults of other people, consistency dictates that we should likewise ignore their praise. If we don't trust their opinion when they think poorly of us, it is intellectually dishonest for us to start valuing their opinion when they think well of us. For this reason, Epictetus tells us that "if someone praises [a Stoic] he laughs to himself at the person who has praised him."[24] Indeed, he goes even further than this in rejecting the admiration of others: "If people think you amount to something, distrust yourself."[25] And the Stoic, besides being leery of the opinions of others, will distrust his opinion of himself: he will be "on guard against himself as an enemy lying in wait."[26]

Other people can also disturb our tranquility by infecting us with undesirable desires. Unwholesome desires, in other words, are like a contagious illness, and in the same way as we should avoid someone afflicted with the flu for fear of catching it ourselves, we should avoid someone afflicted with, say, a craving for fame and fortune. Associate with such people, Seneca says, and we will soon discover in ourselves a similar craving.[27] Seneca also advises us to avoid those "who are melancholy and bewail everything, who find pleasure in every opportunity for complaint," since "the companion who is always upset and bemoans everything is a foe to tranquility."[28]

Most people take the possession of wealth to be a blessing, but the Stoics understood that wealth can disrupt one's tranquility. According to Seneca, the sorrow of not having money is less than the sorrow that comes from losing it. More generally, the less you have, the less anxiety you will experience.[29] The goal with respect to money should therefore be to acquire "an amount that does not descend to poverty, and yet is not far removed from poverty."[30]

On attaining this modest level of affluence, we should, Seneca recommends, "practice poverty." We should, that is, "set aside now and then a number of days during which [we] will be content with the plainest of food, and very little of it, and with rough, coarse clothing, and will ask [ourselves], 'Is this what one used to dread?'"[31] After practicing poverty in this fashion, we will discover that it is not as bad in reality as it appears to our imaginations, and the prospect of being someday plunged into poverty will therefore be less likely to disrupt our tranquility.

It is, by the way, a bit odd that Seneca, one of the wealthiest people of his time, would be so enamored of poverty. He has even been accused of being "history's most notable example of a man who failed to live up to his principles."[32] Seneca responded to the charge of hypocrisy by pointing out that there is nothing wrong with enjoying wealth as long as we do not cling to it. (This thinking is similar to that of Buddha, who, as we saw in Chapter 9, told the wealthy businessman Anathapindika, "It is not life and wealth and power that enslave men, but the cleaving to life and wealth and power.") The Stoics are not opposed to enjoying what life has to offer, including wealth, friendship, and health, but they counsel us to enjoy these things in a manner that does not make us slaves to the enjoyment of them.

The Stoics also counsel us to work at being happy with whatever it is we possess. In other words, we should do what we can to impede the process of psychological adaptation described back in Chapter 5. Along these lines, Marcus advises that when we start taking our possessions for granted, we should think of how much we would crave them if they weren't ours.[33] (Schopenhauer, whose own philosophy of life has a Stoic bent, echoes this advice: instead of dwelling on all the things we don't possess, we should periodically stop to think about how we would feel if we lost the things we do possess.)[34]

Seneca thinks we can make progress in our fight against undesirable desires by adopting a technique taught by the Stoic (or at least Stoic-influenced) philosopher Quintus Sextius: "At the day's end, when he had retired for the night, [Sextius] would interrogate his mind: 'What ailment of yours have you cured today? What failing have you resisted? Where can you show improvement? . . . Could anything be finer than this habit of sifting through the whole day?"[35] Seneca illustrates his own use of this technique.[36] He recalls recent events that disturbed his tranquility and reflects on how, in accordance with Stoic principles, he should have responded to these events. "Denied a place of honour," he says, berating himself, "you began to grow angry with your host, with the master of ceremonies, with the guest who had been placed above you. You lunatic, what difference does it make what part of the couch you put your weight on? Can a cushion add to your honour or your shame?"

In another such exercise, he recalls—again, speaking to himself— that "at the party, certain people made jokes and remarks at your expense which struck home. Remember to keep away from low company." These examples make it clear, by the way, how little human nature has changed in the last two thousand years.

My college students seem to appreciate much of the advice of the Stoics but are puzzled by some aspects of Stoicism. They are, for one thing, puzzled that the Stoics would have as their goal a tranquil life. Why not an exciting life? (This, to be sure, is a criticism not just of Stoicism but of the other Hellenistic philosophies, as well as Hinduism, Taoism, Buddhism, and Christianity as interpreted by St. John of the Cross.) A desire for tranquility seems to be a stage-of-life thing. Many young people actively seek turmoil. If their life becomes tranquil, they do something to shatter the tranquility.

Many of my students hate the idea of "settling for" tran- quility, but then again, they don't want to settle for anything. They imagine that the world will give them what they seek— that they will bend the world to their will. To them, settling is an admission of defeat; it would mean that life has gotten the better of them. But as they gain experience, they typically find that the world not only isn't going to give them what they want but will periodically snatch away what they worked so hard to gain. After years or decades of failure—either total or partial— most people realize that the world isn't going to bend to their will. Coupled with this realization is a decline in their energy level: turmoil is not as tolerable as it once was. Tranquility starts to sound attractive.

The refusal to "settle," by the way, is ridiculous: it is only when you settle that you have a chance of appreciating what you have settled for, and it is only when you gain this appreciation that you have a chance of gaining, if not worldly success, then something even more valuable—satisfaction.

My students are also troubled by what they take to be the emotional coldness—the inhumanity, some would say—of Stoicism. They find one passage from Epictetus to be particularly disturbing: "Never say about anything, 'I have lost it,' but instead, 'I have given it back.' Did your child die? It was given back. Did your wife die? She was given back."[37] They interpret this passage as saying that a Stoic will remain emotionally detached from the people around him: a Stoic husband's attitude toward his wife is not "I love you so much that I would be devastated if I lost you" but rather "I love you, but if anything happened to you, I would be fine." My students question this Stoic love: if you don't go into paroxysms of grief on losing someone, you couldn't truly have loved that person.

This interpretation of Stoicism is, I think, mistaken. In making the above remark, Epictetus isn't suggesting that we should be emotionally distant from people. We should allow intense attachments to form. At the same time, we should realize that there is much in life we cannot control, and that if we try to control things that are beyond our control, we will experience much needless grief and turmoil. Unfortunately, the death of a loved one is often beyond our control.

Indeed, a Stoic attitude with respect to loved ones can result in relations that are deeper and fuller than an un-Stoic attitude. Consider two husbands. One assumes that his wife will always be there for him. This assumption is likely to result in his taking his wife for granted: things he might have done for her or told her today can easily be postponed till tomorrow. If she dies, much of his grief will be an emotional expression of wasted opportunities: "If only I had . . ." A Stoic husband, by way of contrast, won't assume that his wife will be around forever; to the contrary, he will assume that she could be snatched away (by fate) without a moment's warning. For this reason, the Stoic husband won't put off until tomorrow what he could have done today. He will be far less likely to take his wife for granted, and if she is snatched away, he will therefore have fewer regrets about all the things he might have done with and for her: he will, after all, have done them to the extent possible while she was alive.

This aspect of Stoicism has a parallel in Zen Buddhism, which also emphasizes the impermanence of all things in life. Because things can be snatched away without warning, we need to work on enjoying them while we can. Along these lines, writer and Zen practitioner Natalie Goldberg tells a story about how loss is dealt with in Zen. She and other students at a Zen meditation center learned that a fellow Zen practitioner—Chris Pirsig, son of Robert Pirsig, author of *Zen and the Art of Motorcycle Maintenance*—had been stabbed to death for no apparent reason. She waited for her Zen master's daily lecture, on the assumption that he would say something that would "make it all better." His comment: "Human beings have an idea they are very fond of: that we die in old age. This is just an idea. We don't know when our death will come. Chris Pirsig's death has come now. It is a great teaching in impermanence." That was it. No anger, no tears. Goldberg was shocked by her master's apparent indifference to the death.[38]

Stoicism is concerned not so much with dealing with grief as preventing it. If you live the life of a Stoic—or the life of a Zen Buddhist, for that matter—you will enjoy the good things life has to offer while it is possible to do so. When these good things disappear, you will therefore have less cause for grief than if you had assumed that the things in question could be enjoyed forever. You will not plague yourself with "if only" thoughts.

Stoicism doesn't require its followers to live grim, unfeeling lives. It does require them, though, to realize that there is much in life they cannot control, and consequently that many of the things that give them pleasure are transient: possessions will be lost or stolen, friendships will end, loved ones will die. This realization might make them appear emotionally distant, but it also allows them to be emotionally present in the sense that they live "in the moment."

Epicurus founded the school of philosophy named after him. The Epicureans disagreed with the Stoics regarding certain fundamental philosophical doctrines: they rejected, for example, Stoic fatalism. But when we examine their philosophy of life, we find that the Epicureans have much in common with the Stoics.

The Epicureans share, for example, the Stoic goal of tranquility: according to Epicurus, "It is better for you to be free of fear lying upon a pallet, than to have a golden couch and a rich table and be full of trouble."[39] And like the Stoics, they thought we should be suspicious of the desires we find within us: "Every desire must be confronted with this question: what will happen to me, if the object of my desire is accomplished and what if it is not?"[40] The suggestion is that if we ask this question, we will in many cases find that getting what we want will make us no better off than not getting it. Epicurus also agrees with Marcus that rather than pursuing new possessions, we should work to want what we already have: "We should not spoil what we have by desiring what we have not, but remember that what we have too was the gift of fortune."[41]

Epicurus also agrees with the Stoics on the importance, if we seek happiness, of mastering our desires: "Unhappiness comes either through fear or through vain and unbridled desire: but if a man curbs these, he can win for himself the blessedness of understanding."[42] One important part of mastering desire will be mastering our desire for social status. Rather than seeking fame, our goal should be to "live unknown."[43]

Like the Stoics, Epicurus disparages material wealth: "Poverty, when measured by the natural purpose of life, is great wealth, but unlimited wealth is great poverty."[44] Wealth, he argues, rarely compensates one for the drudgery necessary to acquire it.[45] Furthermore, it is difficult to acquire possessions unless one is servile to "mobs or monarchs";[46] consequently, in gaining possessions we generally relinquish our freedom. "Many men," he points out, "when they have acquired riches have not found the escape from their ills but only a change to greater ills."[47]

It should by now be clear that in the same way as upper-case-*S* Stoics were not lowercase-*s* stoics—were not, that is, indifferent to joy, grief, pleasure, and pain—uppercase-*E* Epicureans were not lowercase-*e* epicureans. The dictionary defines an *epicurean* as someone "devoted to the pursuit of sensual pleasure, especially to the enjoyment of good food and comfort." The Epicureans just described hardly meet this definition: in the words of Epicurus, "It is not continuous drinkings and revellings, nor the satisfaction of lusts, nor the enjoyment of fish and other luxuries of the wealthy table, which produce a pleasant life, but sober reasoning, searching out the motives for all choice and avoidance, and banishing mere opinions, to which are due the greatest disturbance of the spirit."[48]

Like the Stoics and Epicureans, the Skeptics valued tranquility, but they offered different advice on how to attain it. Although, as we have seen, the Stoics weren't stoic and the Epicureans weren't epicurean, the Skeptics were in fact skeptical: they thought that the key to a happy, tranquil life is to refuse to form beliefs about the world around us.

Pyrrho of Ellis (c. 360–270 B.C.) founded the Greek school of Skepticism (also known as Pyrrhonism). Five hundred years after Pyrrho, Sextus Empiricus offered a fleshed-out development of Skepticism. Sextus argues that much of the suffering we experience is a consequence of the opinions we hold. Suppose that you are punctured with a needle. You will obviously experience pain. If the needle is wielded by a doctor who is giving you a flu shot at your request, you will accept and tolerate the pain. If, on the other hand, the needle is wielded by an unknown assailant, the actual pain of the needle will be multiplied many times by your sense of outrage at being thus attacked. The physical pain might be identical to that inflicted by the doctor, but the psychic pain will be extreme. (This claim echoes the Stoic claim that what hurts us is not so much the world around us as the thoughts inside our heads.)

Skeptics hope to reduce the amount of pain they experience and gain a measure of tranquility and happiness in their lives by refusing to think that things are bad: "For though [a Skeptic] suffers emotion through his senses, yet because he does not also opine that what he suffers is evil by nature, the emotion he suffers is moderate."[49] In saying this, Sextus is not suggesting that Skepticism allows its followers to live in a perfect world, free of pain and anxiety. Even Skeptics, he admits, will experience cold and thirst. But when they do, because Skeptics don't hold cold or thirst to be bad "by nature," they will experience less pain and anxiety than non-Skeptics in the same circumstances.[50]

Besides withholding our belief about what is good and bad, Skeptics counsel us to withhold our belief about what is desirable and undesirable. After all, as soon as someone allows himself to believe that something is desirable or undesirable, he stirs up for himself, says Sextus, "a flood of evils."[51] If he doesn't get what he wants, "he will be extremely perturbed because of his desire to gain it," and if he does get what he wants, "he will never be at rest owing to the excess of his joy or on account of keeping watch over his acquisition."[52] Consider, by way of illustration, the desire for wealth. According to Sextus, if a man desires wealth but lacks it, he will be doubly perturbed: he will be bothered by his lack of wealth and by the labor necessary to obtain it. And if he succeeds in obtaining wealth, Sextus claims, he will be *triply* perturbed "because he is immoderately overjoyed, and because he toils to ensure that his wealth stays with him, and because he is painfully anxious and dreads the loss of it." By way of contrast, the person who regards wealth as neither desirable nor undesirable "is neither perturbed at its absence nor overjoyed at its presence, but in either case remains unperturbed."[53]

Sextus writes that "it is by pursuing earnestly and with extreme persistence what he himself believes to be good and desirable that each man unwittingly falls into the evil lying next-door."[54] Because of our belief that money is good, for example, we pursue it and transform ourselves into money grubbers. Likewise, our belief that fame is good brings on us that "great evil," the lust for fame, and our belief that pleasure is good brings on us that "depraved condition," a craving for pleasure; if, on the other hand, we declare that "nothing is by nature an object of desire any more than of avoidance," we will live happily and unperturbed.[55]

It is possible, by the way, that in offering this advice, the Skeptics were influenced by Eastern philosophy. There is evidence that Pyrrho accompanied Alexander the Great on his campaigns in the East.[56] And when we examine Eastern philosophy, we find views expressed that resemble those of the Skeptics. Consider, by way of example, the following Buddhist advice on how to attain a tranquil mind: "The remedy . . . is to still the mind, to stop it from making discriminations and nurturing attachments toward certain phenomena and feelings of aversion toward others." Likewise, "one should try to stop the mind from making the kinds of discrimination that lead to craving or attachment."[57] Taken at face value, this sounds a lot like Sextus's recommendation that we withhold our belief about what is desirable and undesirable.

How can we avoid forming beliefs about desirability? For one thing, we can, to the extent possible, ignore the opinions of other people. To a Skeptic, other people are dangerous, since it is they who are primarily responsible for the beliefs we have: they indoctrinate us. Indeed, the path of least resistance is to believe as those around you do. If you share their beliefs, they will admire and welcome you; if you refuse to accept their beliefs, they might ignore you, shun you, or—if they are sufficiently powerful and unenlightened—imprison you or put you to death.

According to Sextus, it is bad enough that listening to other people puts beliefs in our heads; even worse, the beliefs in question will tend to be contradictory. Suppose, then, that we are in the habit, as most people are, of judging whether something is good or bad by whether other people believe it to be good or bad. Because most things are pursued by some people and avoided by others, we will be led by this habit to find something to be both desirable and undesirable—or if not that, we will experience a vexatious puzzlement over who, among these other people, is right. As Sextus puts it, if "a man should assume that everything which is in any way pursued by anyone is good by nature and that everything which is avoided is by nature to be avoided, he will have a life that is unlivable, through being compelled both to pursue and to avoid at the same time the same thing." If, on the other hand, we remember that the mere fact that people desire something doesn't make it desirable, we will have a life "free from perturbation."[58]

Among the other people we shouldn't listen to are philosophers—more precisely, what Sextus calls dogmatic philosophers. These individuals spend their days advising us not to pursue one object but to pursue another as being more noble. They might advise us, for example, to seek virtue rather than wealth or fame. These philosophers—the Stoics and Epicureans are among them—give this advice in the hope that it will reduce men's distress, but, says Sextus, it invariably fails to accomplish this goal: "For just as the man who pursued the first object was distressed, so also he who pursues the second will be distressed, so that the philosopher's discourse creates a new disease in place of the old."[59] If anything, the man might be even more distressed than he was before, since by claiming that virtue is more valuable than wealth, the philosopher is implying that virtue is even more worth troubling yourself to attain than wealth was.[60] Skepticism does not argue for a certain value system; it argues against believing in a particular value system—or believing in anything at all, for that matter.

Another piece of Skeptic advice is that, after using our reason to become Skeptics, we should stop reasoning about the world around us: "Men of talent," says Sextus, will use their intelligence to try to get to the bottom of things, and when they are faced with conflicting views, they will try to determine which is true and which is false, "hoping by the settlement of this question to attain quietude." But according to the "main basic principle" of Skepticism, for every proposition there is an equal and opposite proposition, meaning that we can never get to the bottom of things.[61] It is therefore pointless to try to reason our way into tranquility. Sextus specifically comments on the futility of using reason to control a troubling desire: the person who attempts to do so likely "retains the evil within himself" and is therefore still perturbed. More generally, the person who uses reason to control his desires is "of all men the most unhappy."[62]

Anyone taking to heart the philosophical advice offered in this chapter is likely to be regarded as a bit of an eccentric. If we practice poverty, as Seneca advises, we might walk or take a bus rather than driving our car. "Why isn't he driving?" our neighbors might wonder. If we refuse to allow our picture to be taken for the local newspaper because we want, in accordance with Epicurus's advice, to "live unknown," our neighbors will think us a bit odd. And if we become true Skeptics and doubt everything, we will be thought not just odd but possibly insane.

In the next chapter, we will turn our attention to people who behave eccentrically not as a side effect of their battle against desire but as a primary weapon in their battle against the formation of undesirable desires. The eccentrics in question reason that most of our undesirable desires arise because we care what other people think of us. If we can only stop caring—if we can embrace eccentricity instead of taking shelter in conformity—we can, they think, dramatically increase our chance of finding happiness.

There is some advantage in being the humblest, cheapest, least dignified man in the village, so that the very stable boys shall damn you. Methinks I enjoy that advantage to an unusual extent.

—Henry David Thoreau

TWELVE

# The Eccentrics

Aristotle said that a man who feels no need to live in society must be either a beast or a god.[1] German philosopher Friedrich Nietzsche challenged this dichotomy: a man who feels no need to live in society might instead be *both* a beast *and* a god—might be, as Nietzsche puts it, a philosopher.[2] I agree with this observation; I would quibble, however, with Nietzsche's choice of the word *philosopher* to describe these godly beasts. The philosophers I know feel the need to "live in society" as strongly as anyone. A better name for the third alternative, I think, would be *eccentric*. When a philosopher such as Nietzsche succeeds in living "outside of society," it is not because he is a philosopher but because he is eccentric.

In choosing a lifestyle, most people unhesitatingly conform to the standards of the society in which they live. Conformity represents the path of least resistance. If you conform—if you live the way those around you have chosen to live—they will approve of your lifestyle. (People tend to praise those who resemble them, inasmuch as it is a socially acceptable way to praise themselves.) They will reward you with their admiration and respect—and with some envy thrown in, for good measure.

It is, as I have suggested, only a slight exaggeration to say that people live not for themselves but for other people. For most people, life requires an ongoing series of compromises between what they want for themselves and what other people want and expect of them. Most people thus come to relinquish much of their sovereignty over themselves. They relinquish it to relatives, to neighbors, and even to complete strangers, and they do so because they value highly the admiration of other people and fear their contempt and ridicule.

Eccentrics, on the other hand, refuse to relinquish sovereignty over themselves. They refuse to live for other people. They have their own vision of what is valuable in life and which lifestyles are worth living. If their vision is at odds with the common view, so much the worse for the common view.

Eccentrics refuse to conform to the standards of the society in which they live. What motivates others will not motivate them. They might see no point at all in trying to impress people with a new car or big house. To the contrary, they might argue that anyone who is impressed by such things is simply not worth impressing. (An eccentric might even regard the banged-up old car he drives as a kind of amulet that wards off shallow individuals, with whom he might otherwise have to deal.) Having rejected the trappings of success, eccentrics will typically have less need to prosper financially than their neighbors and in particular will not feel compelled to spend their days doing a job they hate. They will instead spend them doing what they want to do, even though what they want to do pays minimally or not at all.

Eccentrics are worth exploring in this, a book about desire, not because they have mastered desire in general but because they have, to a considerable extent, mastered *social* desire, the desire to win the admiration of those around them. And by overcoming their social desires, eccentrics also subdue many of their material desires: if you don't want to win the admiration of someone who admires people on the basis of what kind of car they drive, you probably won't want the car that would win his admiration.

Not only do eccentrics dislike much of what their neighbors like, but they come up with sensible reasons for disliking it. In doing this, they imply that the likes of their neighbors are foolish, and therefore that their neighbors are foolish to some degree as well. These implications are not lost on their neighbors: the eccentric quickly earns their enmity.

Sometimes people deal with an eccentric by trying to get him to mend his ways and be more like they are. A true eccentric will ignore their advice and in doing so will doubly affront them. In ignoring their advice, the eccentric is demonstrating that he doesn't care what they think. (Telling someone you don't care what he thinks is one of the strongest insults possible.) Furthermore, in ignoring their advice, in not succumbing to social pressure, the eccentric is implying that he is somehow outside—or even worse, above—the "rules" of the society in which he lives. *The rest of us* have to conform to societal expectations. *We* have to work hard to afford the home, car, clothes, and hairstyle necessary to win the admiration of those around us. The eccentric, on the other hand, thinks society's rules do not likewise apply to him. It just isn't fair that we have to obey the rules and he doesn't. Mixed with this feeling of unfairness is a measure of envy: if only we could be as free to live the life of our choosing as the eccentric is!

The neighbors of the eccentric will almost certainly gossip about his foolishness. They might also openly display their disdain for him. They might mock him, only to find that he doesn't seem to mind being mocked. (He might even mock himself in ways they hadn't thought of mocking him.) They might neglect to invite him to gatherings, only to realize that he probably would not have wanted to come even if invited. The neighbors will wait patiently for him to pay a price for his eccentricity—for him to see the foolishness of his ways and ultimately beg for their admiration and respect. The problem is that many eccentrics seem perfectly happy in their eccentricity. This happiness only increases their neighbors' irritation with respect to them.

Some eccentrics avoid the harassment of their fellow beings by removing themselves from society. They might live as hermits in some remote place, or they might continue to live among people but have minimal social contact with them. Many eccentrics, however, do not flee from other people. Instead, they continue to be part of society, while at the same time rejecting societal norms. They know that doing so places them in a minority, but they accept their minority status. When neighbors ridicule them, they shrug it off, realizing that it is the price they must pay to enjoy social freedom. They also realize that fighting back will only incite more neighborly contempt.

In some cases, though, eccentrics do not passively accept their minority status but instead attempt to reform the society in which they live—to make it see the errors of its ways and accept their eccentric values. Let us now turn our attention to two such militant eccentrics, Diogenes of Sinope (412–323 B.C.) and Henry David Thoreau (1817–1862).

Diogenes and Thoreau are both commonly regarded as philosophers and therefore might have been discussed in the previous chapter, in which I considered philosophical advice on desire. The problem is that neither Diogenes nor Thoreau offers a "philosophical" justification of his eccentricity. (Cynicism, the doctrine with which Diogenes is associated, is better described as a lifestyle than as a philosophical theory; according to philosopher Luis E. Navia, Cynicism was not so much a system of ideas as "a *response,* a *reaction,* to those conditions of human existence that the Cynics . . . found unacceptable from the point of view of reason.")[3]

Diogenes and Thoreau do not suggest that we pray, meditate, accept fatalism, or solve a koan to overcome our social and material desires. Instead, they suggest that we watch our neighbors and learn from them. We should look at how they spend their days, at what they call *success*, and, most importantly, at how miserable and desperate they seem. We should examine the contradictions embodied in their lifestyles—the way they work harder, for example, so they can have more leisure time. We should watch as they persist in certain lifestyles even though a growing body of evidence, ignored by them, suggests that the lifestyles in question are taking them no closer to their goals—are, if anything, taking them further away. In particular, we should notice how they stubbornly believe that their next consumer purchase will bring them lasting happiness, even though none of their previous purchases did. We should pay attention to their constant need for external affirmation of their lifestyle and to how they bristle at anyone who suggests that their values are flawed. We should realize that if we care about what these neighbors think of us, we will end up living as they do. And we should ask ourselves this question: is this what we want out of life—to be like *them*?

Diogenes was a student of Antisthenes, founder of the Cynic school of philosophy, who in turn was a student of Socrates. Although Plato was also a student of Socrates, his approach to philosophy was markedly different from that of either Antisthenes or Diogenes. Plato spent his days giving lectures that were long on philosophical theory and short on advice on how to live—lectures that Diogenes dismissed as being a waste of time.[4]

(It is worth noting that Socrates, the intellectual forebear of both Diogenes and Plato, appears to have had a foot in both philosophical camps: he was interested in theoretical philosophy but at the same time lived the life of an eccentric. It is also worth noting that Zeno of Citium, the founder of Stoicism, was a student of Crates, a Cynic; it is in part because of this that one finds an affinity between the Stoics and the Cynics.)

Anyone who chooses an eccentric lifestyle runs the risk of being labeled mad. Indeed, Plato referred to Diogenes as a Socrates gone mad.[5] Because most people are conformists, they have trouble understanding why someone would voluntarily flout social convention and thereby open himself to the disapprobation of society. To be sure, many eccentrics are not that way by choice; instead, they owe their eccentricity to mental illness. Voluntary eccentrics are willing to run the risk of being thought mad because they appreciate the tremendous freedom an eccentric lifestyle can yield: if you are willing to accept "Crazy" as part of your nickname, you can live the life of your own choosing rather than having to conform to the expectations of those around you.

We don't have any writings of Diogenes. We do have descriptions of him, though. He despised wealth and fame, living the simplest life possible. We are told, for instance, that he lived in a tub, although it is not clear exactly what this meant. (Navia argues for a large earthenware barrel.)[6] He held money to be the root of all evil[7] and observed that bad men obey their lusts as servants obey their masters.[8] He argued that his fellow men would be happy if only they would quit their useless toils and live "as nature recommends"; nevertheless, "such is their madness that they choose to be miserable."[9] In defense of a simplified existence, Diogenes pointed out that it is "the privilege of the gods to need nothing and of god-like men to want but little."[10]

Diogenes was renowned for his wit. At one point in his life, he was captured by pirates and auctioned as a slave. When the auctioneer asked him in what he was proficient, Diogenes replied, "In ruling men." He then pointed to an affluent individual in the crowd of buyers and said, "Sell me to this man; he needs a master."[11] On another occasion, someone asked Diogenes why people give money to the lame and blind but not to philosophers. His reply: "Because people worry they may one day be lame or blind, but they never expect that they will someday turn to philosophy."[12]

Diogenes was apparently acquainted with Alexander the Great. Although Alexander was rich, powerful, and famous, Diogenes was unimpressed. On one occasion, Alexander saw Diogenes sunning himself. He walked up, stood over Diogenes, and asked whether there was anything Diogenes wanted, the suggestion being that Alexander would use his power to supply it. Diogenes replied that he wished Alexander would stop blocking his sun.[13] Alexander was impressed by Diogenes's independence: he reportedly said that if he couldn't be Alexander, he would want to be Diogenes.[14]

Diogenes ridiculed men for spending so much time, effort, and money in their quest for sexual gratification. He, by way of contrast, "found Aphrodite everywhere, without expense"— apparently through masturbation. Even fish, noted Diogenes, when they need to eject sperm, find ways to do so without resorting to sexual intercourse, but in this respect, fish are more sensible than men. He further observed that although "men were unwilling to pay out money to have a leg or an arm or any other part of their body rubbed . . . , yet on that one member they spent many talents time and again and some had even risked their lives in the bargain."[15]

Epictetus—who was himself a Stoic but knew and appreciated the Cynics—was asked to advise a person who was thinking about becoming a Cynic. His advice gives us a picture of the Cynic lifestyle. As a Cynic, he said, "you must utterly put away the will to get, and must will to avoid only what lies within the sphere of your will: you must harbour no anger, wrath, envy, pity: a fair maid, a fair name, favourites, or sweet cakes, must mean nothing to you." The Cynic, he says, "must have the spirit of patience in such measure as to seem to the multitude as unfeeling as a stone. Reviling or blows or insults are nothing to him." He describes the true Cynic as "a messenger from God to men concerning things good and evil, to show them that they have gone astray."

A Cynic, according to Epictetus, lacks a house and property, with the exception of one poor cloak. He sleeps on the ground. He has neither a wife nor children to comfort him. Yet, despite lacking all this, the Cynic will claim to lack nothing:

"What do I lack? Am I not quit of pain and fear, am I not free? When has any of you ever seen me failing to get what I will to get, or falling into what I will to avoid?"[16]

Dio Chrysostom, a contemporary of Epictetus who has been described as "a Stoic in theory, a Cynic in practice,"[17] says that Diogenes viewed himself as a physician for the soul. He would go wherever people had assembled, study their desires and ambitions, and by interacting with them, attempt to heal their corrupt souls. He might, for example, approach people who had come to watch an athletic competition and declare himself to be one of the competitors. When they ridiculed this claim and asked against whom he was competing, he would answer, "The noble man holds his hardships to be his greatest antagonists, and with them he is ever wont to battle day and night."[18] The hardships in question include hunger, exile, and the loss of reputation, as well as anger, pain, desire, and fear.[19]

The noble man also battles against pleasure, which, Diogenes observed, "uses no open force but deceives and casts a spell with baneful drugs, just as Homer says Circe drugged the comrades of Odysseus." Pleasure "hatches no single plot but all kinds of plots, and aims to undo men through sight, sound, smell, taste, and touch, with food too, and drink and carnal lust, tempting the waking and the sleeping alike." (In talking this way, Diogenes sounds as though he is anticipating what I have called the BIS.) It is pleasure, he warned us, that "with a stroke of her wand . . . cooly drives her victim into a sort of sty and pens him up, and now from that time forth the man goes on living as a pig or a wolf." Most men lose their battle against pleasure, since "it is impossible to dwell with pleasure or even to dally with her for any length of time without being completely enslaved." "This," Diogenes concluded, "is the contest which I steadfastly maintain, and in which I risk my life against pleasure and hardship, yet not a single wretched mortal gives heed to me, but only to the jumpers and runners and dancers" of the nearby competitions.[20]

Henry David Thoreau was an eccentric, although not to the extent that Diogenes was. For this reason, Thoreau's lifestyle is, for many would-be eccentrics, more plausible as a model than that of Diogenes: people are more open to the idea of abandoning society for a cabin in the woods than for a "tub" in the city.

Thoreau gave evidence of eccentricity shortly after graduating from Harvard in 1837. Jobs were scarce, due to a financial crisis, but Thoreau succeeded in landing a plum teaching position. His employer complained that Thoreau wasn't caning enough students. Thoreau responded by picking six students at random and caning them. He then quit the job, only two weeks after he had begun.[21]

During the rest of his life, Thoreau devoted his energy to avoiding anything resembling what the world would consider success. He ducked work to the extent possible and instead spent his days reading and walking. (When walking, he said, he recovered "the lost child" that he was.)[22] He took steps to reduce his desires, both material and social, to the minimum: "My greatest skill," he boasted, "has been to want but little."[23] These steps culminated in the famous two-year experiment in which he lived in a small cabin on the shores of Walden Pond: "I went to the woods because I wished to live deliberately, to front only the essential facts of life, and see if I could not learn what it had to teach, and not, when I came to die, discover that I had not lived."[24] (Thoreau, by the way, seems to have avoided this last fate; when he died at age forty-four from tuberculosis, friends commented that they had never seen such a peaceful death.)[25]

Thoreau disparaged the values of his neighbors; indeed, much of *Walden* is spent documenting their foolishness. "The twelve labors of Hercules," according to Thoreau, "were trifling in comparison with those which my neighbors have undertaken; for they were only twelve, and had an end; but I could never see that these men slew or captured any monster or finished any labor." And what about the "successful" farmers of his village? "How many a poor immortal soul have I met well nigh crushed and smothered under its load, creeping down the road of life, pushing before it a barn seventy-five feet by forty, its Augean stables never cleansed, and one hundred acres of land, tillage, mowing, pasture, and wood-lot!" His neighbors, Thoreau claimed, led "mean and sneaking lives," lives of "quiet desperation." They were slaves who had themselves as slave drivers.[26]

Thoreau's neighbors were, to his way of thinking, not just wrong, but wrongheaded: "The greater part of what my neighbors call good I believe in my soul to be bad, and if I repent of any thing, it is very likely to be my good behavior. What demon possessed me that I behaved so well?"[27] Elsewhere he wrote that "joy and sorrow, success and failure, grandeur and meanness, and indeed most of the words in the English language do not mean for me what they do for my neighbors."[28] He rejected the common definition of *success:* "If a man has spent all his days about some business by which he has merely got to be rich as it is called: i.e. has got much money, many houses and barns and wood lots, then his life has been a failure, I think."[29]

In putting down his neighbors, Thoreau was not declaring himself to be better than they. The difference was simply that he had seen the light, and they hadn't: "If there are any who think that I am vainglorious, that I set myself up above others and crow over their low estate, let me tell them that I could tell a pitiful story respecting myself as well as them. . . . I could encourage them with a sufficient list of failures, and could flow as humbly as the very gutters."[30]

Although Thoreau was not a hermit—not even during his years at Walden Pond[31]—he had minimal need for social contact. As far as Thoreau was concerned, the costs associated with human contact clearly exceeded the benefits: "My acquaintances will sometimes wonder why I will impoverish myself by living aloof from this or that company, but greater would be the impoverishment if I should associate with them."[32] Elsewhere he commented that "society, man, has no prize to offer me that can tempt me; not one. That which interests a town or city or any large number of men is always something trivial. . . . It is impossible for me to be interested in what interest men generally. Their pursuits and interests seem to me frivolous."[33]

Although Thoreau did not enjoy the company of others, he enjoyed the company of himself.[34] He also felt sorry for people who need people: "Woe to him who wants a companion—for he is unfit to be the companion even to himself."[35]

Thoreau scorned his neighbors' intense desire to conform: "There is a stronger desire to be respectable to one's neighbors than to one's self."[36] But if, like Thoreau, you believe that your neighbors are utterly misguided in how they live their lives, you have but one choice open to you if you are both honest and courageous: you must ignore your neighbors and be your own person; you must decide what life suits *you* best and then set about living it; you must march, as Thoreau put it, to a different drummer.[37]

If Thoreau disapproved of his neighbors' lifestyles, they also disapproved of his. Thoreau realized that his neighbors thought that "it is a mean and unfortunate destiny which makes me walk in these fields and woods so much and sail on this river alone."[38] And it wasn't just Concord's farmers and tradespeople who disapproved of Thoreau, but its intellectuals as well. Ralph Waldo Emerson faulted Thoreau for his lack of ambition.[39] William Ellery Channing said of Thoreau, "I have never been able to understand what he meant by his life."[40] Of course, to a true eccentric, earning the disdain of others or at least puzzling them is a sign of success.

Thoreau rejected the material goods his neighbors worked so hard to obtain: "Most of the luxuries, and many of the so called comforts of life, are not only not indispensable, but positive hindrance to the elevation of mankind. With respect to luxuries and comforts, the wisest have ever lived a more simple and meager life than the poor."[41] More generally, he asserted that "all good things are cheap; all bad are very dear."[42]

He thought it pointless to amass a great fortune, since "superfluous wealth can buy superfluities only."[43] Indeed, from Thoreau's point of view, great wealth isn't just pointless, but evil: "In my experience I have found nothing so truly impoverishing as what is called wealth."[44] He also claimed that "it is fouler and uglier to have too much than not to have enough."[45] We should, he said, "cultivate poverty like a garden herb, like sage."[46]

Thoreau advises us to simplify our diet. During his experiment at Walden Pond, he found he could feed himself for twenty-seven cents per week.[47] Thoreau also advises us to simplify our dwellings. At Walden, he lived in a ten-by-fifteen-foot cabin he built by himself at a cost of $28.12½,[48] but he suspected that even this was more shelter than a sensible person needed. He toyed with the idea of living in a box six feet long and three feet wide. And in case this suggestion sounds impractical, Thoreau reminded us that "many a man is harassed to death to pay the rent of a larger and more luxurious box who would not have frozen to death in such a box as this."[49] Thoreau's box, one imagines, is the New England equivalent of Diogenes's tub.

Thoreau rejected the common view that we should spend our days doing disagreeable labor in order to make a living: "How trivial and uninteresting and wearisome and unsatisfactory are all employments for which men will pay you money! The ways by which you may get money all lead downward."[50] His advice: "You must get your living by loving."[51] According to him, "The aim of the laborer should be, not to get his living, to get 'a good job,' but to perform well a certain work."[52] Thoreau encourages us, when buying things, to think of not their dollar cost but their labor cost—that is, the amount of life we have to give up to obtain the money to buy the thing in question.[53] Of course, if we like what we do for a living, as Thoreau did, we aren't giving up much. In such cases, our paycheck is the icing on the cake.

If we simplify our lives, it won't require much labor to earn our living. Thoreau estimated that he could support himself with six weeks of labor per year,[54] leaving the other forty-six weeks free for more important endeavors, such as being the self-appointed and unpaid inspector of snowstorms and rainstorms.[55] More generally, we can spend the time doing something that ordinary persons are afraid to do—we can chase our dreams. During his time at Walden Pond, wrote Thoreau, "I learned . . . that if one advances confidently in the direction of his dreams, and endeavors to live the life which he has imagined, he will meet with a success unexpected in common hours."[56] And we can spend our days living not just one life but many lives, on an experimental basis. Thoreau, we should remember, left Walden because, he said, he had several more lives to live.[57]

Scottish neuropsychologist David Weeks has probably encountered more eccentrics than any other person. Weeks set out to do a study of eccentricity, only to discover that scientific knowledge about eccentrics was virtually nonexistent. He began working to fill in this gap in our understanding of nonconformity by studying eccentrics of yesterday and today. His conclusions are presented in his and Jamie James's *Eccentrics: A Study of Sanity and Strangeness.*

Weeks discovered that eccentrics are invariably social failures—at least if we use the word *failure* in its conventional sense. At best the world fails to take them seriously, and at worst it ridicules them. Eccentrics also tend to be financial failures, due in part, no doubt, to their lack of social standing. When eccentrics prosper, there are generally two explanations: either they inherited a fortune or they found a way to get rewarded for their obsessive behavior. Weeks turned up one example of the latter: a man who, obsessed with potatoes, became a government potato inspector, a job he carried out with delight.

Weeks came up with a list of characteristics eccentrics tend to share. Most obviously, they are nonconformists. They are also curious, creative, intelligent, idealistic, and opinionated.

And they are obsessive: by definition, eccentrics are passionately devoted to at least one idea, enterprise, or hobby—although according to Weeks, the typical eccentric doesn't stop at one obsession but goes on to develop half a dozen. Whereas the obsessions of people with obsessive-compulsive disorder make them miserable, the obsessions of eccentrics bring them delight.

People who stand out from the crowd pay a price for doing so—a price a true eccentric is perfectly willing to pay. At the same time, many eccentrics have developed techniques to minimize this price. For one thing, they don't try to compete with or seek the approval of those around them. To do so, they realize, is to invite ridicule and abuse. For another thing, as Weeks discovered, most eccentrics have a well-developed and often mischievous sense of humor. Presumably this provides them with an important coping strategy: by making a joke out of their own "failings," they disarm their critics. (It is hard to demean someone who has a self-deprecating sense of humor.) Also, someone able to make light of his failures is unlikely to experience psychological anguish with respect to them. For many eccentrics, the world is a constantly amusing place, and their role in it is one of their greatest sources of amusement.

Although eccentrics are typically failures in the common sense of the word, Weeks found that as a group they are strikingly happy, and their happiness seems to be a result of their nonconformity. Weeks describes them as exhibiting buoyant self-confidence and as being comfortable in their own skins. They also appear far more able than most adults to experience joy. This is in part what makes eccentrics seem childlike: they take obvious and intense delight in things that the rest of us find commonplace or boring. In this respect, they resemble Zen Buddhists who have found enlightenment.

Besides being happy, eccentrics tend to enjoy robust good health. According to Weeks, they visit a doctor much less often than normal people. (Their failure to visit doctors could, of course, be a sign not of good health but of impaired judgment; Weeks considers and rejects this possibility.) They also tend to live to a ripe old age. (Despite his primitive lifestyle, Diogenes lived to nearly ninety.)

Weeks offers an explanation for the health and happiness of eccentrics. Despite their lack of "success," eccentrics live low-stress lives. They simply don't realize that they have "failed," their definition of *success* being so different from the ordinary definition. And even when they fail according to their own definition, they might respond by laughing it off. They don't create stress for themselves by playing the role of victim. They don't spend their days complaining about how unfair the world is or plotting revenge on others. They don't have time for these psychologically harmful activities: they are simply too busy with their various interests. According to Weeks, the low stress of their lives translates into a healthy immune system, which in turn translates into overall health and a long life.

Having said this, I should add that the people who must daily deal with eccentrics—their parents, spouses, or children— might not likewise enjoy life. For unless they too are eccentric, they might feel compelled to spend their days trying to undo the social havoc wreaked by the eccentric "under their care," and their lives might, as a result, be quite stressful.

One suspects that for extreme eccentrics such as Diogenes and Thoreau, conformity is not really an option. They couldn't suppress their eccentricity even if they wanted to. More moderate eccentrics, though, have options available to them.

They can, to begin with, delay the expression of their eccentricity. Weeks discovered a significant number of eccentrics who recognized at an early age their capacity for eccentricity but hid their eccentric tendencies from the world. He found that women eccentrics in particular tend to conform until they have married and raised families; when the nest is empty, they might finally permit themselves the luxury of being different. Other mildly eccentric individuals conform until they are senior citizens. This is a shrewd thing to do, since as people get older, the costs associated with an eccentric lifestyle decline: we tolerate eccentricity in a seventy-year-old better than we tolerate it in a forty-year-old, and we *expect* eccentricity in a ninety-year-old. Many of the elderly realize this and take to eccentricity like a duck to water. At long last they can be themselves, a right they feel they have earned. For these individuals, old age, despite its physical drawbacks, is a time of increased social freedom and diminished social anxiety.

Another option for the moderately eccentric person is to become a low-profile eccentric. Diogenes and Thoreau, as we have seen, openly attacked the values of their neighbors. A low-profile eccentric won't do this: besides not caring what other people think, he won't care to change what they think. He knows that if he openly criticizes his neighbors, it will only make it harder for him to accomplish his primary goal of being left alone to pursue his interests. To accomplish this goal, he will willingly accept a diminished social status and cultivate a sense of humility. He will do his best to convince others that he is not playing the social game and therefore that they need not view him as a social competitor. What he will do, in essence, is roll over and assume a submissive posture, socially speaking. Once people cease to view him as a social competitor, they will feel less threatened by his eccentricity and will be more likely to accept him for who he is.

Suppose someone detects eccentric tendencies in himself and is considering whether to become a "practicing eccentric." He might be tempted to experiment with eccentricity and see whether it works for him—whether the benefits of being an eccentric outweigh the social costs. Such experimentation is risky, however, since the experiment in question is likely to end up on the person's "permanent record." This would not be the case if he experimented with, say, Zen Buddhism or Stoicism. It is possible to "try out" Zen for decades or to read the entire works of Seneca without your neighbors being any the wiser. To try out eccentricity properly, though, you must do so in public. An eccentric who keeps his nonconformity a secret—a closet eccentric, as it were—isn't really practicing an eccentric lifestyle and can't hope to sample the benefits of nonconformity.

This means that if someone's experiment with eccentricity doesn't pan out and he returns to conformity, the world will remember his brief rebellion and will be disinclined to trust him. In dabbling with an eccentric lifestyle, he will have stained his conformist credentials. Indeed, in the business world, where dull gray conformity is typically a key to success, a career can be ruined by a bout of eccentric behavior.

One can become a Zen Buddhist by studying under a Zen master, a Catholic by converting to the religion, or a Stoic by reading the Stoics. Can one likewise "become" an eccentric? French encyclopedist Denis Diderot suggested that if you are not born with a capacity for eccentricity, there is little you can do later in life to develop such a capacity.[58] This is because eccentricity requires a degree of courage and self-reliance that cannot be learned. And in the words of Honoré Daumier, it is "hard being forced to live in a tub if one is not born a Cynic."[59]

David Weeks's findings confirm these observations. The majority of Weeks's eccentrics knew by age eight that they weren't like other people. This suggests that eccentricity is "in the genes," which in turn means that unless you are a born eccentric, it is unlikely that you can choose to become one, the way you can choose to become a Catholic.

Those of us who aren't born eccentrics can nevertheless learn from those who are. Although we can't make ourselves stop caring what other people think, we can work at reducing the number of people whose opinions we value. Although we would be miserable living in a tub in the city or a cabin in the woods, we can resolve that the size of our house will be dictated by our housing needs, not by our social aspirations. More generally, we can adopt a lifestyle that, although far simpler than that of our friends, relatives, and neighbors, isn't so simple that they feel threatened by it.

We can also learn from the way eccentrics respond to their critics. In particular, we can develop a talent for self-deprecation. If someone mocks the way we dress, for example, we might neutralize the criticism by commenting, "If you think this outfit is bad, wait until you see what I wear tomorrow!" If someone points out a failing of ours, we might reply, "Thanks for mentioning it, but to be honest with you, I don't think that particular failing would even make it into my top-five list of character flaws." And to prevent ourselves from taking such criticisms to heart, we can, while giving these self-deprecating replies, add silently to ourselves: "If this person's own life were worth living, he would be so involved in living it that he wouldn't have time to criticize me. If I take his criticisms seriously, my life will become like his, and my life, too, will not be worth living."

More generally, we should work to develop a sense of humor about the world and our place in it. As soon as we start taking ourselves too seriously, we will be at the mercy of those around us. To keep them happy, we will have to form and act on a number of undesirable desires. We will no longer be living the life of our choosing, but the life they want us to live. If we can learn to laugh at ourselves, though, we reduce our chances of falling victim to this kind of social tyranny.

**Content**, *adj.* Having one's desires bounded by what one has (though that may be less than one could have wished); not disturbed by the desire of anything more, or of anything different.

—*Oxford English Dictionary*

# Conclusions

Our desires, as we have seen, have a life of their own. We often don't choose to desire what we desire; instead, we discover desires within us. Even when we consciously form new desires in an utterly rational manner, we usually find, when we examine them, that they are instrumental desires, the satisfaction of which will ultimately enable us to satisfy a desire we didn't choose to have.

Many of our desires can be explained by the presence in us of a biological incentive system, or BIS. The system in question is hardwired into us—part of our circuitry, as it were. We are rewarded with good mental and physical feelings for doing some things and therefore want to do them; we are punished with bad feelings for doing other things and therefore want not to do them. We gained this system through a process of natural selection: our evolutionary ancestors who had certain built-in incentives for action were more likely to survive and reproduce than those who didn't.

Evolutionarily speaking, this way of wanting has served us well. It got us to where we are now, clearly the dominant species on the planet: while other species must adapt to changes in their environment, we have an unprecedented ability to alter our environment so adaptation is not required. But although our way of wanting has enabled us to thrive as a species, it has not, in many cases, allowed us to flourish as individuals.

Many people spend their days unreflectively earning the rewards offered by their BIS: it is, after all, the obvious thing to do. They seek the admiration of others because it feels good to be admired, and to win this admiration they might buy an expensive car and a big house filled with the latest consumer gadgets. If they can't fulfill the desires they form, they feel dissatisfied, and if they are able to fulfill them, they go on to form new desires, and so remain dissatisfied.

Sometimes it dawns on these individuals that they are on a satisfaction treadmill. They realize that the desires they satisfied in the past did not give rise to lasting happiness and that in satisfying these desires they were dealing with the symptoms of the problem of desire, not getting to its roots. They come to realize that there simply has to be more to life than spending one's days earning the rewards offered by one's BIS. They start worrying that the life they are living has no meaning and that they will someday experience Thoreau's nightmare scenario: it will come time to die, and they will realize that they never lived.

In the introduction to this book, I warned readers that I would not provide them with a "magic bullet" they could use to eliminate unwanted desires. It should by now be clear that this warning was justified. Nowhere in the preceding "advice" chapters did we unearth a quick, easy, and surefire way to eliminate objectionable desires.

Another thing to realize is that the different individuals and groups we discussed offer different and in many cases incompatible advice on how to master desire. Some advise us to join a religious community, while others advise us to continue living in "the World" but eschew the admiration of the people around us. Some advise us to pray, meditate, solve koans, or reflect on the possibility of an eternity spent in heaven or a first-rate reincarnation to keep our desires in check. The Stoics, however, reject this advice and suggest instead that we use reason to overcome our propensity to form unwholesome desires. The Skeptics, in turn, reject *this* advice and argue that reasoning about our desires will only serve to disrupt our tranquility. What are we to make of this divergent advice? We cannot possibly follow it all.

I think each of the desire-management strategies described in the preceding chapters is effective. The evidence for this is that those who have adopted any of these strategies have, in many cases, made considerable progress toward mastering their desires. Which strategy a person should adopt depends, I suppose, on that person's personality and circumstances. Someone who recognizes her eccentricity at an early age—a born eccentric—might do well to follow in the footsteps of Thoreau, but someone who, to the contrary, recognizes in herself an intense social need might find it impossible to imitate Thoreau. Someone confident that God exists would do well to pray to Him for help in fighting unwholesome desires, but for an atheist such prayers will be pointless. Someone raised in a Hutterite community would do well, if he wishes to control his desires, to remain in that community; those of us who weren't raised in a Hutterite community lack this option.

If we step back and look at the various strategies for dealing with desire, we find that despite their differences, they share certain insights:

*We shouldn't trust our desires.* Just because we detect a desire within us doesn't mean we should take ownership of it. Many "natural" desires are parasitic: they take up residence in us without being invited, and while within us, try to hijack our plan for living. We should work to rid ourselves of these desires, much as we would try to rid ourselves of a tapeworm.

*We need to be careful about turning to other people for advice on dealing with desires.* Most people, after all, are slaves to their desires and therefore have no helpful advice to offer. (If we tell our friends that we are working to overcome our desire to be rich and famous, they might look at us in blinking incomprehension and conclude that we have been brainwashed by some cult or fallen victim to depression.) The exception to this is if our friends—because, perhaps, we live in a Hutterite community—are like-minded about the importance of mastering desire; in this case, turning to them can help us win our battles against desire. Those who lack enlightened neighbors, friends, and relatives can turn to the writings of Buddha, Epictetus, or Thoreau for moral support.

*Mastering desire will involve a two-stage strategy.* In the first, we try to prevent the onset of unwanted desires: this might mean avoiding certain influences, avoiding certain people whose own desires might be infectious, or maybe even avoiding "the World." In the second stage we try to extinguish those unwanted desires that, despite our attempts to prevent them, arise within us: this might involve praying for help in overcoming a desire or reflecting on how absurd it is for us to have the desire.

*We should work to develop an understanding of desire.* To win a battle, it helps to know the enemy. Anyone wishing to master desire, then, would do well to understand its workings and, more generally, why we want what we want. To develop this understanding, we might meditate, read philosophy, or examine the research of psychologists who have explored the role our unconscious plays in desire formation and the way our evolutionary past affects our behavior. Among the things it will behoove us to understand are these:

- *That our desires generally don't exist in isolation.* Instead they come into existence because of something else we want; they are, in other words, instrumental desires. Furthermore, it is possible for a single desire to give rise to thousands or even millions of these instrumental desires. Desires, in other words, are like microorganisms dropped into a warm, nutrient-rich pond. Left to their own devices, they will reproduce until the pond is a fetid swamp. This in turn suggests that we should be very careful about what "initial" desires we form.

- *That we have multiple sources of desire within us, and they can give rise to conflicting desires.* In particular, our emotions can give rise to a desire that our intellect finds objectionable, and conversely. When this happens, it will be impossible for us to satisfy all our desires.

- *That when it comes to desire formation, our intellect typically plays second fiddle to our emotions.* We gained our ability to reason not so that we could transcend our emotions and the desires to which they give rise but so that we could more effectively satisfy these desires. The intellect is capable of forming desires, but they will typically be less motivated than those formed by the emotions. Indeed, someone who retains his intellect but whose emotions stop giving rise to desires will resemble a depressed individual.

- *That we have the greatest control over the desires that have the least impact on our lives.* If I detect in myself a desire to click my tongue, I can easily extinguish it. But if I discover that I have fallen in love with someone, I might be powerless to fight the feelings I am experiencing.

- *That we have a BIS, and it determines, to a considerable extent, what desires we form.* Suppose our BIS, rather than rewarding us for seeking the company of other people, punished us. It is then unlikely that we would be gregarious. Or suppose our BIS, rather than giving us a reward, in the form of an orgasm, for having sex, punished us with intense pain. We would, under these circumstances, be unlikely to expend effort trying to attract a mate. More generally, if our BIS did not reward us for being social, sexual creatures, our desires would be radically different. In particular, we would have fewer, simpler material desires: most people who want a big house, for example, want it not for its own sake but so that they can win the admiration—or failing that, the envy—of other people.

- *That the "incentive schedule" of our BIS was not devised to encourage us to have a happy, meaningful life.* Our BIS is a consequence of our evolutionary past; we have the BIS we do because our evolutionary ancestors who had it were more likely to survive and reproduce than those who didn't. As long as their unhappiness and their feeling that life is pointless did not affect whether they survived and reproduced—as long as, despite their misery, they ate, drank, evaded predators, and had sex— their misery had no impact on the evolution of the human BIS.

- *That we can choose to forgo the rewards offered by our BIS and to accept its punishments.* Even though we are hungry, we can choose to skip lunch. Even though we feel lustful, we can choose to refrain from having sex. It is because we have multiple sources of desire within us that this is possible: our emotions might push us to eat lunch—those hunger pangs feel bad—but our intellect, if it is sufficiently well developed, might be able to overrule these emotions. Indeed, it should be clear that if we lack a well-developed intellect—if we lack willpower— we will have little chance of mastering our desires. We will instead be like cats, dogs, gerbils, and alligators, doing the bidding of our BIS without second thought.

- *That we are insatiable.* Gaining the object of our desire almost invariably reduces its desirability to us. We experience psychological adaptation: we take the gained object for granted and start feeling dissatisfied. To overcome this feeling, we form a new desire and work to fulfill it, thinking that this time will be different— that this time, gaining the object of our desire will result in lasting satisfaction.

- *That the worst way to deal with our feelings of dissatisfaction is by working to satisfy the desires we find within us.* If we do this, we practically guarantee that we will never experience lasting satisfaction, since the desire we satisfy will quickly be replaced by another desire. Trying to gain satisfaction by working to fulfill the desires that arise within us is like trying to deal with a heroin addiction by working to get a heroin fix. It is better, in the case of heroin, to kick the habit, and better, in the case of desire, to master our desires to the extent possible.

- *That the best way to gain satisfaction—lasting satisfaction— is to change not the world and our position in it but ourselves.* In particular, we should work at wanting what we already have. In doing this, we should remember that in most cases what we have—whether it be our job, our car, our children, or our spouse—is something that we once dreamed of having, or something that someone less fortunate than us presently dreams of having. (Even a paraplegic is living the dream of a quadriplegic, who in turn is living the dream of someone with locked-in syndrome. This last individual is so paralyzed that she can't even speak but instead must blink her eyes to communicate.) We should endeavor to enjoy *this* dream, rather than ignoring it to pursue some other dream.

- *That complete mastery of desire is impossible.* Our goal should not be to eliminate desire altogether; short of committing suicide, that is impossible. Our goal should instead be to attain a degree of mastery over our desires. In particular, rather than simply forming desires in accordance with our evolutionary programming—rather than simply doing the bidding of our BIS—we should, to the extent that we can, take control over the desire formation process.

- *That mastering desire won't be easy.* It will require sustained effort on our part, and there will be setbacks. Having said this, I should add that mastering desire will be less difficult than we might imagine. For one thing, once we come to understand our desires, many of them will simply vanish; they will fall away, as Bhikkhu Bodhi puts it, "like the leaves of a tree, naturally and spontaneously." Furthermore, the effort required to master desire is probably less, all things considered, than the effort we will expend trying to fulfill whatever desires pop into our head. It is true that a person attempting to master desire will have to spend time reflecting on his desires and how best to overcome them and might have to spend some of his free time reading philosophers or meditating. But the alternative approach, working to satisfy a never-ending stream of desires, will be far more arduous. The person taking this last approach might be forced to spend his adult life doing a job he hates so that he can afford the objects of his desires. His days might be frenetic, while the person who works instead to master his desires will enjoy relative tranquility.

Our BIS, as we have seen, was forced on us by our evolutionary past. Furthermore, its incentives are calculated not to encourage us to have happy, meaningful lives but to make us feel perpetually dissatisfied—to want more, no matter how much we have. And to top off our predicament, we cannot escape from our BIS. Like it or not, we must live our lives with its rewards dangling before us and with whispered threats of its punishments. This, unfortunately, is the human condition.

To better understand our predicament, consider the predicament of slaves. They are exploited by their master. He employs an overseer, whose job it is to monitor the slaves' daily activities and reward or punish them in order to induce them to help the master achieve his goals. The incentive system the master imposes on them is non-negotiable, and like it or not, his slaves must spend their lives under this incentive system.

Analogously, we humans have an "evolutionary master"— the evolutionary process that made us who we are. This master seeks to exploit us. His goal is that we survive and reproduce, and to achieve this goal, he employs an overseer—our BIS— who monitors our daily activities and rewards or punishes us to induce us to work on behalf of the evolutionary master—to induce us, in other words, to take the steps necessary to survive and reproduce.

It is one thing to live under an enlightened master who has his slaves' well-being in mind. But our evolutionary master is indifferent to whether we have happy, meaningful lives. He will care only if our misery and sense of futility hinder his pursuit of his own goal that we survive and reproduce. If, for example, we grow so despondent that we become oblivious to his rewards and punishments, he might take steps to ameliorate our living conditions (or rather, to ameliorate the living conditions of our descendants—evolutionary processes take time), but they will be the minimum steps necessary. Then it will be back to exploitation as usual.

One naturally wonders whether it is possible to have a meaningful life under these circumstances. I think it is. Consider, after all, the situation of actual slaves. They may not be able to escape from their master and his system of incentives, but they can form their own personal plan for living and superimpose it over his plan for them. They might, for example, refuse to let their bondage undermine their values. In particular, they might vow to do all they can to help their fellow slaves. This will entail periodically refusing to help their master achieve his goals, since doing so would undermine the goals they have set for themselves, in accordance with their plan for living. If, for example, the master orders them to whip another slave, they will refuse. Of course, if they do this, they will likely be punished by the master's overseer, but this will be a small price to pay in order to have a meaningful life—not meaningful in the cosmic sense, perhaps, but meaningful in the personal sense, and that is arguably what counts.

We "evolutionary slaves" can employ a similar strategy to deal with our circumstances. We can form a personal plan for living and superimpose it over the plan imposed on us by our evolutionary master. If we do this, we will no longer simply be doing his bidding; we will instead be taking our life and doing something with it, something we find meaningful. We will thereby be conferring meaning on our life, to the extent that it is possible to do so.

In forming a life plan, it should be noted, we are cheating our evolutionary master. He gave us the ability to desire because doing so increased his chances of accomplishing his goal that we survive and reproduce. Included in the ability to desire, though, is the ability to choose among options open to us. In particular, we can choose to do something that our BIS will punish us for doing. In forming a life plan, we are, in effect, misusing our ability to choose: we are using it not to accomplish the goals our evolutionary master has set for us but to accomplish other goals we have set for ourselves, goals that are incompatible with his. It may be wrong to cheat our friends and neighbors or even our workplace boss, but cheating our evolutionary master raises, I think, no similar moral issues.

At this point, the reader might expect me to endorse some one life plan as being particularly meaningful. I find that I cannot do so. I think there are many different plans that, if adopted, will confer meaning on one's life. Your plan for living can differ radically from mine, and yet both our lives can be meaningful.

In this book, we have encountered, among the lives we examined, many different life plans—those of Buddha, Merton, Thoreau, and Amish farmers, to name a few. All of these individuals clearly had meaningful lives. Their life plans may not have allowed them to gain worldly success, but they achieved something of even greater value—satisfaction. They did not spend their days wishing they could be someone else, or be themselves living a life other than the one they were living. To the contrary, they embraced their lives and destinies. I also think a life plan can confer meaning without being as exotic as the plans of Buddha, Merton, and the others.

These remarks might make it sound as though I think *any* life plan will confer meaning on a person's life, but this isn't so. I am open to a broad range of life plans. I am even open to life plans, the goals of which are very difficult to attain. Where I would draw the line is at life plans, the goals of which are *impossible* to attain. Adopting such a plan might make it feel to a person as though his life has meaning—indeed, his days will be spent busily pursuing his goals—but if the goals are impossible to reach, all his activity will be futile.

Life is full of instances in which people, because they are thoughtless or misinformed, pursue a goal in a counterproductive way. An acquaintance of mine played a carnival game in which, if you got a hundred points, you could win a grand prize—a television set, I think it was. At first, points were easy to win. As the game progressed, they became harder to win, but he kept on playing, obsessed with winning the prize. Finally, after many hours of playing, and after having spent far more than the television was worth, he figured out that the game was structured so it was impossible to get the hundred points necessary to win. He found a policeman and got his money back.

Unfortunately, this same sort of counterproductive behavior can happen when we plan our lives. Someone might tell us that her goal in life is to gain lasting happiness—an admirable goal, to be sure—and that she plans to achieve this goal by gaining material wealth and social status. In light of the evidence presented in this book, we can ask whether this is a sensible way for her to pursue her goal. The danger is that by pursuing happiness in this way, she is climbing onto a treadmill that will not bring her any closer to her goal. Each thing she buys, each social gain she makes, will only whet her appetite for more things and more social gains.

The day might come when this woman realizes that her life plan is fatally flawed—that she has been playing the equivalent of a carnival game that can't be won—but in this case there will be no policeman to whom she can turn to get back years of misdirected effort. If she is lucky, this realization will come when there is still time for her to modify her life plan— when there is still time for her to salvage some meaning for her existence.

This is what happened to Siddhartha Gautama. He spent the first three decades of his life in the unreflecting pursuit of pleasure until he came to recognize the futility, the pointlessness, of his plan for living. Much the same thing happened to Thomas Merton. Both men subsequently devised new plans for living that could confer meaning on their lives.

Cases in which people, such as the woman described above, form life plans whose goals are impossible to attain are tragic. Almost regardless of her circumstances, the woman had it in her power to live a life filled with contentment and tranquility. She could have taken delight in the most ordinary of events; she could even have experienced joy. She needed only to choose the right life plan. Instead, her life was likely filled with anxiety, envy, bitterness, and discontent (when, for example, she was snubbed when trying to climb into a new social circle or could not afford to buy what she found herself wanting), broken only occasionally by moments of delight (subsequent, perhaps, to a social triumph or to making a significant purchase).

Whether your life is a living heaven or a living hell depends, to a considerable extent, not on your circumstances but on yourself and the degree to which you have mastered your desires. If we take a person whose desires are out of control and give him everything he wants—a big mansion, a private jet, adulatory articles about him in magazines, and a billion dollars in the bank—he will soon be as dissatisfied as he was before we made his dreams come true. If, however, we take a person who is master of his desires and banish him to a desolate island—the way Seneca was banished to a "barren and thorny rock" by Emperor Claudius[1]—he will, despite the privations, probably find more contentment there than the newly minted billionaire will in his luxurious mansion.

In devising a life plan, what should be our grand goal in living? According to the people examined in this book, our goal should not be the attainment of worldly success—the attainment of fame and fortune. It should instead be the attainment of satisfaction. What matters is not a person's absolute level of fame and fortune but whether his level of fame and fortune are sufficient for him—whether he feels satisfied with it. The lower his expectations are with respect to fame and fortune, the easier it will be for him to gain satisfaction.

Someone might argue that worldly success can bring satisfaction—indeed, that the reason people pursue worldly success is so they can become satisfied. But when we look at people who have gained worldly success, we find that their success did not extinguish the feelings of dissatisfaction that drove them to pursue it. In the words of Epicurus, "Nothing satisfies the man who is not satisfied with a little."[2]

Suppose, for the sake of argument, Epicurus is wrong. Suppose we come across a person who, as the result of decades of effort involving unpleasant toil and considerable anxiety, gains worldly success, and suppose that on gaining it he gains lasting satisfaction. This person, despite having gained satisfaction, deserves our pity, for either he could have gained satisfaction with much less effort, or he could not. In the former case, we should pity him for wasting his effort—for working so hard to get something that could easily have been obtained, if only he had mastered his desires. He is like someone who traveled all the way to Tibet to get a certain kind of tea, even though it was readily available at his corner market. And if, turning to the second case, it was impossible for this person to gain satisfaction without first gaining worldly success, we should pity him for being so hard to satisfy. He is like someone who can become healthy only if he undergoes half a dozen operations. If only he could have enjoyed health without all this medical intervention!

I think it *is* possible for a person to gain both satisfaction and worldly success, but usually when this happens, it isn't because his success brought him satisfaction. Instead it might be that the thing that brought him satisfaction also brought him success. This is what happened to Diogenes: his indifference to success, besides enabling him to feel satisfied with his life, made him famous. It is also what happened to Merton, who became famous despite living the life of a Trappist monk. For most of us, though, the choice between worldly success and satisfaction is mutually exclusive. Generally, to gain fame or fortune a person must be driven by ambition, and a driven person is unlikely to feel satisfied with his circumstances.

At this point, someone might comment that if everyone took to heart the advice to stop seeking worldly success and instead seek satisfaction, the world as we know it would grind to a halt. Instead of a world filled with ambitious people, we would have a world full of Thoreaus, Mertons, and Epicuruses. These complacent individuals would be unwilling to put in long hours at jobs they hate. As a result, there would be little progress. There would be no SUVs, no shopping malls, and no mansions.

In response to this criticism, I have two replies. The first is that it is quite unlikely that everyone will take the above advice to heart: across the millennia and across cultures, only a handful of individuals are sufficiently enlightened to recognize that there can and should be more to life than laboring daily in the service of one's BIS. There is little reason to think that this will change in the future. Indeed, in recent decades people have shown, if anything, an increased willingness to comply with the demands of their BIS. My second reply is that even in the unlikely event that we find ourselves living in a world full of Thoreaus, Mertons, and Epicuruses and devoid of SUVs, shopping malls, and mansions, would this be so bad? The above criticism is founded on the premise that worldly success and its trappings are desirable. If we reject this premise—as Thoreau, Merton, and Epicurus surely will—we effectively undermine the criticism.

It is worth noting, by the way, that although Thoreau, Merton, and Epicurus, were not conventionally ambitious— they did not spend their days working to gain fame and fortune— it hardly follows that they were lazy. To the contrary, their days were full of activity they found to be satisfying, even though the activity in question was unlikely to gain them worldly success.

Someone might also object to the advice I have given by pointing out that it is inconsistent for me to talk about choosing a life plan to superimpose over the plan set for us by our evolutionary master. In the foregoing chapters, after all, I have documented the extent to which "our" choices aren't so much made *by* us as they are made *for* us, at an unconscious level. Therefore it follows that any life plan "we" choose won't really be *our* plan, any more than the plan set for us by evolution is our plan. But if it isn't our plan, how can adopting it confer meaning on our lives?

What the person raising this objection is seeking, I think, is a cosmically significant kind of meaning. I don't think such meaning is forthcoming. Seen from the cosmic point of view, our existence is an astounding accident. The universe not only could get along without us but for billions of years did get along. What we must settle for is meaning in some lesser sense—call it personal meaning. In "choosing" a plan of living, I am doing what I want to do with my life, even though the *I* in question is, if psychologists can be believed, something rather mysterious. Will this make my life "genuinely" meaningful? Probably not, but I think it will make it more personally meaningful than if I instead spend my days mindlessly trying to earn the rewards my BIS has to offer and avoid its punishments.

John Stuart Mill wrote that it is better to be a human being dissatisfied than a pig satisfied and better to be Socrates dissatisfied than a fool satisfied. (He adds that "if the fool, or the pig, are of a different opinion, it is because they only know their own side of the question. The other party to the comparison knows both sides.")[3] Mill stops here in his comparisons, but there is one more we can add: it is better to be Socrates satisfied than Socrates dissatisfied. Likewise, it is better to be Merton satisfied, despite having taken a vow of silence, an Amish farmer satisfied, despite not being able to use a cell phone, or Thoreau satisfied, despite living in a 150-square-foot cabin, than to be a billionaire dissatisfied, even though he can speak, can use cell phones, and lives in a huge mansion.

Do you sincerely think that a billionaire or a famous actress is happier than you are, or that having the billionaire's money or actress's fame would make you happier than you currently are? It is true that the billionaire and the actress *look* happy: magazines have such glowing things to say about their luxurious lifestyles. It is also true that the billionaire and actress should in theory *be* happy: they have what most people want. But that is not the question. Rather, the question is, are they *in fact* happier than you? It all depends, I would like to suggest, on how satisfied you, the billionaire, and the actress are with what you've got. If you are more satisfied than they are, then it is entirely possible that they are less happy than you, despite their fame and fortune. And since it is unlikely that the billionaire and the actress would have achieved the success they did if they were easily satisfied, it is likely that you are more satisfied than they are and therefore are happier as well.

It is true that by pursuing material wealth and social status we can earn the rewards offered by our BIS, but it is unlikely that these rewards will fully compensate us for the trouble involved in pursuing them—particularly when we recall how fleeting the rewards are likely to be. Is our goal in life to be rich? Then we would do well to take to heart the Taoist proverb, repeated in many cultures, that "he who knows contentment is rich."[4] Lao Tzu was right, I think, when he claimed that "there is no disaster greater than not being content."[5]

# Notes

## ONE: THE EBB AND FLOW OF DESIRE

1. Seneca, *Letters*, let. IX.
2. La Rochefoucauld, maxim 422.
3. Quoted in Magee, 217.
4. Quoted in Winokur, 245.
5. *Love Lyrics of Ancient Egypt*, 64.
6. Plutarch, 145.
7. Burton, 840.
8. Burton, 798.
9. Pascal, sec. 277.
10. Russell, *Autobiography*, 195–96.
11. Tkacik, A1.
12. Giroux, xxii.
13. Merton, 146.
14. Merton, 236.
15. Merton, 239.
16. Merton, 277.
17. Merton, 398–99.
18. Merton, 225.
19. McMurtry, 145.
20. McMurtry, 147–48.
21. Streitfeld, C1.
22. Thomas, 54.
23. Bodhi, 1.
24. *Laws of Manu*, ch. 6, sec. 1–4.
25. Tolstoy, 15.

26. Tolstoy, 16–17.
27. Tolstoy, 17–18.
28. Bejjani, 1476f.

## TWO: OTHER PEOPLE

1. Aristotle, bk. 1, ch. 2.
2. Plato, "Symposium," 167–68.
3. Johnson, no. 164 (October 12, 1751).
4. Hume, "Enquiry Concerning the Principles of Morals," sec. IX, pt. 1.
5. Trollope, 92–93.
6. Cowen, 154–55.
7. Cicero, 119.
8. Quoted in Schopenhauer, "Wisdom of Life," 58.
9. Rosett, A12.
10. Schopenhauer, "Wisdom of Life," 99.
11. Schopenhauer, "Wisdom of Life," 101.
12. Schopenhauer, "Wisdom of Life," 49.
13. Hobbes, ch. 1, sec 5.
14. Calvin, bk. III, ch. VII, sec. 4.
15. Twain, 345.
16. Bierce, 106.
17. La Rochefoucauld, maxim 256.
18. Schopenhauer, "Counsels and Maxims," 24.
19. La Rochefoucauld, maxim 539.
20. Seneca, *Letters*, let. VI.
21. Schopenhauer, "Counsels and Maxims," 25.
22. Schopenhauer, "Counsels and Maxims," 26.
23. Schopenhauer, "Counsels and Maxims," 30.
24. Diogenes Laertius, "Antisthenes," 7.
25. Mill, *On Liberty*, 76.
26. Carus, 168.
27. La Rochefoucauld, maxim 28.
28. Schoeck, 208.
29. La Rochefoucauld, maxim 19.
30. La Rochefoucauld, maxim 521.
31. Bierce, 106.
32. Schopenhauer, "Wisdom of Life," 15.
33. Schoeck, 4.
34. La Rochefoucauld, maxim 27.

35. Melville, 46.
36. Schoeck, 31.
37. Schoeck, 6.

### THREE: MAPPING OUR DESIRES

1. Schroeder, 5.
2. Frankfurt, 107.

### FOUR: THE WELLSPRINGS OF DESIRE

1. Hume, *Treatise*, bk. 2, pt. 3, sec.3.
2. Minsky, 42.
3. Hume, *Treatise*, bk. 2, pt. 3, sec.3.
4. Hume, *Treatise*, bk. 2, pt. 3, sec.3.

### FIVE: THE PSYCHOLOGY OF DESIRE

1. Brasil-Neto et al., 964f.
2. Libet, 47–51.
3. See, for example, Daniel Dennett's discussion of Libet's work in *Consciousness Explained*, 162–65.
4. See, for example, Haggard and Eimer.
5. Wegner, 2.
6. Banks, 457–58.
7. Banks, 456.
8. Feinberg, 98.
9. Gazzaniga and LeDoux, 146–47.
10. LeDoux, 32.
11. LeDoux, 33.
12. Gazzaniga and LeDoux, 157.
13. See Gazzaniga's "Brain Modularity."
14. Badcock, 22.
15. Wilson, vii.
16. Wilson, 88–89.
17. Wilson, vii.
18. Nisbett and Wilson, 243.
19. Nisbett and Wilson, 243–44.
20. Gilbert and Wilson, 179.
21. Gertner, 46.

22. Gilbert and Wilson, 179–83.

23. Gilbert and Wilson, 186.

24. Gilbert and Wilson, 186–87.

25. See Frederick and Lowenstein.

26. Kahneman, 14.

27. Reber, 13.

28. Zajonc, "Feeling and Thinking: Preferences Need No Inferences," 155.

29. Reber, 13.

30. Wegner, 145.

31. Wegner, 146.

32. Wegner, 171.

33. Wegner, 147.

34. Zajonc, "Feeling and Thinking: Preferences Need No Inferences," 155.

35. Zajonc, "Feeling and Thinking: Closing the Debate over the Independence of Affect," 44.

36. Zajonc, "Feeling and Thinking: Closing the Debate over the Independence of Affect," 31.

37. Carpenter, 539–43.

38. Wegner, 149.

39. Resnik, 5.

40. Resnik, 26–40.

41. Resnik, 11–12.

42. Damasio, 193–94.

43. Damasio, 36.

44. Damasio, 45.

45. Damasio, 49–50.

46. Damasio, xiii.

47. Damasio, 174.

48. Augustine, *Confessions*, bk. 8.

49. Spinoza, 107.

50. Hume, *Treatise*, bk. 2, pt. 3, sec. 3.

51. Hume, *Treatise*, bk. 3, pt. 1, sec.1.

52. Hume, *Treatise*, bk. 2, pt. 3, sec. 3.

53. Schopenhauer, *World as Will and Representation*, 1:290.

54. Schopenhauer, *World as Will and Representation*, 2:210.

55. Schopenhauer, *World as Will and Representation*, 2:205.

56. Huxley, 244.

57. Huxley, 240–44.

58. Quoted in Wegner, 151.

59. Russell, *The Analysis of Mind*, 30–31.

60. Russell, *The Analysis of Mind*, 34.

## SIX: THE EVOLUTION OF DESIRE

1. This is one characterization of what is involved in desiring; see McFarland, 418.
2. Badcock, 125–26.
3. Badcock, 126.
4. James, 387.
5. Colgan, 5.
6. Olds, 319.
7. Valenstein, 67–69.
8. Valenstein, 68.
9. Badcock, 127.
10. Valenstein, 73.
11. See Frijda.
12. Braitenberg, 20.
13. Badcock, 19.
14. *Pinnacles of India's Past*, bk.10, hymn 129.

## SEVEN: THE BIOLOGICAL INCENTIVE SYSTEM

1. Cabanac, 1105.
2. Ornstein, 69.
3. Wagner, 78.
4. Sacks, 97–99.
5. Sacks, 97–111.
6. Clark and Grunstein, 67.

## EIGHT: THE HUMAN CONDITION

1. Carus, 34.

## NINE: RELIGIOUS ADVICE

1. Carus, 39–40.
2. Bodhi, 6–7.
3. Carus, 49.
4. Carus, 50–51.
5. Bodhi, vii.
6. Bodhi, 33.

7. Bodhi, 33.

8. Bodhi, 34.

9. Bodhi, 36.

10. Bodhi, 32, 69.

11. Bodhi, 69.

12. Bodhi, 34.

13. Bodhi, 83–85.

14. Bodhi, 94.

15. Carus, 72–74.

16. Watson, xiii.

17. Lao Tzu, sec. LVI.

18. Goldberg, *Long Quiet Highway*, 146–48.

19. Goldberg, *Long Quiet Highway*, 109.

20. Kornfield, 98–99.

21. Kornfield, 98.

22. Watts, 91–92.

23. Watts, 65–66.

24. Stevens, 70.

25. Stevens, 84.

26. Stevens, 68–69.

27. Stevens, 81.

28. Watts, 87.

29. Watts, 141.

30. Watts, 144.

31. Watts, 148–51.

32. Stevens, 55–56.

33. Stevens, 126ff.

34. Goldberg, *Long Quiet Highway*, 136.

35. Goldberg, "Interview."

36. Goldberg, *Long Quiet Highway*, 86.

37. Stevens, 55–56.

38. Kornfield, xviii.

39. Calvin, bk. III, ch. XX, sec. 8.

40. Luke 16:19–31 (*New English Bible*).

41. Matthew 5:10.

42. Matthew 5:11–12.

43. Ezekiel 1.

44. Revelations 4.

45. Augustine, *City of God*, bk. 22, ch. 30.

46. McDannell and Lang, 60–63.

47. St. John of the Cross, "Sayings," no. 15.

48. St. John of the Cross, "Sayings," no. 78.

49. St. John of the Cross, "Ascent," bk. I, ch. 13, sec. 11.

50. St. John of the Cross, "Sayings," no. 98.

51. St. John of the Cross, "Sayings," no. 72.

52. St. John of the Cross, "Sayings," no. 145.

53. St. John of the Cross, "Sayings," no. 144.

54. St. John of the Cross, "Ascent," bk. I, ch. 11, sec. 4.

55. St. John of the Cross, "Ascent," bk. I, ch. 11, sec. 5.

56. St. John of the Cross, "Ascent," bk. I, ch. 13, sec. 6.

57. Qur'an, ch. 56.

## TEN: RELIGIOUS ADVICE CONTINUED: PROTESTANT SECTS

1. Kraybill, 33. Most of my discussion of the Amish is based on this book.

2. Kraybill, 19.

3. Kraybill, 32.

4. Kraybill, 70.

5. Kraybill, 213.

6. Schopenhauer, "Counsels and Maxims," 21.

7. Kraybill, 137–39.

8. Kraybill, 184.

9. Quoted in Kraybill and Bowman, 33. Most of my discussion of the Hutterites is based on this book.

10. Kraybill and Bowman, 26.

11. Abbott, 100.

12. Andrews, 266–68.

13. Norris, 261.

14. Norris, 256 .

15. Norris, 118.

16. Norris, 117.

17. Norris, 121.

18. Norris, 255.

19. Norris, 262.

20. Quoted in Foster, 89.

21. Foster, 86.

22. Quoted in Foster, 89.

23. Foster, 107.

24. Quoted in Foster, 79.

25. Quoted in Foster, 81.

26. Quoted in Foster, 94.

27. Foster, 95n.68.

28. Foster, 94.

29. Plato, *Plato's Republic*, bk. 1.

## ELEVEN: PHILOSOPHICAL ADVICE

1. Epicurus, "Fragments: Remains Assigned to Certain Books," no. 54.

2. Seneca, *Letters*, let. CVIII.

3. Seneca, *Letters*, let. XC.

4. Clarke, 38.

5. Marcus Aurelius, bk. 7, sec. 55.

6. Marcus Aurelius, bk. 7, sec. 27.

7. Marcus Aurelius, bk. 9, sec. 7.

8. Seneca, "On Tranquillity," pt. II, sec. 4.

9. Seneca, "On the Happy Life," pt. IV, sec. 4.

10. Seneca, "On the Happy Life," pt. IV, sec. 4.

11. Epictetus, *Handbook*, sec. 1.

12. Epictetus, *Handbook*, sec. 2.

13. Epictetus, *Handbook*, sec. 19.

14. Epictetus, *Handbook*, sec. 14.

15. Epictetus, *Handbook*, sec. 8.

16. Seneca, *Letters*, let. XVI.

17. Seneca, "On Anger," bk. II, sec. 13.

18. Seneca, "On Anger," bk. III, sec. 28.

19. Seneca, "On Anger," bk. II, sec. 29.

20. Seneca, "On Anger," bk. III, sec. 13.

21. Epictetus, *Handbook*, sec. 50.

22. Epictetus, *Handbook*, sec. 23.

23. Epictetus, *Handbook*, sec. 20.

24. Epictetus, *Handbook*, sec. 48.

25. Epictetus, *Handbook*, sec. 13.

26. Epictetus, *Handbook*, sec. 48.

27. Seneca, "On Tranquillity," pt. VII, sec. 4.

28. Seneca, "On Tranquillity," pt. VII, sec. 6.

29. Seneca, "On Tranquillity," pt. VIII, sec. 2.

30. Seneca, "On Tranquillity," pt. VIII, sec. 9.

31. Seneca, *Letters*, let. XVIII.

32. Campbell, 14.

33. Marcus Aurelius, bk. 7, sec. 27.

34. Schopenhauer, "Counsels and Maxims," 43–44.

35. Seneca, "On Anger," bk. III, sec. 36.

36. Seneca, "On Anger," bk. III, sec. 37.

37. Epictetus, *Handbook*, sec. 11.

38. Goldberg, *Long Quiet Highway*, xii–xiii.

39. Epicurus, "Fragments: Remains Assigned to Certain Books," no. 48.

40. Epicurus, "Fragments: Vatican Collection," no. LXXI.

41. Epicurus, "Fragments: Vatican Collection," no. XXXV.

42. Epicurus, "Fragments: Remains Assigned to Certain Books," no. 74.

43. Epicurus, "Fragments: Remains Assigned to Certain Books," no. 86.

44. Epicurus, "Fragments: Vatican Collection," no. XXV.

45. Epicurus, "Fragments: Remains Assigned to Certain Books," no. 73.

46. Epicurus, "Fragments: Vatican Collection," no. LXVII.

47. Epicurus, "Fragments: Remains Assigned to Certain Books," no. 72.

48. Epicurus, "Letter to Menoeceus."

49. Sextus Empiricus, "Outlines of Pyrrhonism," bk. III, ch. XXIV.

50. Sextus Empiricus, "Outlines of Pyrrhonism," bk. I, ch. XII.

51. Sextus Empiricus, "Against the Ethicists," 461.

52. Sextus Empiricus, "Against the Ethicists," 441–43.

53. Sextus Empiricus, "Against the Ethicists," 457.

54. Sextus Empiricus, "Against the Ethicists," 445.

55. Sextus Empiricus, "Against the Ethicists," 443–45.

56. Bett, 169.

57. Watson, xx–xxi.

58. Sextus Empiricus, "Against the Ethicists," 441.

59. Sextus Empiricus, "Against the Ethicists," 451.

60. Sextus Empiricus, "Against the Ethicists," 453, 471.

61. Sextus Empiricus, "Outlines of Pyrrhonism," bk. I, ch. VI.

62. Sextus Empiricus, "Against the Ethicists," 491.

## TWELVE: THE ECCENTRICS

1. Aristotle, bk. I, ch. 2.

2. Nietzsche, 1.

3. Navia, viii–ix.

4. Diogenes Laertius, "Diogenes," 27.

5. Diogenes Laertius, "Diogenes," 54.

6. Navia, 22.

7. Diogenes Laertius, "Diogenes," 53.

8. Diogenes Laertius, "Diogenes," 69.

9. Diogenes Laertius, "Diogenes," 73.

10. Diogenes Laertius, "Menedemus," 109.

11. Diogenes Laertius, "Diogenes," 77.

12. Diogenes Laertius, "Diogenes," 57.

13. Diogenes Laertius, "Diogenes," 41.

14. Diogenes Laertius, "Diogenes," 35.

15. Dio Chrysostom, "The Sixth Discourse: Diogenes, or on Tyranny," 261.

16. Epictetus, "Arrian's Discourses of Epictetus," bk. III, ch. XXII.

17. Arnold, 118.

18. Dio Chrysostom, "The Eighth Discourse: Diogenes or On Virtue," 385.

19. Dio Chrysostom, "The Ninth Discourse: Diogenes or the Isthmian Discourse," 409.

20. Dio Chrysostom, "The Eighth Discourse: Diogenes or On Virtue," 391.

21. Richardson, 5–6.

22. Quoted in Richardson, 257.

23. Thoreau, *Thoughts* (July 19, 1851), 1.

24. Thoreau, *Walden*, 61.

25. Richardson, 389.

26. Thoreau, *Walden*, 4.

27. Thoreau, *Walden*, 6.

28. Thoreau, *Thoughts* (October 18, 1856), 7.

29. Quoted in France, 181.

30. Quoted in Richardson, 256–57.

31. Thoreau, *Walden*, 94.

32. Thoreau, *Selected Journals* (December 17, 1851), 142.

33. Thoreau, *Selected Journals* (April 24, 1852), 157.

34. Thoreau, *Walden*, 91.

35. Thoreau, *Thoughts* (June 1850), 83.

36. Thoreau, *Thoughts* (1845–47), 214.

37. Thoreau, *Walden*, 217.

38. Thoreau, *Thoughts* (October 18, 1856), 7.

39. Richardson, 299.

40. Quoted in Richardson, 300.

41. Thoreau, *Walden*, 9.

42. Thoreau, *Thoughts* (March 3, 1841), 205.

43. Thoreau, *Walden*, 220.

44. Thoreau, *Selected Journals* (January 20, 1856), 231.

45. Thoreau, *Selected Journals* (November 18, 1855), 223.

46. Thoreau, *Walden*, 219.

47. Thoreau, *Walden*, 41.

48. Thoreau, *Walden*, 33.

49. Thoreau, *Walden*, 19.

50. Thoreau, *Thoughts* (August 7, 1853), 162.

51. Thoreau, "Life Without Principle," 359.

52. Thoreau, "Life Without Principle," 358.

53. Thoreau, *Walden*, 21.

54. Thoreau, *Walden*, 47.

55. Thoreau, *Selected Journals* (1845–47), 90.

56. Thoreau, *Walden*, 216.

57. Thoreau, *Walden*, 215.

58. Navia, 4.

59. Quoted in Navia, 4.

## THIRTEEN: CONCLUSIONS

1. Seneca, "To Helvia," 439.

2. Epicurus, "Fragments: Remains Assigned to Certain Books," no. 69.

3. Mill, *Utilitarianism*, 10.

4. Lao Tzu, sec. XXXIII.

5. Lao Tzu, sec. XLVI.

# Works Cited

Abbott, Elizabeth. *A History of Celibacy*. New York: Scribner, 1999.

Andrews, Edward Deming. *The People Called Shakers: A Search for the Perfect Society*. New York: Dover, 1953.

Aristotle. "Politics." In *The Basic Works of Aristotle*. New York: Random House, 1941.

Arnold, Edward Vernon. *Roman Stoicism*. Freeport, NY: Books for Libraries Press, 1911.

Augustine, Saint. "City of God." In *Basic Writings of Saint Augustine*. Vol. 2. Edited by Whitney J. Oates. New York: Random House, 1948.

———. *The Confessions of Saint Augustine*. Translated by Edward B. Pusey. New York: Pocket Books, 1951.

Badcock, Christopher. *Evolutionary Psychology: A Critical Introduction*. Cambridge: Polity, 2000.

Banks, Gordon, et al. "The Alien Hand Syndrome: Clinical and Postmortem Findings." *Archives of Neurology* 46 (April 1989): 456–59.

Bejjani, Boulos-Paul, et al. "Transient Acute Depression Induced by High-Frequency Deep-Brain Stimulation." *New England Journal of Medicine* 340 (May 13, 1999): 1476–78.

Bett, Richard. *Pyrrho, His Antecedents, and His Legacy*. New York: Oxford University Press, 2000.

Bierce, Ambrose. *The Unabridged Devil's Dictionary*. Edited by David E. Schultz and S. T. Joshi. Athens: University of Georgia Press, 2000.

Bodhi, Bhikkhu. *The Noble Eightfold Path: Way to the End of Suffering*. Seattle: BPS Pariyatti Editions, 2000.

Braitenberg, Valentino. *Vehicles: Experiments in Synthetic Psychology*. Cambridge, MA: MIT Press, 1984.

Brasil-Neto, Joaquim P., et al. "Focal Transcranial Magnetic Stimulation and Response Bias in a Forced-Choice Task." *Journal of Neurology, Neurosurgery, and Psychiatry* 55 (1992): 964–66.

Burton, Robert. *The Anatomy of Melancholy*. Edited by Floyd Dell and Paul Jordan-Smith. New York: Tudor, 1927.

Cabanac, Michel. "Physiological Role of Pleasure." *Science* 173 (1971): 1103–7.

Calvin, John. *Institutes of the Christian Religion*. Translated by Henry Beveridge. Grand Rapids, MI: Wm. B. Eerdmans, 1998.

Campbell, Robin. Introduction to *Letters from a Stoic*. London: Penguin, 1969.

Carpenter, William Benjamin. *Principles of Mental Psychology*. Tokyo: Maruzen, 1998.

Carus, Paul. *The Gospel of Buddha*. La Salle, IL: Open Court, 1894.

Cicero, Marcus Tullius. "Speech in Defence of Aulus Licinius Archias." In *Orations of Marcus Tullius Cicero*. Translated by Charles Duke Yonge. Revised edition. London: Colonial Press, 1900.

Clark, William R., and Michael Grunstein. *Are We Hardwired? The Role of Genes in Human Behavior*. New York: Oxford University Press, 2000.

Clarke, M. L. *The Roman Mind: Studies in the History of Thought from Cicero to Marcus Aurelius*. New York: W. W. Norton, 1968.

Colgan, Patrick. *Animal Motivation*. London: Chapman and Hall, 1989.

Cowen, Tyler. *What Price Fame?* Cambridge, MA: Harvard University Press, 2000.

Damasio, Antonio R. *Descartes' Error: Emotion, Reason, and the Human Brain*. New York: G. P. Putnam's Sons, 1994.

Dennett, Daniel C. *Consciousness Explained*. Boston: Little, Brown, 1991.

Dio Chrysostom. "The Eighth Discourse: Diogenes or on Virtue." In *Dio Chrysostom*. Vol. I. Translated by J. W. Cohoon. Cambridge, MA: Harvard University Press, 1961.

———. "The Ninth Discourse: Diogenes or the Isthmian Discourse." In *Dio Chrysostom*. Vol. I. Translated by J. W. Cohoon. Cambridge, MA: Harvard University Press, 1961.

———. "The Sixth Discourse: Diogenes, or on Tyranny." In *Dio Chrysostom*. Vol. I. Translated by J. W. Cohoon. Cambridge, MA: Harvard University Press, 1961.

Diogenes Laertius. "Antisthenes." In *Lives of Eminent Philosophers*. Vol. II. Translated by R. D. Hicks. Cambridge, MA: Harvard University Press, 1942.

———. "Diogenes." In *Lives of Eminent Philosophers*. Vol. II. Translated by R. D. Hicks. Cambridge, MA: Harvard University Press, 1942.

———. "Menedemus." In *Lives of Eminent Philosophers*. Vol. II. Translated by R. D. Hicks. Cambridge, MA: Harvard University Press, 1942.

Epictetus. *The Handbook (The Encheiridion)*. Translated by Nicholas White. Indianapolis: Hackett, 1983.

———. "Arrian's Discourses of Epictetus." In *The Stoic and Epicurean Philosophers*. Edited by Whitney J. Oates. New York: The Modern Library, 1940.

Epicurus. "Fragments: Remains Assigned to Certain Books." In *The Stoic and Epicurean Philosophers*. Edited by Whitney J. Oates. New York: The Modern Library, 1940.

———. "Fragments: Vatican Collection." In *The Stoic and Epicurean Philosophers*. Edited by Whitney J. Oates. New York: The Modern Library, 1940.

———. "Letter to Menoeceus." In *The Stoic and Epicurean Philosophers*. Edited by Whitney J. Oates. New York: The Modern Library, 1940.

Feinberg, Todd E. *Altered Egos: How the Brain Creates the Self.* New York: Oxford University Press, 2001.

Foster, Lawrence. *Religion and Sexuality: The Shakers, the Mormons, and the Oneida Community.* Urbana: University of Illinois Press, 1984.

France, Peter. *Hermits: The Insights of Solitude.* London: Chatto and Windus, 1996.

Frankfurt, Harry G. "Necessity and Desire." In *The Importance of What We Care About: Philosophical Essays.* Cambridge: Cambridge University Press, 1988.

Frederick, Shane, and George Loewenstein. "Hedonic Adaptation." In *Well-Being: The Foundations of Hedonic Psychology.* Edited by Daniel Kahneman, Ed Diener, and Norbert Schwarz. New York: Russell Sage Foundation, 1999.

Frijda, Nico H. "Emotions in Robots." In *Comparative Approaches to Cognitive Science.* Edited by Herbert L. Roitblat and Jean-Arcady Meyer. Cambridge, MA: MIT Press, 1995.

Gazzaniga, Michael S. "Brain Modularity: Towards a Philosophy of Conscious Experience." In *Consciousness in Contemporary Science.* Edited by A. J. Marcel and E. Bisiach. Oxford: Clarendon Press, 1988.

Gazzaniga, Michael S., and Joseph E. LeDoux. *The Integrated Mind.* New York: Plenum Press, 1978.

Gertner, Jon. "The Futile Pursuit of Happiness." *New York Times Magazine,* September 7, 2003, 44–91.

Gilbert, Daniel T., and Timothy D. Wilson. "Miswanting: Some Problems in the Forecasting of Future Affective States." In *Feeling and Thinking: The Role of Affect in Social Cognition.* Edited by Joseph P. Forgas. New York: Cambridge University Press, 2000.

Giroux, Robert. Introduction to *The Seven Storey Mountain,* by Thomas Merton. San Diego: Harcourt Brace, 1998.

Goldberg, Natalie. "Interview." Included on *Long Quiet Highway: A Memoir on Zen in America and the Writing Life.* Boulder, CO: Sounds True, 2000. Sound recording.

———. *Long Quiet Highway: Waking Up in America.* New York: Bantam, 1993.

Haggard, Patrick, and Martin Eimer. "On the Relation Between Brain Potentials and the Awareness of Voluntary Movements." *Experimental Brain Research* 126 (1999): 128–33.

Hobbes, Thomas. *On the Citizen.* Edited and translated by Richard Tuck and Michael Silverthorne. Cambridge: Cambridge University Press, 1998.

Hume, David. "An Enquiry Concerning the Principles of Morals." In *Enquiries: Concerning the Human Understanding and Concerning the Principles of Morals.* Edited by L. A. Selby-Bigge. Westport, CT: Greenwood Press, 1946.

———. *A Treatise of Human Nature.* Edited by David Fate Norton and Mary J. Norton. Oxford: Oxford University Press, 2000.

Huxley, Thomas Henry. "On the Hypothesis That Animals Are Automata, and Its History." In *Method and Results.* New York: D. Appleton, 1897.

James, William. *The Principles of Psychology.* Vol. II. New York: Dover, 1950.

John of the Cross, Saint. "Ascent of Mt. Carmel." In *The Collected Works of Saint John of the Cross.* Translated by Kieran Kavanaugh and Otilio Rodriguez. Washington, D.C.: ICS Publications, 1991.

———. "Sayings of Light and Love." In *The Collected Works of Saint John of the Cross.* Translated by Kieran Kavanaugh and Otilio Rodriguez. Washington, D.C.: ICS Publications, 1991.

Johnson, Samuel. "The Rambler." *The Yale Edition of the Works of Samuel Johnson.* Vol. V. New Haven: Yale University Press, 1969.

Kahneman, Daniel. "Objective Happiness." In *Well-Being: The Foundations of Hedonic Psychology.* Edited by Daniel Kahneman, Ed Diener, and Norbert Schwarz. New York: Russell Sage Foundation, 1999.

Kornfield, Jack. *After the Ecstasy, the Laundry: How the Heart Grows Wise on the Spiritual Path.* New York: Bantam, 2000.

Kraybill, Donald B. *The Riddle of Amish Culture.* Baltimore: Johns Hopkins University Press, 2001.

Kraybill, Donald B., and Carl F. Bowman. *On the Backroad to Heaven: Old Order Hutterites, Mennonites, Amish, and Brethren.* Baltimore: Johns Hopkins University Press, 2001.

La Rochefoucauld, François duc de. *Maxims.* Translated by Leonard Tancock. London: Penguin, 1959.

Lao Tzu. *Tao Te Ching.* Translated by D. C. Lau. New York: Penguin, 1963.

*Laws of Manu.* Translated by G. Bühler. Delhi: Motilal Banarsidass, 1964.

LeDoux, Joseph. *The Emotional Brain: The Mysterious Underpinnings of Emotional Life.* New York: Simon and Schuster, 1996.

Libet, Benjamin. "Do We Have Free Will?" In *The Volitional Brain: Towards a Neuroscience of Free Will.* Edited by Benjamin Libet, Anthony Freeman, and Keith Sutherland. Thorverton, UK: Imprint Academic, 1999.

*Love Lyrics of Ancient Egypt.* Translated by Barbara Hughes Fowler. Chapel Hill: University of North Carolina Press, 1994.

Magee, Bryan. *The Philosophy of Schopenhauer.* Oxford: Clarendon Press, 1983.

Marcus Aurelius. *Meditations.* Translated by Maxwell Staniforth. London: Penguin, 1964.

McDannell, Colleen, and Bernhard Lang. *Heaven: A History.* New Haven: Yale University Press, 1988.

McFarland, David. "Opportunity Versus Goals in Robots, Animals, and People." In *Comparative Approaches to Cognitive Science.* Edited by Herbert L. Roitblat and Jean-Arcady Meyer. Cambridge, MA: MIT Press, 1995.

McMurtry, Larry. *Walter Benjamin at the Dairy Queen: Reflections at Sixty and Beyond.* New York: Simon and Schuster, 1999.

Melville, Herman. "Billy Budd." In *Billy Budd and the Piazza Tales.* Garden City, NY: Doubleday, 1961.

Merton, Thomas. *The Seven Storey Mountain.* San Diego: Harcourt Brace, 1948.

Mill, John Stuart. *On Liberty.* Edited by Elizabeth Rapaport. Indianapolis: Hackett, 1978.

———. *Utilitarianism.* Edited by George Sher. Indianapolis: Hackett, 1979.

Minsky, Marvin. *The Society of Mind.* New York: Simon and Schuster, 1985.

Navia, Luis E. *Diogenes of Sinope: The Man in the Tub.* Westport, CT: Greenwood Press, 1998.

*New English Bible with the Apocrypha.* New York: Oxford University Press, 1961.

Nietzsche, Friedrich. *The Twilight of the Idols.* Translated by Anthony M. Ludovici. New York: Russell and Russell, 1964.

Nisbett, Richard E., and Timothy DeCamp Wilson. "Telling More than We Can Know: Verbal Reports on Mental Processes." *Psychological Review* 84 (May 1977): 231–59.

Norris, Kathleen. *The Cloister Walk.* New York: Riverhead Books, 1996.

Olds, James. "Self-Stimulation of the Brain: Its Use to Study Local Effects of Hunger, Sex, and Drugs." *Science* 127 (February 14, 1958): 315–24.

Ornstein, Robert. *The Evolution of Consciousness: Of Darwin, Freud, and Cranial Fire: The Origins of the Way We Think.* New York: Prentice Hall, 1991.

Pascal, Blaise. *Pascal's Pensées.* New York: E. P. Dutton, 1958.

*Pinnacles of India's Past: Selections from the Rgveda.* Translated by Walter H. Maurer. Philadelphia: John Benjamins, 1986.

Plato. *Plato's Republic.* Translated by G. M. A. Grube. Indianapolis: Hackett, 1974.

———. "Symposium." In *The Portable Plato.* Translated by Benjamin Jowett. New York: Penguin, 1948.

Plutarch. "Life of Demetrius." In *Plutarch's Lives.* Vol. V. Translated by John Dryden. New York: Bigelow, Brown and Co., 1900.

*Qur'an: The Eternal Revelation Vouchsafed to Muhammad, the Seal of the Prophets.* Translated by Muhammad Zafrulla Khan. New York: Olive Branch Press, 1997.

Reber, Arthur S. *Implicit Learning and Tacit Knowledge: An Essay on the Cognitive Unconscious.* New York: Oxford University Press, 1993.

Resnik, Michael D. *Choices: An Introduction to Decision Theory.* Minneapolis: University of Minnesota Press, 1987.

Richardson, Robert D. *Henry Thoreau: A Life of the Mind.* Berkeley: University of California Press, 1986.

Rosett, Claudia. "Turkmenbashi: Megalomaniac, Tyrant, and 'Ally.'" *Wall Street Journal,* August 29, 2002, A12.

Russell, Bertrand. *Analysis of Mind.* London: George Allen and Unwin, 1921.

———. *Autobiography of Bertrand Russell: 1872–World War I.* New York: Bantam, 1968.

Sacks, Oliver. *The Man Who Mistook His Wife for a Hat and Other Clinical Tales.* New York: Summit, 1985.

Schoeck, Helmut. *Envy: A Theory of Social Behavior.* Translated by Michael Glenny and Betty Ross. Indianapolis: Liberty Press, 1987.

Schopenhauer, Arthur. "Counsels and Maxims." In *The Wisdom of Life and Counsels and Maxims.* Translated by T. Bailey Saunders. Amherst, NY: Prometheus, 1995.

———. "The Wisdom of Life." In *The Wisdom of Life and Counsels and Maxims.* Translated by T. Bailey Saunders. Amherst, NY: Prometheus, 1995.

———. *The World as Will and Representation.* Translated by E. F. J. Payne. New York: Dover, 1969.

Schroeder, Timothy. *Three Faces of Desire.* New York: Oxford University Press, 2004.

Seneca. "On Anger." In *Moral and Political Essays.* Translated by John M. Cooper and J. F. Procopé. Cambridge: Cambridge University Press, 1995.

———. "On the Happy Life." In *Moral Essays.* Vol. II. Translated by John W. Basore. Cambridge, MA: Harvard University Press, 1932.

———. "To Helvia on Consolation." In *Moral Essays.* Vol. II. Translated by John W. Basore. Cambridge, MA: Harvard University Press, 1932.

———. *Letters from a Stoic.* Translated by Robin Campbell. London: Penguin, 1969.

———. "On Tranquillity of Mind." In *Moral Essays.* Vol. II. Translated by John W. Basore. Cambridge, MA: Harvard University Press, 1932.

Sextus Empiricus. "Against the Ethicists." In *Sextus Empiricus.* Vol. III. Translated by R. G. Bury. Cambridge, MA: Harvard University Press, 1967.

———. "Outlines of Pyrrhonism." In *Sextus Empiricus.* Vol. I. Translated by R. G. Bury. Cambridge, MA.: Harvard University Press, 1967.

Spinoza, Benedictus de. *Ethics.* Oxford: Oxford University Press, 2000.

Stevens, John. *Three Zen Masters: Ikkyū, Hakuin, and Ryōkan*. New York: Kodansha International, 1993.

Streitfeld, David. "The Yellowed Prose of Texas ." *Washington Post*, April 6, 1999, C1.

Thomas, Edward J. *The Life of Buddha as Legend and History*. London: Routledge and Kegan Paul, 1949.

Thoreau, Henry D. "Life Without Principle." In *Thoreau: Walden and Other Writings*. New York: Bantam, 1962.

———. *The Selected Journals of Henry David Thoreau*. Edited by Carl Bode. New York: New American Library, 1967.

———. *The Thoughts of Thoreau*. Edited by Edwin Way Teale. New York: Dodd, Mead, 1962.

———. "Walden." In *Walden and Resistance to Civil Government*. Second edition. Edited by William Rossi. New York: W. W. Norton, 1992.

Tkacik, Maureen. "Films, Rap Stars Inspire Kids." *Wall Street Journal*, January 25, 2002, A1.

Tolstoy, Leo. "A Confession." In *A Confession, The Gospel in Brief, and What I Believe*. Translated by Aylmer Maude. London: Oxford University Press, 1940.

Trollope, Anthony. *Autobiography*. London: Oxford University Press, 1974.

Twain, Mark [Samuel Clemens]. *Mark Twain's Notebook*. New York: Harper and Brothers, 1935.

Valenstein, Elliot S. *Brain Control: A Critical Examination of Brain Stimulation and Psychosurgery*. New York: John Wiley and Sons, 1973.

Wagner, Hugh. *The Psychobiology of Human Motivation*. London: Routledge, 1999.

Watson, Burton. Introduction to *The Zen Teachings of Master Lin-Chi*. Boston: Shambhala, 1993.

Watts, Alan W. *The Way of Zen*. New York: Vintage, 1989.

Wegner, Daniel M. *The Illusion of Conscious Will*. Cambridge, MA: MIT Press, 2002.

Wilson, Timothy D. *Strangers to Ourselves: Discovering the Adaptive Unconscious*. Cambridge, MA: Harvard University Press, 2002.

Winokur, Jon, ed. *The Portable Curmudgeon*. New York: New American Library, 1987.

Zajonc, Robert B. "Feeling and Thinking: Closing the Debate over the Independence of Affect." In *Feeling and Thinking: The Role of Affect in Social Cognition*. Edited by Joseph P. Forgas. New York: Cambridge University Press, 2000.

———. "Feeling and Thinking: Preferences Need No Inferences." *American Psychologist* 35 (February 1980): 151–75.

# Index